REDEFINING RACE

REDEFINING RACE

Asian American Panethnicity and Shifting Ethnic Boundaries

Dina G. Okamoto

Russell Sage Foundation
New York

The Russell Sage Foundation

The Russell Sage Foundation, one of the oldest of America's general purpose foundations, was established in 1907 by Mrs. Margaret Olivia Sage for "the improvement of social and living conditions in the United States." The Foundation seeks to fulfill this mandate by fostering the development and dissemination of knowledge about the country's political, social, and economic problems. While the Foundation endeavors to assure the accuracy and objectivity of each book it publishes, the conclusions and interpretations in Russell Sage Foundation publications are those of the authors and not of the Foundation, its Trustees, or its staff. Publication by Russell Sage, therefore, does not imply Foundation endorsement.

BOARD OF TRUSTEES
Robert E. Denham, Chair

Larry M. Bartels
Kenneth D. Brody
Karen S. Cook
W. Bowman Cutter III

Sheldon Danziger
Kathryn Edin
Lawrence F. Katz
Nicholas Lemann

Sara S. McLanahan
Claude M. Steele
Shelley E. Taylor
Richard H. Thaler

Library of Congress Cataloging-in-Publication Data

Okamoto, Dina G.
  Redefining race : Asian American panethnicity and shifting ethnic boundaries / Dina G. Okamoto.
    pages cm
  Includes bibliographical references and index.
  ISBN 978-0-87154-676-0 (pbk. : alk. paper)—ISBN 978-1-61044-845-1 (ebook)
  1. Asian Americans. 2. Ethnicity—United States. 3. Group identity—United States. I. Title.
  E184.A75O37 2014
  305.895'073--dc23   2014018102

Copyright © 2014 by Russell Sage Foundation. All rights reserved. Printed in the United States of America. No part of this publication may be reproduced, stored in a retrieval system, or transmitted in any form or by any means, electronic, mechanical, photocopying, recording, or otherwise, without the prior written permission of the publisher.

Reproduction by the United States Government in whole or in part is permitted for any purpose.

The paper used in this publication meets the minimum requirements of American National Standard for Information Sciences—Permanence of Paper for Printed Library Materials. ANSI Z39.48-1992.

Text design by Suzanne Nichols.

RUSSELL SAGE FOUNDATION
112 East 64th Street, New York, New York 10065
10 9 8 7 6 5 4 3 2 1

Contents

	List of Tables and Figures	vii
	About the Author	xi
	Acknowledgments	xiii
Chapter 1	Introduction: Ethnic Boundary Change and Panethnicity	1
Chapter 2	Beginnings: The Durability of Ethnic Boundaries in the Pre-1963 Era	26
Chapter 3	The Emergence of Organizational Panethnicity	53
Chapter 4	The Ethnic-Panethnic Dynamics of Collective Action	85
Chapter 5	Ethnic Organizations and the Flexibility of Group Boundaries	112
Chapter 6	Panethnicity and Beyond	145
Appendix A	Variable Construction and Tables	159
Appendix B	Data Collection	169
	Notes	175
	References	203
	Index	233

List of Tables and Figures

Table 1.1	Asian American Population, by Decade, 1980–2010	17
Table 1.2	Socioeconomic Indicators for Asian Ethnic Groups, 2010	18
Table 2.1	The Asian Population in the United States, 1910–1960, by Ethnic Group	30
Table 3.1	Types and Examples of Panethnic Organizations in Operation, 1970–2000	57
Table 3.2	Top Thirty Metropolitan Areas with the Largest Asian American Populations in 1990	63
Table 3.3	Asians in Professional and Nonprofessional Occupations, 1960 and 2000	68
Table 3.4	Labor Market Segregation and Competition in Metropolitan Areas, by Levels of Panethnic Organizational Formation, 2000	69
Table 3.5	The Effects of Racial Competition and Segregation on the Formation of Pan-Asian Organizations, 1970–1998	71
Table 4.1	The Effects of Ethnic Organizations on the Rate of Pan-Asian Collective Action Events, 1970–1998	101
Table 4.2	The Effects of Ethnic Events on the Rate of Pan-Asian Collective Action Events, 1970–1998	102

Table 4.3	The Effects of Interethnic Labor Market Segregation on the Rate of Pan-Asian Collective Action Events, 1970–1998	104
Table 4.4	The Effects of Labor Market Segregation on the Rate of Pan-Asian Collective Action Events, 1970–1998	104
Table 5.1	Characteristics of Leaders of San Francisco Bay Area Ethnic Organizations	115
Table 5.2	Racial and Ethnic Population of San Francisco and Oakland, California, 2010	116
Table A.1	The Independent Variables Used in the Regression Analyses	160
Table A.2	Zero-Inflated Poisson (ZIP) Regression Models Estimating the Effects of Independent Variables on the Formation of Pan-Asian Organizations, 1970–1998	163
Table A.3	The Effects of Ethnic-Specific Variables on the Formation of Pan-Asian Organizations, 1970–1998	164
Table A.4	The Effects of Interethnic Competition and Segregation on the Rate of Pan-Asian Collective Events, 1970–1998	165
Table A.5	The Effects of Interracial Competition and Segregation on the Rate of Pan-Asian Collective Action Events, 1970–1998	166
Table A.6	Characteristics of Asian Ethnic Organizations by Boundary-Related Activity	167
Table A.7	The Effects of Panethnic Organizing on the Panethnic Identity	168
Table A.8	The Effects of Panethnic Organizing on Political Participation	168

Figure 1.1	The Broad Social Conditions Leading to the Emergence of Panethnicity	12
Figure 1.2	The Competition and Segregation Models	13
Figure 1.3	The Proximate Factors Encouraging Panethnic Activity in the Post–Civil Rights Era	16
Figure 2.1	Immigration to the United States, by Global Region, 1960–2009	47
Figure 2.2	Asian Immigration to the United States, by Ethnic Group, 1960–2009	48
Figure 2.3	The Race Question on the 1980 Census Form	49
Figure 3.1	The Number of Asian, Latino, and Black Panethnic Organizations Formed per 100,000 Asians, Latinos, and Blacks, Respectively, 1970–2000	56
Figure 3.2	National Pan-Asian Organizational Foundings, 1970–1988	60
Figure 3.3	The Segregation and Competition Models: Local Conditions and Mechanisms for the Emergence of Panethnicity	64
Figure 3.4	Predicted Probabilities for the Formation of Panethnic Organizations, by Level of Racial Segregation in the Labor Market	72
Figure 3.5	Predicted Probabilities for the Formation of Panethnic Organizations, by Ethnic Segregation in the Labor Market	73
Figure 3.6	Opposing Effects of Ethnic and Racial Occupational Segregation on Panethnicity	75
Figure 4.1	African American and Pan-Asian Protest Events in the Post–Civil Rights Era, per 100,000, by Decade	89

Figure 4.2	Ethnic and Panethnic Collective Action Events Involving Asian Americans, 1970–1998	90
Figure 5.1	Practices of San Francisco and Oakland Ethnic Organizations Related to Expanding Boundaries	120
Figure 5.2	Ethnic Leaders' Narratives to Explain Why They Maintained Ethnic Boundaries	125
Figure 5.3	Assimilation Narratives and Program Activities Used by Ethnic Leaders to Manage Organizational Shifts Toward Panethnicity	129
Figure 6.1	The Mediating Conditions and Mechanisms That Encourage Panethnic Organizing	147

About the Author

DINA G. OKAMOTO is associate professor of sociology and Director of the Center for Research on Race and Ethnicity in Society (CRRES) at Indiana University.

Acknowledgments

THIS BOOK BEGAN as a kernel of an idea at the University of Arizona, and its writing and completion would not have been possible without the support and encouragement of many colleagues, friends, and family members. I am especially grateful to Michael Hechter, who convinced me that panethnicity was a topic worth pursuing and pushed me to sharpen my theoretical arguments. He also asked me the hard questions throughout the development of the book, yet continued to be encouraging. I am also indebted to Sarah Soule, Stephen Cornell, Sun-Ki Chai, Lynn Smith-Lovin, Doug McAdam, Woody Powell, and Paula England, who supported my work and helped me to develop as a scholar while at Arizona.

Some of the material in this book has appeared elsewhere in published articles, but the overarching theoretical framework I present here is new, which reflects the development of my thinking on the topic. Additionally, the context within which I place this work is new, specifically in regard to how panethnicity relates to both assimilation and racialization theories. Writing this book has forced me to revisit my published work, develop new ideas, expand my analyses, and come to understand all of the pieces as part of a larger project.

I was fortunate to spend more than ten years at the University of California–Davis, where I received mentorship, support, and friendship from a number of colleagues and graduate students. I am particularly indebted to Mary Jackman, who provided me with constructive feedback on my work and helped me to become a better thinker and writer. I especially want to thank Erin Hamilton, Vicki Smith, Ming-cheng Lo, Drew Halfmann, Michael McQuarrie, and Bruce Haynes, each of whom read chapters of the book or spent time talking with me about formative ideas for the book. Valerie Feldman, Cassie Hartzog, Kim Ebert, Melanie Jones Gast, David Orzechowicz, Stephanie Deliganis, Emerald Nguyen, Jesse Rude, and Andre Lee also deserve much thanks for commenting on early chapter drafts and/or helping with the data collection process.

My research for this book benefited from generous funding support from the National Science Foundation and UC Davis. I am also grateful to have been a visiting scholar at the Russell Sage Foundation (RSF) and the Center for Advanced Studies in the Behavioral Sciences (CASBS) at Stanford. The book was in its infancy when I was at RSF, and I could not have completed it without the generous support of Eric Wanner, Sheldon Danziger, Aixa Cintron-Velez, and Suzanne Nichols at the foundation. A special thanks to Suzanne, who was a wonderful editor and encouraged me throughout the entire process. I especially thank RSF visiting scholars Eddie Telles, Ruth Milkman, Mignon Moore, Ingrid Banks, Greg Duncan, Rose Razaghian, Ira Katznelson, and Carol Worthman for the time they took to engage with me about my work. At CASBS, Tyrone Forman, Amanda Lewis, Michael Hechter, and John Mollenkopf carefully read several chapters from the manuscript and pushed me to clarify my concepts, argumentation, and evidence. I thank them for their wisdom and friendship. I also received excellent feedback from other CASBS fellows, including Kathleen Gerson, Barbie Zelizer, William Roy, William Darity, Arlene Saxonhouse, Rachel Prentice, Nancy Kollman, Jing Tsu, Carolyn Becker, Daniel Hallin, and Zach Shore.

Over the years I have presented pieces of this work at various institutions. I received especially useful feedback from the talks I gave at Stanford University, Indiana University, UC Berkeley, the Graduate Center of the City University of New York (CUNY), and New York University. I also thank Mignon Moore, Rhacel Parrenas, Prudence Carter, Rima Wilkes, and Pawan Dhingra for reading earlier versions of the book and providing honest and helpful feedback. Irene Bloemraad and Taeku Lee were careful reviewers of the book, and I could not have asked for more insightful and detailed comments; their contributions pushed the book in the right directions, and for that I am grateful. I am also deeply indebted to Jenny Irons for reading the entire book manuscript at the last hour, pushing me to forge my contribution and make it to the proverbial finish line. I thank my colleagues at my new institution, Indiana University, for giving me the time and space to finish the book manuscript and for providing a stimulating intellectual environment in which to work.

Many other colleagues and friends provided words of advice and support along the way, including: Irenee Beattie, Ada Chu, Angie Chung, Nancy Foner, Bill Ong Hing, Tomás Jiménez, Michael Jones-Correa, Jane Junn, Karyn Lacy, Helen Marrow, Monica McDermott, David Meyer, Cristina Mora, Susan Olzak, Michael Omi, Lisa Pearce, Karthick Ramakrishnan, Steliana Schmidel, David Takeuchi, Linda Tropp, Vivian Tseng, Karolyn Tyson, Nella Van Dyke, Janelle Wong, and Amy Yamashita.

I thank my parents for being an inspiration for this work and for their steadfast encouragement of my intellectual pursuits, and my brother Duane for his listening ear as I made my way through the different stages of the book. I especially thank Chris Pelton. I would not have been able to finish the book had it not been for his endless support during the many times I wanted to give up and his constant understanding when I had to work another late night. And finally, Maya and Frida have kept me grounded and often remind me that each day is filled with new possibilities.

Bloomington, IN
May 2014

Chapter 1 | Introduction: Ethnic Boundary Change and Panethnicity

IN JUNE 2012, the Pew Research Center issued a major report, "The Rise of Asian Americans," on the demographics and attitudes of the Asian population in twenty-first-century America.[1] Based on a nationally representative survey, the report noted that Asian Americans are the "highest-income, best-educated and fastest-growing racial group in the United States" and that, as a group, Asians are more likely to marry across racial lines, live in racially mixed neighborhoods, and place more value than other Americans do on marriage, parenthood, hard work, and career success. The report highlighted the economic success and social assimilation of Asian Americans and emphasized that three-fourths of this population is foreign-born, suggesting that Asian Americans as a group are exceptional. The national media picked up the story and focused on the achievement and integration of Asian Americans.

Within days of the report's release, over thirty key Asian American advocacy organizations contested the report's portrayal of the Asian population as a monolithic model minority with few challenges. Community leaders explained that Asians have been erroneously understood as a model minority since the 1960s.[2] The lack of attention to significant disparities within and between various Asian subgroups and the dearth of data beyond East Asian groups have produced an inaccurate representation of the Asian American community, leading to misinformation among policymakers, institutional stakeholders, and the larger public. The full Pew report examined demographic and social differences among six different Asian national-origin groups—Chinese, Filipino, Japanese, Vietnamese, Korean, and Indian—but according to scholars and community leaders, it failed to discuss the role played by U.S. immigration and foreign policies in selecting educated migrants and refugees from Asia and also neglected the continuing economic and social inequality experienced by Asian ethnic groups, especially Southeast Asians, Filipinos, and South Asians.[3]

The Pew report and the uproar it created among Asian American community leaders, organizations, and their members reflected the fact that, on the one hand, the label "Asian American" is commonplace and accepted in contemporary American society, but on the other hand, it is also contested and problematic.[4] Today the panethnic label is regularly used in the media, in household surveys and textbooks, on job applications and college admissions forms, and in the names of organizations to represent a population that shares a racial background. But before 1968 the category and identity of "Asian American" did not exist. We often forget that the ethnic and national-origin groups racially categorized as Asian American have no natural or biological affinity. The first wave of immigrants arriving in the United States from China, Japan, and Korea did not form alliances or cooperate, nor did they adopt an ideology and narrative about a shared history. Instead, they built separate ethnic communities and depended on their own systems of social and economic support. So how did distinct ethnic groups with cross-cutting differences and contentious histories come to cooperate and build a shared identity? Under what conditions did group boundaries shift and change? And what is the nature of ethnic boundaries? Are they static or dynamic, layered or uniform, flexible or durable?

This book addresses these questions by investigating *panethnicity*, the process through which multiple ethnic groups relax and widen their boundaries to forge a new, broader grouping and identity. Clearly, distinct ethnic and immigrant groups can be part of the same racial, religious, or territorial category, and they may subscribe to or act upon expansive identities and labels. When different ethnic groups come to share interests and a collective history and build institutions and identities across ethnic or cultural boundaries, the result is panethnicity.

In the American context, this boundary shifting has taken place among immigrant groups who arrived in the United States with regional, ethnic, and language differences.[5] Over time group boundaries expanded to encompass a broader array of ethnic groups: Poles, Italians, and Greeks became European and later white ethnics[6]; Mexicans, Puerto Ricans, and Cubans became Hispanic or Latino[7]; and Chinese, Japanese, and Koreans became Asian American.[8] And yet, these boundary expansions, at least among contemporary immigrant groups, cannot easily be equated with assimilation, the process in which ethnicity declines in importance and salience. Members of these panethnic groups have typically retained meaningful ethnic boundaries.

Asian Americans, in particular, provide a compelling case for the study of boundary change given their recent status as the fastest-growing immigrant group in the United States, which suggests their growing influence and prominence. Additionally, the extensive diversity within the category of "Asian" by national origin, language, culture, complexion, class, and religion further complicates the panethnic group formation process. As past scholars have noted, the Asian American population is far from homogeneous; in fact, it has been characterized as reflecting "heterogeneity, hybridity, and multiplicity."[9] But one element that particularly sets the Asian case apart from others is the unique nature of past antagonistic histories between Asian countries. The relations among Asian ethnic groups' in the United States were initially hostile, in part because of homeland politics. Japan's colonization of Korea in the early 1900s, the ongoing conflicts between Japan and China, and Japanese war crimes during World War II in China, Korea, Southeast Asia, and the Philippines influenced several generations, and those who immigrated to the United States brought memories of the war and colonization with them.[10] Nevertheless, decades later, Asian-origin groups developed a new, broader identity and a collective history in the United States, built shared institutions, and organized their communities under a panethnic banner.[11]

The development of an Asian American label and identity in the post–civil rights era may not be surprising to some because of the prevalence of racial categories and the continuing salience of race in contemporary U.S. society. But such a sentiment reflects the embedded and taken-for-granted nature of Asian American identity within American culture and society today. Such a view also presumes that racial categories assigned by the state align or correspond with actual group identities and behavior. When distinct groups enter a new society through immigration or conquest and are labeled as sharing the same ethnic, linguistic, or racial grouping, it is assumed that the process of group formation will be unremarkable. These groups, however, though deemed part of the same social category, may not necessarily see themselves as sharing similar interests, conditions, or outcomes. In the United States, immigrants from distinct groups are typically viewed as belonging to a larger racial category—as Asian, Latino, black, or white—and despite their allegiance to their homeland cultures and dialects, they must work to understand themselves as members of a single racial group. In many ways, it is part of the assimilation process whereby group members adapt to social schemas and contexts in American society.[12] But we must remember that racial group formation and identity do not occur naturally. The main contribution of this book is to interrogate the use of an Asian American panethnic label and identity, and demonstrate that panethnicity is not a natural outcome or process, but a social achievement.

Scholars have focused on the key role of racialization in shaping panethnic identities and group formation. Such explanations look at the ways in which social institutions categorize and treat individuals on the basis of race, leading immigrants and ethnic group members to form new panethnic identities.[13] Because ideas about race are deeply rooted in American culture and ideology, racialization is constant and recurring: institutions' regular use of racial categories reinforces and legitimizes them, and individuals' everyday interactions not only are shaped by racial ideologies but often reproduce them.[14] The implication is that racialization imposes racial categories on distinct ethnic groups through macro- and micro-level processes and erases ethnic boundaries, encouraging Asian Americans to identify and organize themselves along panethnic lines.

And yet, as shown by the recent reaction of Asian American advocacy organizations to the Pew report, panethnicity is far more complicated. Clearly, the use of racial categories by the state, mainstream institutions, and individuals provides the logic and motivation for panethnic group formation, but other conditions and processes mediate the translation of the broader forces of racialization into panethnicity. Here I build on past work by scholars who have interrogated the category of "Asian American" and provided a nuanced understanding of Asian American organizing.[15] In further unpacking the group formation process for Asian Americans, this book advances our theoretical understanding of panethnicity (1) by focusing on meso-level conditions to explain the emergent variation in panethnic activity over the post-1968 era, when Asian ethnic groups took up and used the panethnic label and identity to organize in the public arena and form institutions; and (2) by expanding how we think about ethnic boundaries to see them as layered and mutualistic rather than as competing, a view that has broader implications for ethnic boundary change and assimilation.

Redefining Race forges new ground by arguing that when Asian Americans adopted a panethnic label and organized to challenge inequalities and build new communities during the post-1968 era, they did so not simply because the state had assigned them to a racial category that encouraged the expansion of group boundaries. Instead, Asian ethnic groups organized along panethnic lines when they were configured in ways that reinforced racial group boundaries and generated shared interests, identities, and statuses across ethnic, linguistic, and cultural lines. In particular, segregation—when distinct ethnic groups comprising a racial label or category are spatially concentrated within labor markets—created a context where group members could interact, develop shared interests and experiences, and build trust and solidarity across ethnic lines. The segregation of different Asian-origin groups in the same jobs, occupations, and industries increased panethnic group solidarity, especially when the institutional arrangements reinforced unequal access to resources and opportunities and disadvantaged group members.[16] But those who participated in panethnic efforts were not solely drawn from segregated workplace or industry settings or from ethnic enclaves. Labor market segregation also produced a social reality consistent with a pan-Asian ideology that community leaders and organizers drew on when articulating needs and developing new organizations and campaigns.[17] Without the community leaders who constructed pan-Asian narratives, shepherded ethnic group interests, and prioritized inclusive programs, panethnic organizing would not have been realized within the context of segregation.

Additionally, the racial segregation patterns in local labor markets reflected the fact that Asian ethnic groups were segregated from whites and, to some degree, from one another. Segregation among Asian-origin groups contributed to the development of strong ethnic communities and organizations, which ultimately benefited pan-Asian organizing efforts. Thus, a key mediating factor was the presence of organized ethnic groups that encouraged panethnic efforts. Organizing along ethnic lines could have detracted from panethnic organizing, but instead, the assertion of ethnic boundaries actually *encouraged* panethnicity. The boundaries between Asian ethnic groups—between Chinese, Japanese, Filipinos, Koreans, Vietnamese, and Indians—proved to be layered and flexible, allowing for ethnic ties to enhance panethnic efforts. This mutuality further informs our understanding of group boundaries and the conditions under which they expand, illuminating the concept of panethnicity itself. It challenges standard assimilation frameworks that claim panethnicity is simply reflective of assimilation—the erosion or attenuation of ethnic distinctions as ethnic groups become part of a larger panethnic group.

In examining the conditions that give rise to cooperation and collective action among different ethnic groups, this book illuminates the layered, multifaceted nature of panethnicity. It puts forth the *racialized boundary framework*—the argument that ethnic boundaries are not static but dynamic and layered, such that panethnic identities are taken up in certain times and places and not only are multiple affiliations possible, but they can coexist and even enhance one another. Recognizing the layered and flexible nature of boundaries is important because it disrupts the idea of race as bounded and durable. Yet, at the same time, ethnic and racial groups are structured by the social reality of race embedded within institutions and everyday interactions, a reality in which resources and privileges are provided for groups near the top of the racial hierarchy and closed off for those at the bottom. This framework also posits that social conditions within local areas mediate broader racialization processes, demographic shifts, and political opportunities. Structural conditions and cultural narratives that foster intergroup relations and ties and help to generate a collective identity and status across ethnic groups go a long way toward explaining the emergence of panethnicity. Before groups can respond in panethnic ways to assigned categories, group interests and identities need to have been constructed across ethnic, linguistic, and cultural lines. Local conditions—specifically, racial segregation, ethnic organizing, and active leaders—can facilitate the panethnic organizing process among Asian Americans as they redefine race by creating new communities that span ethnic lines, break down racial stereotypes, and challenge unfair treatment.

ETHNICITY AS BOUNDARY PROCESS

Early theorists initially viewed ethnic boundaries as fundamental and immutable. The intensity and meaning of ethnic attachments stemmed from the cultural content of ethnic group membership, such as shared customs and historical experiences.[18] An individual who had been designated as part of an ethnic group could not switch, change, or negotiate ethnic identity because it was part of his or her genetic makeup, something that was in a person's blood. Today ethnicity is understood as socially constructed and at least somewhat malleable.[19] In defining ethnicity as "a subjective belief in common descent," Max Weber emphasized the notion that ethnic attachments are based not on blood ties but on a *belief* in blood relationships, or on what people perceive to be true in terms of common descent.[20] Other scholars have added to this definition to include shared kinship and ancestry, a common history, and symbols that capture the core of the group's identity.[21] This conception of ethnicity reflects a process where group members define their own self-concepts, histories, and identities, suggesting that ethnic boundaries are not rigidly ascribed.

Fredrik Barth was among the first to advocate for the study of "the ethnic boundary that defines the group."[22] He recognized that even though the social and cultural features associated with certain groups may change over time, ethnic boundaries remain intact and continue to distinguish between insiders and outsiders. Following Barth, scholars have claimed that ethnicity is best conceived as an emergent boundary with both symbolic and social aspects.[23] Ethnic boundaries are symbolic in that they are used to make distinctions between people, socially defining who or what belongs in which category.[24] Such distinctions can generate feelings of similarity (or difference) and group membership. Ethnic boundaries are also social boundaries because they are associated with patterns of exclusion, inequality, and discrimination. To the extent that valuable resources are generated within the group, ethnic boundaries can protect these resources by preserving their use for in-group members.[25] They can also be used, however, as a device to maintain exclusion from material resources and preserve social privileges.

In sum, ethnic boundaries, though socially constructed, are meaningful because of the social and symbolic differences they enact.

DEFINING PANETHNICITY

We can understand *panethnic* boundaries as similar to ethnic boundaries, especially in regard to their ability to shift and change and their power as a broader social grouping that marks insiders and outsiders. But the uniqueness of panethnicity lies in the fact that not only are ethnic identities maintained but they are necessary for the success and longevity of the broader grouping.[26] Along with building commonality across different ethnic groups, maintaining diversity and recognizing ethnic distinctions are inherently part of the panethnic process. Panethnic community leaders and activists must work to negotiate, maintain, and sometimes mute ethnic group interests for the good of the larger collective. This diversity principle and balancing act may occur within the context of ethnicity and ethnic boundaries, but it is central to panethnicity.

Some groups engage in widening ethnic group boundaries to form a new, broader grouping and identity primarily as a political strategy, while for others the aim is to establish a cultural identity. Groups organizing along panethnic lines as a political strategy learn that this often generates strength in numbers, which is required in a crowded political field where many interest groups are making demands of public officials and policymakers.[27] Speaking out as Asian Americans rather than as Koreans or Vietnamese may garner more attention on the national public stage simply because of the larger numbers affiliated with the panethnic grouping.[28] Likewise, claims by a Latino or Hispanic organization are likely to be recognized by policymakers and the national press even when Salvadoran and Puerto Rican organizations have already been organizing around similar issues, but on a lesser scale and perhaps with fewer ties to broader communities. The downside of enacting panethnicity solely as a political strategy, however, is that it can often be fleeting. Groups may act in unison during a political campaign to achieve a clear goal that requires the participation of multiple groups, yet in people's daily lives the ties between ethnic groups may be quite weak.

For some individuals, panethnic identity is an integral part of their self-definition, shaping their everyday interactions and influencing important life decisions. Some individuals in the United States adopt a panethnic identity because it enables them to feel like they are part of a larger cultural group whose shared experiences help them navigate educational institutions, workplaces, neighborhoods, and everyday life.[29] Their personal experiences of being seen and understood as part of a racial category, such as Asian or Latino, and being stereotyped—as foreign, as a model minority, as undocumented—contribute to the building of a cultural community.[30] For some, adopting a panethnic identity also represents a form of resistance or opposition to the typically white, middle-class American mainstream.[31] For others, on the other hand, identifying as Latino or Asian is a way to keep outsiders from racializing them as black. In New York City, for example, Puerto Ricans identify as Latino and Nigerians as African because of the misperceptions and negative stereotypes associated with African Americans.[32]

With their focus on understanding how and to what extent immigrants have been incorporated into host societies, assimilation scholars have often interpreted the development of panethnicity as part of the assimilation process.[33] Rethinking traditional assimilation theory, Richard Alba and Victor Nee define assimilation as the attenuation of ethnic boundaries and suggest that Asian and Latino immigrants become part of mainstream society as their ethnic origins become less important in daily life and as dominant group members come to see the social differences between themselves and new immigrants as diminishing.[34] In this view, when ethnic group members identify as Latino or Hispanic instead of Cuban or Mexican, or as Asian American instead of Korean or Vietnamese, assimilation is taking place. The adoption of a panethnic identity is equated with the erosion of ethnic distinctions, such that becoming Asian American means that the ethnic boundaries between Chinese, Japanese, Koreans, and other Asian-origin groups are declining in importance and salience.

Other scholars understand assimilation as a "segmented" process where the adaptation of immigrants and their children can take different pathways, depending on their experiences with racial discrimination and the amount of human capital they bring with them. Scholars using the segmented assimilation framework have suggested that those who lose their ethnic distinctiveness and adopt a panethnic identity are at risk of being downwardly mobile.[35] Those who identify with the panethnic identity of black or Latino are likely to be treated as a racial minority and to suffer the disadvantages of weaker ties to the immigrant community, which can often serve to protect coethnics in the face of racial discrimination and inequality.[36] Choosing a panethnic identity such as black or Latino seems to rule out the importance of an ethnic or national-origin one and is associated with a bumpy and uneven process of incorporation into mainstream American society. Thus, within both of these assimilation frameworks, ethnic and panethnic identities are conceived of as mutually exclusive or as operating like a seesaw, where the assertion of one is associated with the decline of the other.

For the most part, I do not quarrel with conceptions of panethnicity as a socially constructed political and cultural identity. Clearly, people can take up these identities and use them when needed (that is, to advocate for a panethnic claim), and these identities are certainly salient in the daily lives of some people. I also recognize that panethnicity is part of a broader assimilation process that occurs over time and across generations. "Asian American" and "Latino/Hispanic" are terms or categories made in the United States; for new immigrants to accept such a label is one step in the assimilation process—one where immigrants become racial minorities and eventually, over time, a part of the larger mainstream. However, I build on past notions of panethnicity and argue that ethnic group boundaries expand to create a new, broader identity not simply as part of an assimilation process—that is, not just because the distinctiveness of ethnic groups wanes as they become part of a larger panethnic group. Instead, ethnic group boundaries can be both durable and permeable; when ethnic group boundaries widen to include others, those boundaries are not displaced, and in some cases, they are actually strengthened. Additionally, organizing along ethnic lines neither attenuates nor diminishes panethnicity and can even facilitate it. So while panethnicity may result from assimilation over time and generations, it does not necessarily reflect the demise of ethnic boundaries. The recognition of ethnic diversity and the preservation of ethnic boundaries is one of the hallmarks of panethnicity in the United States, and this book shows how and when this is possible.

THEORIZING BOUNDARY SHIFTS

Standard explanations for how distinct ethnic groups come together to produce a larger, composite group emphasize the state's minority- or majority-making strategies.[37] In the United States, broad identities that transcend ethnic or national-origin boundaries emanate from state-imposed economic and political systems as well as from the dominant group's conceptions of minority groups.[38] Michael Omi and Howard Winant explain that racial formation takes place through the state's macro-level racial projects of developing and enforcing laws based on racial differences and creating official racial categories to enumerate the population, divide up voting districts, and allocate governmental resources.[39] There is also a micro level component to the racial formation process. The state's racial projects reinforce the idea of race as a real biological difference at the micro level when individuals enter into everyday interactions in a social world where race and ethnicity are salient markers.[40] The perceptions and schemas that individuals develop can shape whether they take up racial labels, when they use them, the extent to which these labels organize their daily lives, and whether the ethnic groups that make up a larger racial, regional, or cultural category come to redefine themselves as part of a broader grouping.

The assignment of racial labels by the state and the larger society is a *racialized* process because it classifies groups of people into categories based on physical and cultural differences that are assumed to have a biological basis.[41] Racial groups are viewed and treated as homogeneous with little or no recognition of their differences—in tribe, ethnicity, national origin, immigration history, and culture. Racialization is also in many ways a relational boundary process: how one group is racialized is inextricably linked to how other groups are racialized. Asians in particular have been defined and racialized, relative to blacks and whites, as foreigners (compared to blacks, who are native-born and accepted as American) and as inferior (compared to whites, who are superior in social worth).[42] This racial triangulation matters because the racialization of Asian Americans affects the opportunities, constraints, and possibilities not only for Asian Americans but also for whites, blacks, and Latinos.[43]

In the United States racial categories are also significant because they are organized hierarchically: whites are at or near the top, enjoying social, economic, and political privileges, and below them are other racial minority groups, some of which suffer systematic social, economic, and political disadvantages that have significant implications for their life chances.[44] Moreover, the ways in which the state ascribes racial categories to distinct ethnic groups—how the U.S. government constructs policies and distributes resources along racial lines—influences how groups organize and how they eventually come to see themselves. African Americans, Asians, and Latinos did not enter the United States as clearly formed racial groups, but state policies and political institutions provided new incentives and motivations for each group to draw certain types of boundaries across ethnic, religious, linguistic, and cultural lines.[45] The salience of group boundaries has been shaped by whether current groupings will be useful vehicles for political competition. Groups learn that organizing along particular lines that are recognizable to the state can bring visibility to their claims and interests, as well as social, economic, and political benefits.

In her seminal study on the topic, Yen Le Espiritu argues that it was not simply state-ascribed labels that led Asian Americans to identify as a panethnic group.[46] Ascription by individuals through anti-Asian violence was a key manifestation of the racialization process. Espiritu uses the Vincent Chin case to illustrate how racialized threats encouraged Asian Americans to organize for justice and social change on a panethnic basis rather than along ethnic lines. In the early 1980s, Vincent Chin was attacked and killed by two white autoworkers in Detroit. They had mistaken Chin, a Chinese American, for a Japanese national and blamed him for the job layoffs in the area.[47] Because distinctions based on ethnicity, nativity, and generation had made no difference to Chin's murderers when they attacked him, all Asian ethnicities felt under threat. When Asian ethnic groups were racialized by others (that is, when racial status was made salient), they began to recognize their shared status and common fate and to work across ethnic lines to organize protests and create civil rights organizations.

In the United States, then, past accounts of boundary expansion have argued that when societies are organized on the basis of race—when social and political institutions *and* the public culture adopt racial boundaries as real—this provides the logic for the construction of panethnic identities.[48] The state plays a key role in implementing racialized policies or sanctioning racial discrimination, and individuals racialize others through key interactions. The overarching power of race compels ethnic group members to see themselves as part of a racial group when navigating mainstream institutions and everyday life. Put more positively, ethnic group members often respond to the constraints of racial boundaries by reshaping their identities to be based on a shared history and culture. In challenging racial categories by attaching new meanings to them, ethnic groups thus redefine race.[49] Their panethnic identities are formed through the interaction between the labels ascribed to them by others and their own assertions about a shared history and experience.

Beyond racialization, the expansion of group boundaries during the post–civil rights era was undoubtedly influenced by the rapid social and political changes in the 1960s (see figure 1.1).[50] Social movements forged by African Americans, women, and students challenged the status quo and the white power structure through political organizing, providing a model for social change.[51] To present itself as a democratic world power in the face of stark racial inequalities at home, the U.S. government extended citizenship and civil rights to all groups, thus generating new social, economic, and political opportunities for racial minorities.[52] The United States also abandoned its discriminatory immigration policies and opened the door to all nations, which resulted in diverse streams from around the world.[53] Social movements, federal policy adjustments, and demographic and political shifts contributed to new political rights and a growing and diverse Asian American population, but panethnicity, I argue, was not a natural outgrowth or result; panethnicity had to be achieved and negotiated. As other scholars have noted, the "identity-to-politics link"—the im-

Figure 1.1 The Broad Social Conditions Leading to the Emergence of Panethnicity

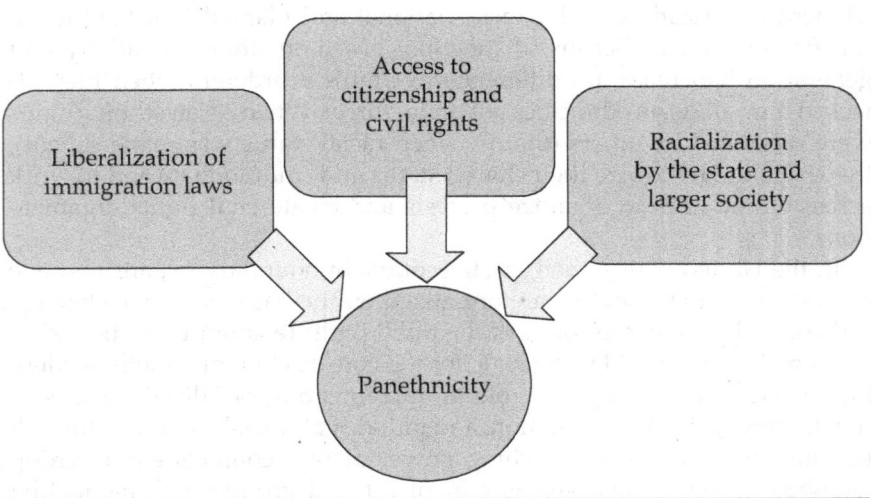

Source: Author's calculations.

plied linkage between demographic categories and a collective group politics—is a complicated and uneven process.[54]

Explanations that point solely to racialization by the state and everyday individuals or the political opportunities unleashed by new federal policies are problematic because they assume that groups will respond to these factors in kind: once policies and categories are set, groups are expected to fall into line accordingly. If this were the case, however, we would see panethnicity everywhere around us. But to the contrary, as we will see throughout the book, panethnicity in the post-1968 era was the exception rather than the rule. Instead of attributing interests and agency to racial groups and assuming these groups are durable, concrete, and bounded entities, a more dynamic understanding of the emergence of panethnic categories is warranted. By distinguishing between groups and categories in our analyses, we can interrogate the relation between them—that is, the extent to which categories and groups correspond and the conditions under which they do so.[55] We can also begin to think about how individual and organizational actors interact with and use these categories, and we can focus on the processes through which ethnicity and race become manifested as categories, institutional forms, or organizational routines.[56] This book makes the case that the broad social forces of political opportunities and an increase in the Asian American population provided the possibility for panethnicity, but to understand when and how ethnic group members acted on the racialized boundaries imposed upon them and challenged established notions of race and racial inequalities, we need to focus on the local conditions and processes that shape the way these groups view and interact with one another.

THE RACIALIZED BOUNDARY FRAMEWORK

The racialized boundary framework advanced in this book suggests that socially constructed categories such as "Asian American" need to be propped up by structural conditions that encourage group formation and by narratives that are used and reproduced by leaders and organizations. Meso-level theories of ethnic conflict and solicarity address the particular ways in which ethnic groups are structured—as concentrated/segmented or as diffuse/integrated—and the impact of these structures on how group members organize, interact, and interpret their interests (for a visual heuristic, see figure 1.2). Such theoretical models focus on gleaning insights from local conditions about the mechanisms through which ethnic group members organize as a larger collective and about the creation and enforcement of ethnic group boundaries.[57] Standard threat and competition models, for example, suggest that because economic and demographic shifts in local areas encourage intergroup contact and competition, ethnic groups engage in collective efforts to exclude others from access to good neighborhoods, schools, and other desired resources, thereby maintaining

Figure 1.2 The Competition and Segregation Models

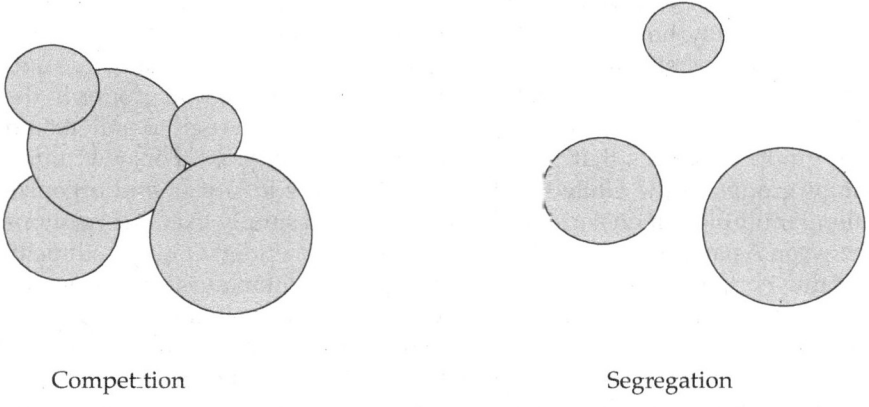

Competition　　　　　　　　　　　　　Segregation

Source: Author's calculations.

or improving their position in the social hierarchy.[58] A number of studies have found support for competition as a key mechanism that heightens group boundaries and results in ethnic collective action.[59] In this case, ethnic group boundaries should expand when Asian ethnic groups, competing with other racial groups for material and symbolic resources, engage in panethnic efforts in order to be a competitive force.

The competition model is useful, but instead I draw upon a segregation model, which suggests that the structural context of segregation, by enabling the development of interethnic ties, trust, and shared interests, facilitates group solidarity. According to this model, the segregation of different social and symbolic groups through institutional arrangements such as occupational segregation facilitates minority group formation and results in ethnic collective action.[60] The centralized workplaces and cooperative work strategies that characterize segregated ethnic labor markets contribute to high levels of interaction among group members, who come to depend on one another for successful work outcomes, thus reinforcing ethnic boundaries.[61] In addition, ethnic solidarity intensifies when ethnic group members have sole access to particular jobs, occupations, and industries because of closed social networks.[62] These dynamics contribute to shared interests and experiences and provide a basis for group solidarity, especially if discrimination—which disadvantages group members by restricting their access to resources and opportunities—is just as responsible for such occupational segregation as ethnic preference. Applying this model to panethnicity, Asian ethnic groups' experience of racial segregation should reinforce the boundary between "us" and "them" (that is, between Asians and other racial groups) and foster common interests and identities across ethnic lines, leading them to see themselves as part of a larger group (Asian Americans) and to engage in panethnic group action.

Additionally, how Asian ethnic groups are organized or distributed in a local labor market relative to one another should matter for panethnic outcomes. Because past research has primarily focused on racial groups in the United States, current theoretical models have not been used to understand the group dynamics that play out *within racial categories*. For new immigrant groups in the United States that can create identities and organize along multiple dimensions, it is not sufficient to simply examine relations between Asians and whites, blacks, or Latinos. To understand panethnicity we must pay attention to how the ethnic groups within racial categories are structured and what the resulting dynamics between them look like. The concentration of Asian ethnic groups in different parts of local labor markets should reinforce ethnic symbols, practices, and beliefs and increase ethnic solidarity. Yet this same dynamic is likely to make it difficult for interaction and trust to develop across ethnic lines, hindering panethnicity.

Beyond the mechanisms of interethnic interaction and the building of network ties and trust, I also argue that the structural condition of racial segregation has produced a social reality, which enables community leaders and activists to build and reproduce a narrative about experiences of inequality and unfair treatment among Asian Americans. To counter the "model minority" stereotype that all Asians are high-achieving, activists and organizers during the post–civil rights era drew upon the fact that Asian ethnic groups were concentrated in low-skilled jobs without access to affordable housing, workplace rights, and health care, and successfully promoted an Asian American identity when forming organizations and engaging in protests.[63] They also highlighted the fact that Asian Americans were not fully integrated into the American mainstream because they continued to be viewed as foreigners with divided loyalties. These leaders were also important as key actors who shaped the interests of community members, and negotiated and navigated the panethnic work. They constructed and reinforced a pan-Asian narrative about the shared social and political histories and experiences of Asian Americans, but they also recognized the diversity of needs and interests among the different national-origin groups when organizing protests and civic actions in the public arena.

Ethnic organizing is another structural condition that has encouraged Asian American panethnicity. Organizing along ethnic lines not only benefits the ethnic community but also provides an infrastructure for ethnic groups working together to support one another's causes or to bolster a broader panethnic effort. *Ethnic organizations* have been central in providing the foundation needed to generate the support of different Asian-origin communities, and *ethnic events* have reinforced the ethnic solidarity so crucial to building a strong pan-Asian community. At times, ethnic organizations have also expanded their boundaries to include other Asian-origin groups as members and constituents in their programs and community served. This mutuality between ethnicity and panethnicity demonstrates the flexible, layered nature of ethnic boundaries, such that organizing along ethnic lines does not diminish but actually enhances panethnic collective action.

Put simply, the racialized boundary framework advanced in this book argues that a structure and narrative must be in place to facilitate panethnic organizing, and it identifies three key social conditions in generating a collective panethnic identity that can cut across language, citizenship, national origin, and phenotype—racial segregation, ethnic organizing, and active leaders. Figure 1.3 depicts how the broader social conditions shown in figure 1.1. are mediated by these proximate social conditions to produce panethnicity.

Figure 1.3 The Proximate Factors Encouraging Panethnic Activity in the Post–Civil Rights Era

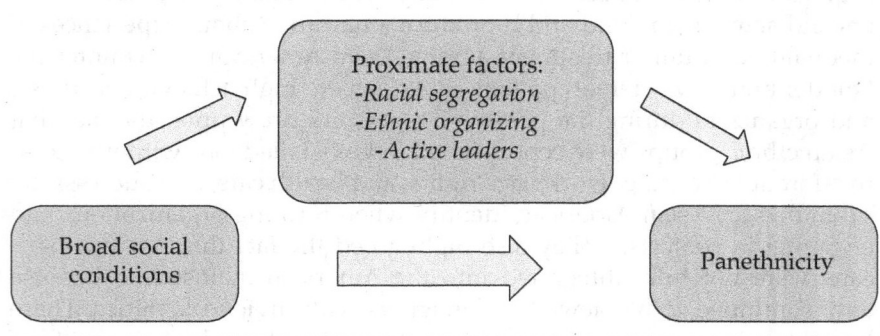

Source: Author's calculations.

ASIAN AMERICANS IN THE UNITED STATES

The label of "Asian American" is used to describe more than forty-five Asian-origin groups, from countries ranging from Bangladesh to Vietnam to South Korea, that differ in terms of culture, language, religion, and even appearance.[64] As the size of the Asian American population has steadily grown over the last twenty-five years, it has become more visible and influential within U.S. society. In 1970 Asian Americans made up only 1.4 percent of the total U.S. population, and as shown in table 1.1, none of the six largest Asian ethnic groups—Chinese, Japanese, Filipino, Asian Indian, Korean, and Vietnamese—had reached 1 million in population. By 2000 Asian Americans made up 4.2 percent of the U.S. population, which translated into 12 million people.[65] In 2010 Asian Americans were the fastest-growing racial group in the United States, they made up the largest share of recent immigrants, and they had a total population of over 17 million.[66]

Nearly two-thirds of the Asian population in the United States today is foreign-born, which complicates the possibility of panethnicity in the contemporary context. Immigrants from different parts of Asia arrive in the United States with their own languages, cultural traditions, and religious beliefs. Generational differences are also prevalent among these groups, and simply finding commonalities within ethnic groups can often be challenging.[67] Referring to the traditional values of the first generation, Tom, a U.S.-born Korean American organizational leader, explained (with a chuckle because of its familiarity as a topic within the Korean community), "It does create a barrier for us. We try to work with it the best we

Table 1.1 Asian American Population, by Decade, 1980–2010

	1980	1990	2000	2010
Chinese	806,040	1,645,472	2,445,363	4,010,114
Filipino	774,652	1,406,770	2,364,815	3,416,840
Indian	361,531	815,447	1,899,599	3,183,063
Japanese	700,974	847,562	1,148,932	1,304,286
Korean	354,593	798,849	1,228,427	1,706,822
Vietnamese	261,729	614,547	1,223,736	1,737,433
Other Asian	—	779,991	1,623,020	2,353,507
Total	3,259,519	8,554,110	12,223,370	17,927,506

Source: See US census reports from Barnes and Bennett (2002, Table 4, p. 9), Gibson and Jung (2002, Table C1 and C3), and Hoeffel et al. (2012, Table 5, p. 14).
Note: U.S. census, 100-percent data. No data are reported for the "Other Asian" category in 1980 because no other Asian ethnic categories were enumerated as part of the race question. In 1990, "Other Asian" was calculated to include Cambodian, Hmong, Laotian, Thai, and other Asian. In 2000 and 2010, totals reported are for Asian alone or in combination with one or more races, and "Other Asian" includes Bangladeshi Cambodian, Hmong, Indonesian, Laotian, Malaysian, Pakistani, Sri Lankan, Taiwanese, Thai, and other Asian.

can, and recognizing that they are also a part of the community is important, and trying to change it is challenging, difficult, and damn near impossible!" Panethnic collaboration and cooperation among second-generation Asian Americans coming of age in many different Asian-origin groups may be somewhat easier because they have the shared experience of growing up in the United States. The second generation shares a language and culture, as well as an understanding of how to organize communities and navigate the political arena, but they still must work across ethnic, generational, and class lines when engaging in panethnic efforts.[68]

Although the majority of Asians in the United States are foreign-born, there is clear variation among the six largest Asian subgroups: Koreans have the highest percentage of foreign-born (72 percent), and the Japanese have the lowest (37 percent). Table 1.2 demonstrates that there are also major socioeconomic differences among some of the Asian ethnic groups. Median household income ranges from $45,980 (Koreans) to $65,700 (Indians), and poverty rates vary as well, with Filipinos experiencing the lowest rates and Koreans the highest. For nearly all of the national-origin groups, nearly half of the adult population has received a college education with the exception of the Vietnamese adult population, only one-quarter of whom have received a B.A. degree or higher. This internal diversity of Asian America—which would be even greater if data were included on additional Asian-origin groups—and the widespread use of the racial category of Asian by government institutions represent a point

Table 1.2 Socioeconomic Indicators for Asian Ethnic Groups, 2010

	Median Household Income	Poverty Rate	B.A. Degree or Higher
Chinese	$65,129	13.8%	50.7%
Filipino	$78,202	6.1	48.5
Indian	$90,711	8.5	70.8
Japanese	$64,551	8.0	47.3
Korean	$50,316	15.8	52.8
Vietnamese	$52,153	15.6	25.1

Source: U.S. Census, 2010 American Community Survey, Selected Population Profiles, S0201.
Note: All indicators are based on respondents who chose a single race category.

of conflict where ethnic group members must negotiate their differences and the groupings imposed on them by the state to create a meaningful community.

This increasing diversity of Asian newcomers has presented a challenge for the formation of a broader collective identity, especially considering that ethnic groups also differ in terms of type of entry, which often is associated with differences in social and human capital.[69] Starting in 1968, immigration flows from East and South Asia have been primarily dictated by immigration policies that emphasize family reunification and occupational demands for low- and high-wage sectors in the United States, such as agriculture, health, engineering, and technology. Meanwhile, those who arrived from Vietnam, Laos, and Cambodia in the 1970s and 1980s entered as refugees due to the political turmoil in Southeast Asia.[70] These variegated flows have contributed to an informal hierarchy within the Asian American population determined by length of time national-origin groups have been in the United States, what immigrants brought with them (education, job skills, financial capital), and the status of the different countries of origin. These immigration and refugee flows also produce different historical and material conditions, which affect whether and how Asian-origin groups are incorporated, accepted, or resisted as part of a larger panethnic community.[71]

Because of their extensive histories in the United States and relatively high levels of human capital, the Chinese and Japanese have been considered the most established groups. Southeast Asians (Vietnamese, Cambodian, Laotian, Hmong), the newest and least assimilated group, are typically located at the bottom of the hierarchy, which further complicates the possibilities of panethnicity. Koreans, Filipinos, and South Asians are located in the middle because of their histories in the United States before 1968 and their higher levels of human capital. This hierarchy may shift as the number of Japanese immigrants continues to decline and as the number of Indian immigrants with occupational skills and high levels of education continues to grow. Countries such as Hong Kong, South Korea, Singapore, and Taiwan are now known for their advanced, high-income economies and highly educated workforces. While they remain the world's fastest-growing developed economies, in recent years attention has shifted toward China and India. The rapid economic transformation of these two countries has increased their status within the international system, and arguably, the status of these groups in the United States has risen accordingly.

In addition to the social and economic hierarchies within the Asian American population, the view of Asian Americans as a model minority that has successfully assimilated into the American mainstream adds complexity to understanding boundary expansion. Asians as a group have made considerable economic and educational gains, even reaching parity or superseding whites on several measures of socioeconomic status.[72] And today Asian Americans make up nearly one-fourth of the student populations at several elite colleges and universities, including Stanford, Harvard, and MIT. The representation of Asian Americans at UC Berkeley and UCLA is even higher, at almost half of the student population.[73] Asian Americans are also doing well in occupational attainment. Nearly half (47 percent) of all Asians work in management and professional occupations, such as financial managers, engineers, teachers, and registered nurses.[74]

But if Asians have successfully assimilated, their ethnic boundaries should be diminishing and they should be an integral part of the American mainstream. As we will see, what the model minority stereotype overlooks is the low level of education among recent arrivals from China and Southeast Asia. New research shows that mobility is possible within one generation, but the fact that not all Asian Americans are at the top of the educational and labor market structures has implications for an expression of panethnic identity that distinguishes Asian Americans from the mainstream.[75] With their increasing numbers and diversity, the conditions under which group boundaries between Asian ethnic groups expand will continue to be a key issue for understanding immigrant incorporation and group formation.

THE ORGANIZATION OF THE BOOK

In terms of what is to come, the following chapters elaborate on the racialized boundary framework as a way of understanding why Asian Americans took up a panethnic label and identity during the post-1968 era. Chapter 2 provides the historical context within which we can understand the widening of ethnic group boundaries. The exclusion of Asian immigrants from social and political citizenship during the pre-1968 era created a durable boundary between Asians and whites. At the same time, racial oppression, the hierarchical structure of work, and antagonistic relations among Asian countries reinforced ethnic boundaries, which hindered the emergence of panethnicity. The strength and durability of ethnic boundaries during this era was reflected in how Asian immigrants developed their own systems of support and primarily organized their communities along ethnic lines. These group boundaries began to loosen during the post-1968 era, in part because of the broader social and political changes of the late 1960s, which brought new social and political rights to a growing, diverse Asian population and also gave rise to the Asian American movement. These conditions undoubtedly set the stage for further panethnic activity in the contemporary period, but as I argue throughout the book, panethnicity was neither a given nor an automatic result of these conditions. Providing this early history is important because many presume that Asian immigrants entered the United States as an already formed racial group with shared interests. In emphasizing that this was not the case, chapter 2 not only demonstrates how panethnicity was shaped by broader social conditions, but also describes it as a deliberate social process with different contributing actors, including the state, student activists, community leaders, and ethnic group members themselves.

The next three chapters focus on the evolution of panethnicity in organizational and collective arenas in the post-1968 era and the conditions under which ethnic group boundaries expanded for Asian Americans. By deliberately focusing on organizational and collective forms of panethnicity, we can empirically "see" group boundaries in action. While racial attitudes and ethnic identities provide insights into the potential tensions and alliances between groups and the extent to which racial or ethnic boundaries are viewed as durable or flexible, attitudes and identities do not necessarily translate into behaviors.[76] Individuals engaged in collective panethnic efforts—that is, working across ethnic lines in pursuit of a common goal, such as challenging discriminatory action or forming a community organization—are asserting group boundaries and redefining racial categories.[77] Additionally, collective and organizational activity that cross ethnic lines must be coordinated and purposeful; group members must build interethnic relations and work together to ensure that the needs and demands of the different Asian ethnic communities are being met. Whether organizing a public event or working with others in an organizational context, group members must devote considerable time and effort to planning and coordination, and oftentimes, they must also participate in intensive outreach efforts to secure the support of in- and out-group members. In short, collective and organizational panethnicity are deliberate accomplishments.

The data I draw on in these chapters come largely from original data sets. The first data set documents the formation of national organizations serving the Asian American community in the United States from 1970 to 2000. The *Encyclopedia of Associations* (*EA*), a comprehensive public directory of nonprofit organizations, was the main source of information about when new organizations entered the field, how organizational characteristics changed over time, and when organizations ceased to exist.[78] Asian ethnic and pan-Asian organizations were located in different regions and metropolitan areas of the United States and served or advocated for ethnic-specific and broader Asian American communities. To construct the second data set, I gathered information on protest and civic activity involving Asian Americans from national newspapers from 1970 to 1998.[79] Newspaper data are useful for providing the "hard news"—the facts related to who, what, when, where, and why—and detailing how groups organize themselves, advocate, and make claims.[80] I searched in the *Los Angeles Times*, the *New York Times*, and the *Chicago Tribune* for accounts of collective ethnic and panethnic action events—protests, demonstrations, campaigns, public celebrations—across the United States over a nearly three-decade period in which Asian-origin groups were engaged in such coordinated group action.

The organization and event data sets both provide conservative estimates of pan-Asian activity: *EA* only captures the formation of large, established organizations operating at the national level, and major mainstream newspapers report on publicly visible events that are potentially relevant for social and political change.[81] Thus, for my purposes, these data sets capture the organizations and events that serve as leading indicators of the level of Asian American panethnicity across the United States and can provide insights into panethnic boundary formation, but they are by no means comprehensive or exhaustive in measuring panethnic activity in all of its diverse forms. We might think of the formation of national organizations as a top-down process initiated and carried out by elites, and of collective action as a grassroots process that develops from within the larger community. But the distinction is not always clear-cut: many national organizations began as grassroots initiatives with a handful of volunteers (chapter 3), and some of the leaders and activists who had a hand in organizing the masses to engage in protest and civic actions were part of the political and educational elite (chapter 4).

In chapters 3 and 4, I discuss the ways in which ethnic identities were transformed into panethnic ones through collective organizing efforts during the post–civil rights era. Building upon the founding moments of social movement activism that contributed to the formation of new panethnic organizations (chapter 2), chapter 3 describes the development of the national pan-Asian organizational field in the United States and emphasizes that after 1970 new organizations began to focus on serving a broader Asian American community rather than advancing cross-cultural education and trade, as their predecessors had done. Beyond the broad social and political opportunities that emerged in the post-1968 era thanks to civil rights, citizenship, and immigration legislation, local conditions also shaped the ability of Asian ethnic groups to organize along panethnic lines. Specifically, interracial contact and competition did not activate panethnic boundaries, but when Asians found themselves clustered together in the occupational structure, they began to form panethnic organizations. While racial segregation produced shared interests, network ties, and trust among Asian ethnic groups, leaders also played an important role in developing and reinforcing the pan-Asian narrative, which was critical to generating and sustaining panethnicity.

Chapter 4 elaborates on the dynamic nature of ethnic boundaries by highlighting the fact that while Asian Americans were engaging in panethnic collective action during the post-1968 era, they were also organizing along ethnic lines in the public arena. Importantly, ethnicity and panethnicity not only coexisted but were complementary, as one facilitated the other. In addition to illustrating the layered nature of ethnic boundaries, this chapter also highlights the ways in which leaders constructed and reproduced panethnic narratives at collective action events that emphasized the social and political commonalities among Asian Americans yet recognized the diversity of needs and interests across ethnic groups.

Throughout the book, I also draw on interviews with fifty leaders, staff members, and program directors from forty community-based nonprofit organizations representing Japanese, Chinese, Filipino, Korean, Southeast Asian, and Asian Indian populations and pan-Asian organizations serving multiple Asian-origin groups in San Francisco and Oakland. Additionally, I use information from public documents on both the organizations in my sample and organizations in the broader San Francisco Bay Area, including program fliers, annual reports, press releases, newspaper articles, newsletters, and online organizational materials.[82] I use pseudonyms to protect the identities of the organizations and organizational leaders I interviewed, but I refer to the actual names of organizations and leaders when I cite publicly available documents, such as websites or newspaper articles.

The interviews, which were conducted in 2003–2004, provide insights into how community leaders think about ethnic and panethnic boundaries: who they view as part of the pan-Asian community, when and why they engage in panethnic efforts, what narratives they use when adopting new panethnic practices, and what factors hinder interethnic cooperation. Many of the subjects had worked in the community-based organization (CBO) nonprofit sector for over twenty years and were able to provide detailed retrospective information about the origins of the organization, shifts in its mission and programs, and changes in the Asian American community. The interview and documentary data also allowed me to move beyond panethnic organizations and events on the national stage and focus on the practices of local community-based organizations to gain a sense of the flexibility and reach of ethnic boundaries. The San Francisco–Oakland area provided a useful context for this study given its history of Asian American immigration, activism, and progressive politics. But while we would expect panethnicity to flourish in the Bay Area—and to some extent it does—panethnicity is a process that must be negotiated, developed, and maintained.

Chapter 5 draws most heavily on the interview and documentary data and further investigates the processes that encourage group boundaries to widen by taking a closer look at the organizational landscape in San Francisco and Oakland. It emphasizes the key role that leaders play in prioritizing panethnic programs, building ties with other ethnic communities, and supporting one another's causes, while at the same time working to maintain ethnic boundaries, all of which contributes to the larger purpose of panethnicity: recognizing ethnic diversity while creating a common panethnic boundary. This chapter also shows the impact of the panethnic model—which is now generally accepted by mainstream institutions and ethnic communities—on ethnic organizations and the ways in which leaders of ethnic organizations have framed the transition to panethnic practices. Organizational practices and leader narratives not only reveal who is part of the panethnic community but they also provide insights into the flexibility and durability of ethnic group boundaries.

Finally, in chapter 6 I address the broader implications of this work for understanding boundary processes by discussing how the theoretical ideas presented here relate to other groups, both within and outside the United States. In hopes of providing some direction for future research, I also consider questions that remain about boundary expansion and assimilation, the relationship between organizing and identity, and the durability of race.

A NOTE ON LANGUAGE AND CONCEPTS

Throughout the book I use the terms "ethnic" and "national origin" interchangeably, though I recognize that in some instances an ethnic group is not also a national-origin group—for example, the ethnic Chinese from Vietnam and the Hmong from Laos. Also, I often use "racial" and "panethnic" to describe the same group. "Racial" refers to groups that have been racially categorized in U.S. society, such as Asian, Latino, black, and white. Because these racial categories continue to be used by social institutions and remain significant in access to rewards and opportunities, and ultimately life chances, I use them here too. "Panethnic" refers to a grouping or category that is defined by the group itself, within the constraints imposed by the larger society. Ethnic group members, by taking part in creating their own collective histories, cultures, and identities, are challenging and redefining current notions of race, despite the fact that group boundaries are often set by the larger society, and serve as reminders of group positions within the racial hierarchy. I use the overarching term "community" to refer to a grouping of people who may or may not share a communal relationship or belief in a shared history and culture. At times, "community" refers to a population, category, or group, and it may not yet be clear whether group members actually understand themselves as part of a broader grouping. Communities need not be unified and cohesive, but they may be identified by certain cultural, ethnic, or religious markers. At times, in the following chapters, I also discuss panethnicity as identity, even though my data are about panethnicity as activity, practice, and narrative. I do not have original data on the strength and meanings that individuals attribute to their own identities. Instead, I examine social action at the collective and organizational levels, and use theory and past research to guide how actions relate to identity. I also draw upon leaders' narratives and organization documents to understand how a collective identity—a connection with a broader category or community—is formed, expressed, and deployed.[83]

Focusing on panethnicity in the United States as a way to understand group boundary formation is useful because it is a social phenomenon that will likely endure in the United States and beyond, owing to the forces of globalization, immigration, and the static nature of social hierarchies based on race, ethnicity, language, or culture. As immigrants from Asia, Africa, and Latin America enter the United States, Europe, and other parts of the world, they are likely to be categorized according to race, skin color, language, or appearance even if they see themselves as Chinese, Nigerian, Mexican, or Iranian. The insights provided in this book about the mechanisms and processes that encourage distinct ethnic, linguistic, and cultural groups to form and organize around a broader identity, such as European, Latino, Yoruba, or Muslim, have many implications for group formation processes, immigrant integration, and intergroup relations. More generally, a greater understanding of how group boundaries expand has implications for inequality because social groupings are often associated with ranking systems and inequality, and when group boundaries shift and change, it is possible for minority groups to disrupt this process.

Chapter 2 | Beginnings: The Durability of Ethnic Boundaries in the Pre-1968 Era

EARLY IMMIGRANTS FROM Asia arrived in the United States with identities linked to nation, region, dialect, hometown, and clan. Japanese immigrants arrived from prefectures such as Kumamoto, Hiroshima, and Yamaguchi, and the Chinese who migrated to the United States were either Punti or Hakka, groups associated with differences in dialect, appearance, and region.[1] They organized by developing associations and engaging in collective efforts based on finer group distinctions, and eventually they widened their boundaries to form ethnic groups. Asian immigrants viewed each other as ethnically distinct, and as we will see, some Asian-origin groups made deliberate efforts to differentiate themselves from one another. But the larger society perceived these newcomers as the same—as Orientals, Asiatics, Mongolians, and, ultimately, non-whites.

In 1790 American policymakers deemed that only "free white persons" had access to citizenship through naturalization, and in 1870 the Naturalization Act was amended to include blacks but not Asian immigrants.[2] In response, Asians did not further expand their ethnic boundaries to protest their political exclusion. Instead, they attempted to cross ethnic boundaries as individuals, by contesting U.S. citizenship law and the definition of whiteness. Asian immigrants initiated legal challenges from 1887 to 1923, culminating in two key U.S. Supreme Court decisions in *Ozawa v. United States* (1922) and *United States v. Bhagat Singh Thind* (1923). The Court eventually struck down these boundary-crossing efforts and interpreted the law as extending citizenship rights only to "white men from Europe and their descendants."[3] Although these decisions were made in regard to Japanese and Indian immigrants, the Court applied its rulings to other

Asians as well, bolstered by the logic of racial exclusion used in the Immigration Act of 1917, which had prohibited immigrants residing in the "Asiatic Barred Zone" from legal entry into the United States.[4] The U.S. Supreme Court decisions essentially categorized immigrants from Japan, China, India, Thailand, Vietnam, and Malaysia together as unassimilable noncitizens.[5] Soon after, in 1924, the Immigration and Nationality Act excluded all persons ineligible for citizenship from entry into the United States, thereby cutting off immigration from other Asian countries not named as part of the Asiatic Barred Zone (namely Japan) and further solidifying the racial category of "Asian" and the boundary between Asians and whites.[6]

For the most part, Asian immigrants faced economic and political exclusion during the pre-1968 era. Despite federal and local laws that restricted access to citizenship and civil rights, prohibited property ownership, and barred entry into skilled trades, Asian immigrants found creative ways to survive and build communities.[7] While U.S.-born Asians had more rights than their immigrant parents, they were still treated as second-class citizens and often faced economic and social exclusion on the basis of their race and "foreignness."[8] Threat and racialization explanations for panethnicity suggest that when the state and larger society treat different ethnic groups as a racial category, not making distinctions based on national origin or immigrant status, and threatens a group's livelihood, ethnic boundaries should expand and groups should organize on a panethnic basis. Yet exclusionary treatment, such as the restriction of their social, economic, and political rights, did not generate panethnicity among Asian ethnic groups; instead, ethnic boundaries remained durable.

This chapter provides a historical context within which to understand the emergence of panethnicity among Asian Americans in the contemporary era. It elaborates on the divisions that Asian immigrants experienced along national-origin lines during the early period of Asian immigration in the United States from the late 1800s to the mid-1900s, a period I refer to as "the pre-1968 era." Social conditions during this period reinforced ethnic boundaries and hindered interethnic cooperation. Divide-and-conquer strategies were enacted by employers, threats of replacement and exclusion emanating from the white power structure, and relations between home countries were antagonistic, making it difficult for Asian ethnic groups to create a shared identity. The dramatic social and political changes in the late 1960s helped to loosen ethnic boundaries and give rise to the Asian American movement and pan-Asian ideology, which Asian Americans drew on later in this era when organizing in the public arena to call attention to the issues faced by their communities. The social conditions that arose out of the expansion of civil rights, citizenship, and immigration policies set the stage and provided the logic and motivation for immigrant groups to organize along a broader group boundary.

THE DURABILITY OF ETHNIC BOUNDARIES
Demand for Immigrant Labor and Eventual Exclusion

The first Asian immigrants arrived in the United States in successive waves and were primarily regarded as labor, not as full citizens. When employers needed laborers in the factories and fields, they welcomed immigrants with open arms. But when white workers and local residents viewed the newcomers as competitors for scarce resources, such as jobs, nativist campaigns for immigrant exclusion erupted, leading policymakers to pass exclusion legislation and employers to recruit new groups to fill labor demand. This pattern of labor demand, immigrant supply, economic threat, and eventual exclusion, which I elaborate on in this chapter, continued through the early 1900s. Looking at how these dynamics shaped immigration flows as well as the ways in which Asian-origin groups related to one another helps us to understand the durability of ethnic boundaries during the pre-1968 era.

The Chinese provide a useful example of labor demand and eventual exclusion. Chinese immigrants first arrived in the United States to seek their fortunes during the California Gold Rush of the mid-nineteenth century. While the vast majority of Chinese settled in California, they also lived and worked in the Pacific Northwest, the Southwest, the East Coast, and the South.[9] They were first recruited to work on the construction of the transcontinental railroad, and in the late 1800s white employers began to hire Chinese labor in industries such as farming and manufacturing. Employers believed that the new immigrants were easier to control and could be used as strikebreakers to quash white and black workers' demands for higher wages.[10]

Eventually, the presence of Chinese laborers combined with a weakened economy to give rise to a fervent anti-Chinese movement on the East and West Coasts.[11] White workers claimed that the Chinese were unfair competitors and feared that their entry into skilled trades such as cigar and shoe manufacture would lead to the demise of American workers and their families.[12] In 1878, a report by the California State Senate Committee on Chinese Immigration, stated that "the Chinese are ... able to underbid the whites in every kind of labor. They can be hired in masses; they can be managed and controlled like unthinking slaves."[13] Politicians agreed and also claimed that the new immigrants were a threat to American ways of life. Because of their non-Christian religious beliefs, their use of opium, and their "strange" foods, non-Western clothing, and distinctive appearance, Chinese immigrants were viewed as heathens.[14] The larger public believed they were un-American, unassimilable, and genetically unsuited for American life.[15] Exclusionists also emphasized that Chinese women—deemed "prostitutes" by government officials—were a significant source of disease and posed a threat to the health of American families.[16] Given such arguments, excluding the Chinese on the basis of culture, economics, and health made sense to policymakers. In 1882 Congress passed the Chinese Exclusion Act, which barred Chinese laborers from entering the United States and allowed only selected classes of Chinese immigrants to apply for admission.[17] In 1884 the act was amended so that no Chinese could legally enter the United States. Without Chinese women immigrating to the United States, families could not settle, reproduce, and build productive communities. Once considered "one of the most worthy of our newly adopted citizens," the Chinese were no longer welcome.[18]

Japanese immigrants and smaller numbers of Korean and Asian Indian immigrants entered the United States during the height of the Chinese exclusion movement in the late 1800s. Initially, they were welcomed as cheap labor in the agriculture, fishing, and railroad construction industries. Like the Chinese, they faced limited opportunities within as well as outside of these industries. Soon white workers began to regard Japanese laborers as economic competitors; given Japan's increasing geopolitical power and the increasing number of Japanese immigrants who purchased land to farm in Western states, white hostilities began to grow.[19] The press did its part to heighten xenophobic fears. The *San Francisco Chronicle* participated in an anti-Japanese campaign for over a year and published inflammatory headlines such as "The Yellow Peril—How Japanese Crowd Out the White Race" and "The Japanese Invasion, The Problem of the Hour."[20]

With the success of the Chinese Exclusion Act, white workers formed organizations whose main purpose was to organize and lobby for the exclusion of all Asian laborers. In 1905 a coalition of over sixty labor unions formed the Japanese and Korean Exclusion League in San Francisco. Ironically, the main leaders were immigrants themselves, but of European descent. Members of the American Federation of Labor (AFL), a powerful U.S. labor union, unanimously passed a resolution supporting the goals of the newly formed exclusion league, concurring that "the Mongolian and Caucasian races can never assimilate," and "the presence of these Mongolian-Malay and Hindoo peons in any great number among us will deteriorate the American standard of living."[21] For the leaders and members of the Japanese and Korean Exclusion League and the AFL, all Asian immigrants were similar because they held the same lowly position as

Table 2.1 The Asian Population in the United States, 1910–1960, by Ethnic Group

	Japanese	Chinese	Filipino	Indian	Korean
1910	72,157	71,531	160	2,545	462
1920	111,010	61,639	5,603	2,507	1,224
1930	138,834	74,954	45,208	3,130	1,860
1940	126,947	77,504	45,563	2,405	1,711
1950	141,768	117,629	61,636	—	—
1960	464,332	237,292	176,310	—	—

Source: Gibson and Jung (2002).

cheap laborers who threatened the strength of white labor. Under pressure from labor unions, the Gentlemen's Agreement of 1907 and 1908 barred the entry of Japanese laborers into the United States.[22] Korean and Indian laborers continued to arrive after 1908, and Filipinos entered unskilled jobs in agriculture, mining, and domestic service in larger numbers after the Immigration Acts of 1917 and 1924 cut off immigration from the rest of Asia.[23]

Filipinos, like the other Asian immigrants before them, came to the United States in the 1920s to fulfill the needs of employers in domestic service, fisheries, and agriculture in California and the Pacific Northwest.[24] Table 2.1 displays the growth in their numbers after 1910. Even though Filipinos competed with Mexicans and other Asian ethnic groups for farm work, white workers perceived them as a competitive threat. The California Building Trades Council fueled perceptions of widespread job competition and falsely charged that Filipinos were "forcing their way into the building industry, many of them working as engineers, painters, electricians, carpenters' helpers, and laborers."[25] This led to local practices of exclusion. The California Joint Immigration Committee, the American Federation of Labor, and the American Legion all passed resolutions for Filipino exclusion in the late 1920s.[26] Despite anti-Filipino sentiment, Filipino immigrants could not be excluded from the United States because inhabitants of the territories ceded from Spain in 1898—Guam, Puerto Rico, and the Philippines—were U.S. nationals who could move freely to and from the U.S. mainland but did not have citizenship rights. Filipino laborers could be excluded only if independence was granted to the Philippines. Congress deliberated about the issue and likened Filipinos to Chinese and Japanese immigrants, eventually supporting exclusion. In 1934, with the support of an unlikely coalition comprising nativists and Filipino nationalists, Congress passed the Tydings-McDuffie Act (the Philippine Independence Act), which established the Philippines as a commonwealth and classified Filipino immigrants as aliens who could legally be excluded from the United States.[27]

This process of *replacement and succession* shaped the interethnic relations among Asian immigrants. On the one hand, because immigrant groups arrived successively in the United States, one after the other, direct interethnic competition was not initially prevalent. Instead, white workers campaigned for the exclusion of these groups and often racialized them in different ways. The Chinese were portrayed as heathens, the Japanese as colonizers, and the Filipinos as dependents due to their semicolonial status.[28] These actions reinforced ethnic boundaries between Asian immigrant groups while also strengthening the boundary between whites and Asians. On the other hand, while exclusionary legislation kept new immigrants from arriving, many Asian immigrants remained in the United States and at times were forced to work in the same industries and locales as other Asian ethnic groups. Despite their proximity to one another, working in the same jobs under the same poor conditions, *the division of labor*—the way in which ethnic groups were organized in relation to one another in the factories and fields—reinforced ethnic boundaries by keeping Asians from recognizing their shared interests.

Ethnic Divisions of Labor and Ethnic Competition

Organizing large numbers of workers across ethnic lines to participate in labor strikes would have been an effective strategy to negotiate with growers and other employers for higher wages and better working conditions in the pre-1968 period. The divisive work conditions and the hierarchical structure of work, however, hindered any such panethnic organizing as employers often pitted different Asian ethnic groups against one another in the factories and fields. In the early 1900s, the Japanese were brought in to replace and undercut Chinese laborers on the sugar plantations of Hawaii.[29] Soon after their arrival, Japanese laborers began to agitate against owners because of the low wages and harsh working conditions. They became known as troublemakers: by 1910 they had organized forty labor strikes and cost plantation owners an estimated $2 million.[30] A local newspaper with plantation interests in mind encouraged the threat of replacement to keep the Japanese in line: "To discharge every Jap and put in newly-imported laborers of another race would be a most impressive object lesson to the little brown men on all the plantations."[31] Plantation owners recruited Filipinos, Puerto Ricans, Portuguese, and Spanish workers to Hawaii to counter the demands of the

Japanese.[32] Although these ethnic groups worked on the same plantations, employers continued to separate them and maintain an ethnic division of labor by paying different wages for the same work.[33] For example, the Japanese were paid $18 a month while the Portuguese and Puerto Ricans received $22.50 for the same amount of work.[34] This tactic led to animosity between the groups, which was exactly what the employers desired: laborers who were in conflict with one another could not collectively organize and rise up against owners. The agriculture, fishing, and lumber industries depended on the labor of hundreds of workers, and a work stoppage would have represented a significant loss to owners.

Interethnic relations during this period must also be understood within a broader power structure which heightened Asian immigrants' fear of exclusion. During the anti-Chinese movement, the Japanese feared that they would be identified with the Chinese and targeted for exclusion. To counter anti-Japanese sentiment, Japanese immigrant leaders attempted to improve the conditions of the Japanese community so that whites would accept them.[35] They encouraged their community members to adopt the Western style of dress, learn English, and embrace American customs to distinguish themselves from the Chinese.[36] Japanese men would often be seen in jackets and ties while Chinese men wore queues and traditional Chinese dress. In addition to encouraging assimilation, Japanese immigrant leaders launched intensive anti–Chinese gambling campaigns to eradicate the influence and "moral corruption" of the Chinese. One effective tactic used to discourage the Japanese from gambling in Chinatown was social ostracism. Japanese gamblers were turned over to the police, their names were published in local newspapers, and Japanese boardinghouses were prohibited from accommodating them.[37] These anti–Chinese gambling campaigns served to eliminate "the unsavory feature of Japanese immigrant life" and, more importantly, maintained a distinction between the Japanese and Chinese that was visible to white elites.[38]

Whites not only were in charge of making decisions about immigration and exclusion policy but they also dominated the political economy.[39] Agriculture was a major industry on the West Coast, and whites, who occupied the top position in the racial hierarchy, owned virtually all of the land. They did not allow immigrant tenant farmers and sharecroppers much autonomy in cultivating, harvesting, shipping, and marketing crops. In addition, there were few desirable options for Asian immigrants outside of agricultural labor. Under such conditions, the need for survival and the threat of replacement led each Asian ethnic group to fend for itself. Relations between Asian ethnic groups in the early 1900s can be characterized as *competitive* because the structure of work and the racial hierarchy reinforced one another.

To illustrate this point, after the Gentlemen's Agreement in 1907 and 1908 created a shortage of Japanese laborers, white employers recruited Indian and Filipino immigrants into the agriculture industry.[40] Indians worked for lower wages than the Japanese, and before long their numbers were steadily increasing. This shift concerned Japanese tenant farmers, who feared that white landowners would eventually replace Japanese workers with Indians.[41] In response, the Japanese organized a community-wide campaign to encourage the employment of more Japanese field hands and characterized Indians as "the enemy of our working class countrymen." Although the Japanese were well below whites in the racial hierarchy, they viewed themselves as occupying a position above all other Asian "races" and desired to maintain such a position.

In the 1920s, when Alien Land Laws constrained the ability of the Japanese to own and lease land, and the Immigration Acts of 1917 and 1924 cut off immigration from Asia, an influx of new labor from the Philippines arrived to work in the fields of the San Joaquin Valley and other parts of California.[42] The Japanese viewed these newcomers as a "racial menace" and a threat to their position in the economic order. To preserve their position above Filipinos, the Japanese invoked a racial ideology derived from Imperialist Japan. In the 1930s, an editorial in *Nichibei Shinbun,* one of the largest and most influential Japanese American newspapers, clearly expressed this ideology:

> The Japanese race, possessing superior racial traits unparalleled in the world, is destined for ceaseless development and prosperity. On the other hand, those people [Filipinos], whose homeland contents itself with being a third-class nation ... would see nothing but poverty and misery in their lives. If their lazy blood becomes part of the Japanese race through interracial marriage, it would eventually offset the racial superiority of the Japanese.[43]

Instead of organizing with Filipinos and Indians to fight against white landowners, the Japanese worked to maintain a racial hierarchy with white elites in the top stratum, Japanese tenant farmers in the middle, and Filipino and Indian laborers at the bottom.[44] Not surprisingly, Asian ethnic groups saw themselves as different "races" and often worked to distinguish themselves from one another. They feared exclusion and removal, and to maintain their position in the racial hierarchy and gain whites' favor they distinguished themselves and even denigrated other ethnic groups. Not allowing Asian immigrants to naturalize as U.S. citizens because of their foreignness and constructing racialized images of and ideologies about Asian immigrants relative to whites and blacks—what Claire Jean Kim refers to as civic ostracism and relative valorization—secured a cheap immigrant labor supply without political rights. Not surprisingly, this broader context of Asian vulnerability and white oppression hindered Asian interethnic solidarity and cooperation.[45]

Hostile Relations Between Homeland Countries

Strained relations between home countries and the broader context of racial oppression also shaped interethnic relations among Asian-origin groups, making it difficult for groups to see possibilities beyond ethnic boundaries. For Korean immigrants in the United States, Japan's colonization of Korea in the early 1900s had left them without a nation and home.[46] Under Japanese rule, Koreans experienced repressive conditions. With their countrymen stripped of their land and culture, Korean immigrants had no choice but to remain in the United States. While they continued to make a living in the United States, as farmers and field hands, many Koreans contributed a portion of their wages to the independence movement.[47] Korean immigrants also organized their families around the movement, as parents enrolled their children in Korean schools and sent them to Korean churches. These two key institutions were the basis for Korean cultural identity and nationalistic education.[48]

Not surprisingly, the situation abroad strained relations and reinforced group boundaries between the Koreans and Japanese living in the United States. Korean immigrants did not typically socialize with Japanese in the United States, and even in times of need, Koreans refused help from the Japanese. When the building that housed the Korean Mutual Assistance Association was destroyed in the 1906 San Francisco earthquake, the association announced that it did not want any assistance from the Japanese: "We are calling your attention to the fact that we are anti-Japanese, so we shall not accept any relief fund from the Japanese consulate. We shall reject any interference of Japanese authorities in our community affairs in any manner. No matter how great a plight we are in, we must always refuse Japanese help. We'd rather die free than under Japanese jurisdiction."[49]

Koreans were not the only group to express hostility toward the Japanese. Japan's increasing aggression toward China affected relations between Chinese and Japanese immigrants in the United States. Seeking control and influence over territories in East Asia, Japan invaded and occupied China after colonizing Korea. Reflecting the Chinese view of Japanese immigrants in the United States, the *Chinese-Western Daily*, a Chinese newspaper based in San Francisco, claimed that the bias toward the Japanese exacted through the Alien Land Laws was due to "the shameless greedy nature of the Japanese, who regarding California as a good place for colonization, seized land ... and swindled for any profit."[50] The hostilities between Japan and China continued through the 1930s, and at the height of the war effort against Japan in 1937, Chinatown communities organized massive campaigns to raise funds to send to China and participated in rallies to stop the shipment of American scrap metal to Japan.[51] Chinese schools in San Francisco held demonstrations and marches where students sang the Chinese anthem and speakers encouraged students to do their part for China.[52]

In defense of Japan's actions in Korea and China, the Japanese in the United States asserted a strong national identity. With funding from the Japanese government, Japanese language schools took up a nationalistic agenda and sponsored educational programs about Japanese policies in East Asia, as well as its history, society, and ideology.[53] Organizations such as the Japanese Chamber of Commerce in Los Angeles distributed political pamphlets explaining Japan's position toward China.[54]

The conflict between homeland countries had a profound effect on relations between Asian immigrants in the United States. Even though Japan's occupation of Korea and China was not soon forgotten by Chinese and Korean immigrants, the experience of oppression in their homelands was not enough for them to band together against the Japanese. For Chinese and Korean immigrants, any such effort would have been secondary to the larger struggle of simply surviving and sending funds back to their families and relatives, in the hope of one day returning to their homeland.

Asian ethnic groups often shared the same grievances about wages, working conditions, and survival, but they did not develop a common strategy or identity. If they did recognize their common plight, they chose to solve their problems using their own strategies. At times, Asian ethnic groups organized together, but these coalitions were few compared to the strikes and boycotts organized along ethnic lines.[55] It was unlikely that a panethnic narrative would emerge considering that there was no history of prolonged interethnic cooperation among Asian ethnic groups; the ethnic divisions of labor constructed by employers to maintain power and control, whites' dominance of the political economy, and the lack of civil rights for Asians had all served to heighten ethnic rather than racial boundaries.[56] Fearing replacement, exclusion, and removal, immigrant groups ended up fending for themselves instead of banding together as one. Since Asian immigrants were newcomers, they were also learning how to simply survive and adapt to American ways of life. They did not develop cooperative ties with other ethnic communities but instead found ways to create separate ethnic communities within a society that was largely hostile.

ORGANIZATIONAL LIFE AND EARLY FORMS OF RESISTANCE

During the early twentieth century, Asian immigrant laborers—Chinese, Japanese, Koreans, Indians, and Filipinos—organized their communities along ethnic lines, segregated from the rest of the larger society.[57] Mostly men, they initially had difficulty finding housing, as the Alien Land Laws, restrictive covenants, and local residents made it clear that newcomers were not welcome.[58] They settled among coethnics in rural farming communities in California and in cities such as New York and San Francisco.[59]

Despite the fact that separate, concentrated areas of Indians were perceived as filthy, poverty-ridden urban slums, which marked their residents as undesirable "others," the social organization of these ethnic communities provided an important basis for social support and collective organizing.[60] Asian immigrants lacked social and political rights, but they were able to organize their own communities to address issues related to working conditions and homeland politics. Some collective efforts were formed along class and occupational lines, but they often coincided with ethnicity.

Chinatowns in San Francisco, Los Angeles, Portland, Chicago, New York, and Boston emerged in the mid to late 1800s, well before other Asian immigrant enclaves. When the anti-Chinese movement forced Chinese laborers out of the general labor market and skilled trades, they began to open up small businesses, such as laundries and grocery stores, and to manufacture cigars, shoes, and clothing.[61] Unlike many immigrant ghettos, Chinatowns were largely self-supporting: governing associations and businesses in the Chinese community supplied jobs, economic aid, social service, and protection.[62] Chinese immigrants organized themselves along family or clan lines, which were based on last names; each Chinese immigrant also belonged to a *huiguan*, an association based on regional districts of Kwangtung Province.[63] These district and family associations focused on the well-being of the entire community and often served as de facto governments within Chinatowns.[64] The Chinese Consolidated Benevolent Association directly governed the different district associations and functioned as a benevolent and protective organization, often representing the Chinese community to outsiders.[65] Various *tongs*, or fraternal organizations, and guilds were also formed in Chinatowns to protect the economic interests of workers.[66]

After the Chinese Exclusion Act of 1882 was passed, the Chinese population significantly declined. For the newer, younger immigrants who remained in the United States, regional and clan loyalties became less important than they were for the older generation and ethnicity emerged as a shared identity.[67] In 1904 the Chinese Exclusion Act was extended, and in response, the Chinese abroad participated in a movement to protest the poor treatment of the Chinese in the United States and boycotted American goods in August 1905.[68] Companies in major Chinese cities such as Shanghai and Canton canceled orders for American goods, and people across China refused to purchase American products. With the support of immigrant and ethnic organizations in the United States, Chinese Americans also joined the movement by publicly speaking out against Chinese exclusion, sending funds abroad in support of their countrymen, and publishing materials about the boycott movement.[69]

Despite interethnic tensions, Japanese, Korean, and Indian immigrants settled in and near established Chinatowns in the early 1900s because of the low rents and available services.[70] With the growing number of Japanese laborers in the United States, separate ethnic economies in San Francisco, Los Angeles, and Seattle—Japanese-owned hotels, boardinghouses, restaurants, and grocery stores—developed to fulfill their needs.[71] Japanese immigrants initially organized themselves according to old homeland regions because doing so was familiar, but also because cities, villages, and neighborhoods were often too small to provide the basis for viable organizations.[72] These prefectural associations provided economic aid and social events for the community and were the primary association group larger than the family. Soon, ethnic newspapers, professional associations, churches, and other businesses evolved in the areas known as Japantown and Little Tokyo.

Since agriculture played such a large role in the immigrant economy, the Japanese also formed agricultural associations in the early 1900s to maintain their position in the California produce sector.[73] These associations, representing extensive networks within the Japanese community, disseminated information about new farming techniques, purchased supplies in bulk from wholesalers, and collectively set the wages for farmworkers.[74] Other Japanese associations were formed in urban areas to protect the community's economic interests and sustain ethnic solidarity. In response to the increasing anti-Japanese sentiment, Japanese immigrants formed the United Japanese Deliberative Council of America, a network of eleven affiliated local councils throughout California.[75] When the Gentlemen's Agreement between the United States and Japan was struck in 1908, the Japanese consulate general founded the Japanese Association of America (JAA) to keep track of all Japanese in the United States and to protect their rights.[76] In theory, all Japanese residents, despite their village and prefecture differences, were members of the organization.

The Korean community also organized itself largely on the basis of ethnicity. Beginning in the early 1900s, the Korean community was highly involved in the movement to free Korea from Japan's domination and formed churches, organizations, and schools to preserve a Korean national identity and serve as patriotic forums.[77] The Korean National Association (KNA) was created in 1909 to coordinate the resistance efforts of several different nationalist organizations and eventually became the key organization of the nationalist movement.[78] The KNA set up Korean language schools and published textbooks, collected funds, and organized rallies for the Korean independence movement, all with the goal of maintaining a strong Korean national identity.[79] The organization also supported military training centers that prepared young men for battle with the Japanese.[80] The churches established by Koreans in the United States served not only as places of worship and social support but as venues for discussing politics, raising funds, and organizing support for the Korean independence struggle.[81]

Dora Yum Kim, a Korean immigrant who was born in 1921, described what the Korean Methodist Church—the first Korean church in the United States (formed in 1905)—meant in her life as she was growing up in San Francisco: "I remember the church on the Powell Street. It was really much more than a church. It was a social center, it was the only place that the Koreans could get together for support or socializing. . . . At church, there seemed to be two topics of conversation. People talked about each other . . . and told stories about Japanese occupation."[82] Dora's narrative highlights the importance of the Korean church in bringing the community together on an ethnic basis.

Like the Japanese, Filipino laborers settled near Chinatowns because they provided access to boardinghouses, restaurants, and other services.[83] Filipinos resided in hotels and boardinghouses between seasonal work within informal ethnic enclaves that provided both comfort and protection. Soon, Filipinos created their own services, such as barbershops, restaurants, and pool halls. However, Manilatowns lacked the stability and permanency of Chinatowns and Japantowns. Part of this was due to racial discrimination in the housing market, which prevented their enclaves from becoming stable neighborhoods.[84] Koreans and Asian Indians did not have their own separate ethnic economies and communities because of their smaller numbers. Korean immigrants opened up small businesses in Chinatowns, selling ginseng or operating small restaurants. In California agricultural areas, such as Marysville and the Imperial Valley, Punjabis lived in areas near Chinese and Japanese immigrants.[85] Indian immigrants were mostly agricultural laborers and farmers, but some owned grocery stores, bars, and boardinghouses in both rural and urban areas and served as contacts for laborers when they came through town.[86]

Violent attacks and riots against Indian workers in the early 1900s in the Pacific Northwest and California led Muslims, Hindus, and Sikhs to establish protective organizations, such as the Hindustani Welfare Reform Society in central California.[87] After race riots in Watsonville and Stockton, where white mobs attacked Filipino agricultural laborers and destroyed their living quarters, the majority of Filipino associations were established on the basis of ethnicity rather than kin or province.[88] During the same period, Punjabis in the United States formed the Gadar Party; located in San Francisco, it focused on Indian independence from British rule. Immigrant laborers, farmers, and students participated in the movement, and by many accounts, they were more militant than their compatriots in India.[89] They raised funds, delivered political lectures, and started a weekly newspaper called *Gadar*, which disseminated their revolutionary message throughout the Americas, Asia, and Europe.[90]

Despite the social organization of Asian immigrant communities, Asians were unable to challenge discriminatory treatment through formal means. One strategy was to withhold their much-needed labor in return for better working conditions and wages, but such efforts were not always successful because American employers often found other sources of labor with which to replace the striking workers. A more viable strategy for increasing their status and worth in the United States was to improve the conditions in their homelands; many Asian immigrants believed that their fortunes in the United States were tied to the strength of their homelands in the international arena.[91] These movements increased the national consciousness of Asian ethnic groups in the United States, raised their sense of cultural pride, and demonstrated that they were capable of working effectively with their countrymen abroad to achieve greater rights. In the early 1900s, virtually all of the protests, boycotts, strikes, and political movements were organized along ethnic lines and shaped by national-origin interests.

Even though they shared experiences of exclusion, Asian immigrants developed and largely depended on their own systems of social and economic support within their own separate communities. Over time, immigrant organizations were established along ethnic instead of kin, region, or dialect lines. Central in providing aid and support to newcomers, these ethnic organizations represented the foundation upon which panethnic organizations were later built. Shaped by each group's unique history of immigration and U.S. relations with its country of origin, many ethnic organizations in the early 1900s were formed to promote homeland solidarity. As can be seen in the social organization of the different ethnic groups during this period, ethnic boundaries remained salient in the face of racial discrimination, xenophobic attitudes, and federal immigration legislation that treated them as a unified group.

THE INFLUENCE OF WAR AND SHIFTING BOUNDARIES

World War II reshaped the experiences of Asian immigrants and was a watershed event that had larger implications for the expansion of ethnic group boundaries. Japan's bombing of Pearl Harbor in 1941 significantly changed the social and economic world of Japanese Americans residing on the U.S. mainland.[92] President Franklin D. Roosevelt issued Executive Order 9066, which allowed the military to take action to safeguard the American people.[93] Under military orders, approximately 120,000 Japanese Americans—citizens and noncitizens alike—were forcibly relocated, bringing only what they could carry with them to assembly centers and internment camps in remote, unpopulated areas in California, Idaho, Wyoming, Utah, Arizona, Colorado, and Arkansas.[94] Not only were their homes, possessions, and other property taken from them, but Japanese Americans also lost their freedom.[95]

The war with Japan affected the status of other Asian ethnic groups besides the Japanese. Once referred to as the "heathen Chinee," the Chinese were now seen as noble peasants or resisters of Japanese aggression.[96] Despite this shift, the Chinese community was fearful that they would be mistaken for Japanese and become targets of anti-Japanese violence. Chinese shopkeepers put up signs in their shop windows that read THIS IS A CHINESE SHOP, while individuals wore buttons that read I AM CHINESE.[97] Confined for decades in a Chinese ethnic labor market comprised mainly of restaurants and laundries, Chinese workers suddenly found new employment opportunities in the defense industries, shipyards, airplane factories, craft occupations, and even some professional and technical occupations.[98]

The politics of the war led to further changes in the lives of Asian Americans as the U.S. government expanded the rights of many Asian-origin groups. In 1943, the Chinese Exclusion Act was finally repealed due to Japanese propaganda condemning the United States for its discriminatory laws, pressure from Chinese American organizations, and China's status as an ally in World War.[99] Naturalization rights were also extended to the Chinese.[100] During the same period, the California attorney general reinterpreted the land laws and decided that Filipinos would be allowed to lease land and encouraged them to take over the holdings of the Japanese who were being interned. Employment opportunities also expanded for Filipinos as they became farmers and entered jobs in shipyards. Soon after, Congress passed a law that extended citizenship to Filipino immigrants and permitted the annual entry of one hundred Filipino immigrants. That same year, Congress allowed India to have a small immigration quota and granted Indians naturalization rights in exchange for Indian cooperation in the war effort against Japan.[101] Even though Korean nationalists supported U.S. military efforts against Japan, U.S. government policies failed to distinguish Koreans from the Japanese and classified Korean immigrants as subjects of Japan.

By the 1960s, the U.S. social and political landscape had significantly changed. Japan had surrendered to the United States in 1945, ending World War II, and in the decades that followed the federal government extended citizenship and property ownership rights to Asian Americans and other racial minorities. The Civil Rights Act of 1964 ended racial segregation and promised to provide equal opportunity and affirmative action to ensure the full participation in American society of racial minorities as well as women and the disabled.[102] Seeking to further establish the United States as a democratic world power, Congress passed the Immigration and Nationality Act of 1965, which abolished national-origin quotas and allowed entry to immigrants from all nations. Although the new immigration policy implemented in 1968 was intended to remedy past discrimination against Southern, Central, and Eastern Europeans, who faced restrictions stemming from the Immigration Act of 1924, what resulted was a dramatic surge in immigration from Asia as well as Latin America, Africa, and the Caribbean.[103] With a changing social landscape, Asian immigrants were gaining access to new economic and political rights, which would shape the ways they responded to adversity and inequality in the new era.

THE EMERGENCE OF A PANETHNIC MOVEMENT AND IDENTITY

The late 1960s and early 1970s marked the starting point of sustained Asian American panethnic collective action to combat racial oppression and secure social and economic rights for the larger Asian American community.[104] The panethnic category and identity originated from student and community activists who recognized their unique position as Asian Americans when they engaged in the antiwar, women's, black power, and other social movements of the late 1960s.[105] Asian American activists began to build a political movement based on the shared oppression experienced by all Asian ethnicities. Rejecting the label of "Oriental," they defined the movement as Asian American, a term that represented an inclusive effort to construct an expansive panethnic identity among diverse Asian ethnic groups.[106] This redefinition of the Asian American community also emphasized that political change would come from the construction of democratic organizations and the active participation of group members.[107]

Many of the social movements of this period were associated with political action that was used to advance the interests of group members who shared a common, marginalized identity. Participants in the women's and black power movements were able to transform their low-status positions by drawing attention to the creation and legitimation of their new identities. An emerging main goal for social movements was to gain recognition for stigmatized or new social identities that reflected the shared histories and struggles of group members.[108] A key aspect of the Chicano, black power, and Native American movements was their recognition and affirmation of a cultural identity.[109] Asian Americans were undoubtedly influenced by these social movements and their own participation in them, but as we will see, the Asian American panethnic identity was also shaped by their unique experiences as Asians in the United States.

Radical Politics and a New Racial Solidarity

The Asian American Political Alliance (AAPA), one of the first pan-Asian organizations to adopt a pan-Asian ideology, was formed in May 1968 at the University of California at Berkeley. The organization brought East Asian groups together to increase the effectiveness and political visibility of their activism and to radicalize other Asians.[110] Like many panethnic organizations that were formed in support of the Asian American movement, AAPA explicitly rejected the strategy of assimilation as a way to address racial inequality; instead, it adopted a racial paradigm that emphasized the continuing political and economic salience of racial categories.[111] The AAPA played a key role in the first large-scale protest involving Asian Americans, which took place in 1968: Asian American college students participated in mass strikes, rallies, and sit-ins with African American, Chicano, and Native American students as part of the Third World Liberation Front (TWLF), protesting against the lack of diversity in the university curriculum.[112] Anti-imperialist resistance movements in Asia, Africa, and Latin America provided the backdrop to radical politics in the United States, and the black power movement popularized the concept of "internal colonialism," which explicitly linked the oppression of Third World peoples abroad with those on American soil.[113] Over the course of several months, more than 10,000 students took part in the demands for establishing ethnic studies programs, hiring faculty of color, and implementing open admissions for students of color at San Francisco State College and UC Berkeley. Hundreds of students were arrested by police in riot gear, and at one point near the end of the struggle the National Guard was dispatched to maintain martial law. In the end, the students achieved their collective goals: ethnic studies programs were implemented at both universities.

For many students, this was the first time they had participated in non-institutional political action. Floyd Huen, a first-generation Chinese American and UC Berkeley student who became active in community politics, recalled what the strike meant to minority students:

> The Third World Strike represented the convergence of this identity movement with the educational mission of the University, and the common status of all minorities in the U.S. affected by racist attitudes and racist curriculums in history, sociology, and political science. For me, it was the high point of my time at UC Berkeley—the Strike was led by a determined group of minority youth committed to bringing important change to the University, the flagship of higher education in the State. It represented solidarity in action based on shared values, and allowed comradeship to develop in the midst of a common struggle.[114]

With this success, Asian American college students and activists began to develop a new movement to address racial oppression and aid their relatively poor communities, which were experiencing substandard housing, police harassment, lack of access to health care, and labor discrimination.[115] Influenced by the revolutionary ideas of Malcolm X, Stokely Carmichael, Frantz Fanon, Che Guevara, and Mao Tse-tung, Asian activists aimed to serve the people and enact social change through political means.[116] They were also radicalized through their participation in the antiwar movement. In the early 1970s, the mainstream antiwar movement emphasized bringing the troops home from Vietnam, but Asian American activists declared that the war was racist and unjust and that the United States was an imperialist force abroad as well as at home. The colonization of the Philippines, the occupation of Okinawa, and the Korean War were all instances of U.S. imperialism in Asia, they argued, and the Vietnam War was yet another.[117] Asian American antiwar activists also brought attention to U.S. racism and genocide in Vietnam and asserted racial commonality with the Vietnamese people.[118] To reflect this shared racial status, activists created political antiwar flyers displaying a picture of a Vietnamese peasant. The caption on the flyers stated: "This is a gook. Or a jap, slope, chink . . . is it true what they do to people who look like me?"[119]

Understanding the war in racist and anti-imperialist terms led them to build a multiethnic racial solidarity among Asians to fight against injustices experienced by Asians abroad and in the United States instead of developing assimilationist strategies.[120]

In addition to forming panethnic organizations in the early 1970s such as Asian Media Collective, Asian Women United, and Bay Area Asian Coalition Against the War, Asian American activists also contributed to the movement by developing newspapers and magazines. Traditional ethnic presses were important sources of information about homeland politics but tended to neglect political issues within the U.S. context, such as civil rights, the Vietnam War, and ethnic studies.[121] College students and activists launched their own publications such as *Gidra, Bridge, Asian Expressions, Rodan,* and *Insight,* which focused on the empowerment of Asian Americans and addressed issues such as drug abuse in the Asian American community, the antiwar movement, prison conditions in the United States, and Third World oppression in Africa.[122] According to longtime activist Bob Hsiang, these magazines and newspapers were "crucial in establishing a new method for analyzing society and establishing models for revolutionary changes and self-determination."[123] Students and activists created their own media outlets to express, share, record, and disseminate their ideas, thoughts, and understandings of the world as Asian Americans. Their magazines and newspapers incorporated art, especially poetry and drawing, and were crucial to articulating a nascent Asian American identity and the political goals of the movement.[124]

The emerging Asian American movement paved the way for panethnic community organizing during the post-1968 era. In particular, the International Hotel anti-eviction movement was a key point in collective organizing among Asian Americans. Beginning in the early 1900s, the I-Hotel in San Francisco had been home to generations of Filipino immigrant laborers who worked in local canneries, farms, and factories, and it became a symbol of their struggle and history.[125] In 1968 the owners of the hotel wanted to evict the tenants—mostly elderly Filipinos and Chinese—and tear down the building to make way for a parking lot. After much deliberation, an agreement was struck in 1969: the tenants were allowed to stay, but would be responsible for all repairs. Saving the I-Hotel was the first campaign to bring larger numbers of Asian American students into the community. Activist groups that promoted radical ideologies about social change, including the Asian Community Center, Everybody's Bookstore, the Red Guards/I Wor Kuen/Chinese Progressive Association, the Kearny Street Workshop, and the I-Hotel Tenants Association, housed their organizations in the storefronts of the I-Hotel.[126]

After several years of legal action and organized protests from the Filipino, Chinese, and Japanese communities and a coalition of progressive groups ranging from affordable housing to gay and lesbian advocates, a major protest to keep the I-Hotel was organized in August 1977.[127] Thousands of people formed a barrier around the block to prevent the forced eviction of the tenants. Three hundred police dressed in riot gear eventually took over the building and evicted over fifty residents. The building was torn down later that year. Even though the community efforts had failed, the collective action process reinforced a new Asian American identity.[128] New and stronger networks had been built between ethnic groups. Through coordinating action and sharing experiences, Asian-origin groups realized their commonalities and the potential for change.[129]

College students and community activists developed an all-encompassing panethnic label and identity which constituted one strategy to enact social change and redefine Asian communities. But not all Asians supported this strategy. Assimilationists opposed a panethnic categorization and instead encouraged group members to embrace an American identity. For example, the Japanese American Citizens League (JACL), a highly influential organization within the Japanese American community, advocated for assimilation and worked to highlight the patriotic citizenship of Japanese Americans and to portray Japanese culture as compatible with American values. They allied with white conservatives, seeking to gain racial equality by collaborating with whites and arguing for the extension of the privileges of whiteness to Japanese Americans.[130] New immigrants also did not identify with the new panethnic label and identity, nor did many first- and second-generation Chinese, Japanese, and Korean Americans who strongly identified with their national-origin identities. In fact, many second-generation Chinese were torn between being Chinese or American, and identifying as Asian American held little interest.[131] During the late 1960s and early 1970s, panethnicity emerged from a select group of individuals—college students and community activists—and then later in the post-1968 era was appropriated and used by others within the Asian American community who tended to have much less radical ideas about racial inequality and oppression and who used the label for funding and organizing purposes.

New immigration flows from different parts of Asia and the increasing diversity of newcomers to the United States presented a challenge for the formation of a broader collective identity, but by the mid-1980s panethnicity was well established as an organizing principle for building a community among groups with different ethnic origins. This institutional logic of panethnicity was adopted by ethnic groups when organizing and making collective claims, as evidenced by the creation of panethnic organizations and institutions as well as the visibility of protests and demonstrations under a pan-Asian banner.[132] Among 117 advocacy groups serving the Asian American community across the nation in 1984, more than half were pan-Asian.[133] Consequently, new immigrants often found themselves dealing with institutions that used panethnicity as the central way to organize and categorize people from different parts of Asia.[134]

The next section elaborates on the broad social changes enacted by the state that enhanced the logic for organizing on a panethnic basis during the post-1968 era, but as we will see in later chapters, these social conditions at the macro level are just one piece of understanding the larger puzzle of panethnicity.

THE PREDOMINANCE OF RACE IN THE NEW ERA

Asian Americans continued to use the panethnic label in the new era in part because the broad social and political changes in the United States reinforced race as a central organizing principle. Before 1968, immigration and race narratives had been largely distinct because the great majority of immigrants originated from Europe.[135] Immigrants from Poland, Italy, and Bulgaria were considered low-status, but they were never viewed as nonwhite.[136] The "race problem" in the United States had related solely to African Americans, who suffered from deep forms of institutionalized racism.[137] But with new demographic shifts, specifically the increasing proportion of immigrants to the United States from non-European countries, racial minority status became more tightly linked with immigrants, and the state played a key role in this racialization.[138]

The new demographic landscape in the United States resulted from the 1965 Immigration and Nationality Act, which eliminated national-origin quotas in the admission process. The new policy was significant because it allowed 20,000 immigrants from each country annually and removed the ban on Asian entry to the United States that had been in place since 1924. For the first time in nearly four decades, Asian immigrants were able to freely migrate to the United States. The result of the new legislation was a marked increase in immigrants from Asia, Africa, and Latin America.[139] Figure 2.1 shows that between 1960 and 1968, the largest number of immigrants to the United States originated from Europe. In the following decade, immigrants from Asia and Latin America were the most predominant, with the largest numbers arriving from Asia. Between 1980 and 1989, the numbers of Asian and Latino immigrants nearly doubled, totaling 4 million. Figure 2.2 depicts the increasing numbers of Asian immigrants from diverse national-origin and socioeconomic backgrounds

Figure 2.1 Immigration to the United States, by Global Region, 1960–2009

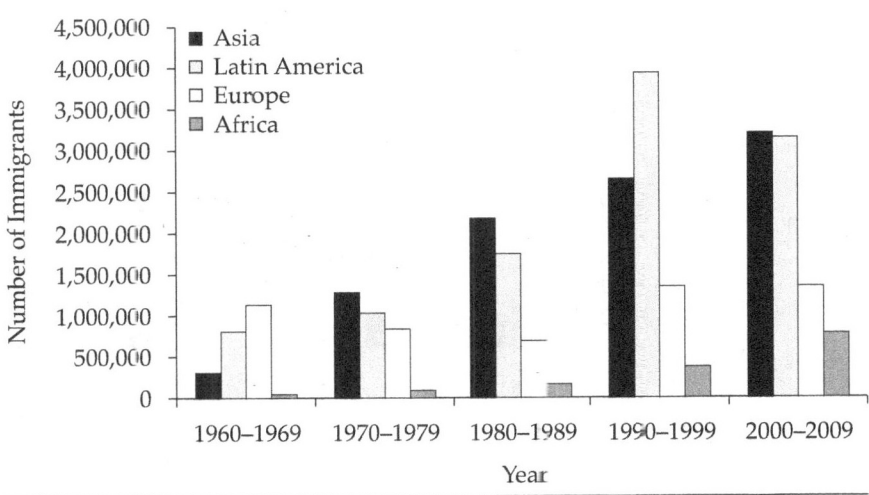

Source: U.S. Department of Homeland Security (2010).
Note: The Asian region includes China, Hong Kong, India, Japan, Korea, the Philippines, Taiwan, Vietnam, and "other Asia." The Latin American region includes Mexico, Central America, and South America.

who migrated to the United States from China, Korea, Japan, Taiwan, India, Vietnam, and the Philippines.

Despite the growing diversity of the Asian population in the United States, the federal government collapsed national-origin groups into an official racial category. Before 1970, the U.S. Census Bureau categorized Asian ethnic groups as different "races." In 1860 the racial category of Chinese first appeared on the U.S. census, and then, in 1870, the Japanese were identified.[140] The 1910 census enumerated Filipinos, Hindus, and Koreans for the first time, but by 1950 the only Asian ethnic groups identified were Chinese, Japanese, and Filipino.[141] The racial category of Asian/Pacific Islander was used for the first time in 1980 census reports, reflecting the Directive on Race and Ethnic Standards for Federal Statistics and Administrative Reporting.[142] Released in 1977 by the U.S. Census Bureau, this directive designated Asian/Pacific Islander as one of four official racial categories—along with black, white, and Native American or Alaskan Native and the ethnic category of Hispanic—to be used by federal agencies.[143] The shift was primarily a result of civil rights legislation: federal agencies needed a standard system for collecting data on access to hous-

Figure 2.2 Asian Immigration to the United States, by Ethnic Group, 1960–2009

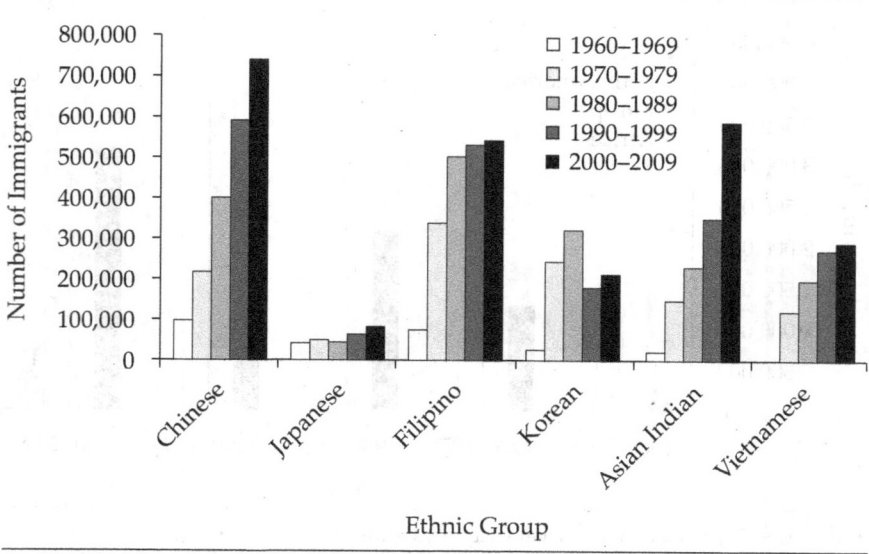

Source: U.S. Department of Homeland Security (2010).
Note: "Chinese" includes immigrants from China, Hong Kong, and Taiwan.

ing, employment, education, and other institutional arenas so that they could enforce equal opportunity and affirmative action policies.[144]

In providing the basis for the distribution of federal and state resources to disadvantaged ethnic and racial communities, this official racial classification system also had an impact on how public policy was approached, designed, and implemented. Even though nine ethnic categories—Chinese, Japanese, Filipino, Korean, Vietnamese, Asian Indian, Hawaiian, Guamanian, and Samoan—were included on official census questionnaires in 1980, researchers, businesses, public agencies, educational institutions, foundations, hospitals, and industry adopted the *racial* category of Asian (as well as black, white, and Hispanic) when collecting data, awarding grants, and allocating resources (see figure 2.3). Racial categories were also included as part of standard identification questions on administrative forms and household surveys.[145] Over time, the use of racial categories by mainstream institutions became institutionalized and were taken for granted in everyday interactions.[146]

The fact that public and private institutions adopted racial categories and often operated on racial assumptions sometimes resulted in harmful consequences. For example, two influential community foundations, the

Figure 2.3   The Race Question on the 1980 Census Form

3. Sex Fill ONE circle for each person.	○ Male ○ Female
4. Race Fill ONE circle for the race that the person considers himself/herself to be If Indian (Amer.), print the name of the enrolled or principal tribe ⟶ If Other Asian or Pacific Islander (API), print one group, for example: Hmong, Fijian, Laotian, Thai, Tongan, Pakistani, Cambodian, and so on ⟶ If Other race, print race ⟶	○ White ○ Black or Negro ○ Indian (Amer.) [Print the name of the enrolled or principal tribe] ⌐ ¬ ○ Eskimo ○ Aleut Asian or Pacific Islander (API) ○ Chinese ○ Japanese ○ Filipino ○ Asian Indian ○ Hawaiian ○ Samoan ○ Korean ○ Guamanian ○ Vietnamese ○ Other API ⌐ ¬ ○ Other race (print race)
5. Age and year of birth	a Age b Year of birth

Source: U.S. Census Bureau.

San Francisco Foundation (SFF) and the Cleveland Foundation (CF), implicitly used racial categories when making decisions about which nonprofit projects or programs to fund to address the needs of the disadvantaged, and often did not recognize the internal diversity within the Asian American community.[147] In fact, foundation trustees claimed that the plethora of small ethnic businesses in Chinatown and other ethnic enclaves was evidence that the Asian population did not have significant social needs. Yet in reality, the Asian population was dealing with health care access, language needs, poverty, and culture shock.[148] Additionally, community foundations did not recognize the complexity that arises when multiple Asian-origin groups work together.[149] These funders viewed Asian Americans as having inherent commonalities that did not need to be developed, negotiated, and managed. As one agency director noted, foundations "aren't good at knowing ... how delicate those links are."[150] Instead of funding panethnic efforts, foundations prioritized projects involving more than one *racial* group, such as those with Asian and Latino collaborators. In their eyes, diversity could only be defined as racial, not as ethnic. These public foundations committed to diversity and improving the lives of low-income and needy populations could not see beyond the racial categories that had become more or less institutionalized further elucidates the complicated nature of panethnicity.

Some Asian ethnic groups have resisted the fact that mainstream institutions place distinct groups under one category.[151] Clearly, racializing ethnic groups can introduce problems of stereotyping and misinformation about different Asian-origin communities. Despite the potential pitfalls of racialization, the pan-Asian concept was used extensively by professional and community spokespersons to lobby and organize for the welfare and rights of Asian Americans in the 1990s and 2000s, and it has been promoted not only by nonprofit organizations but also by political parties, churches, and schools.[152] Social workers and community leaders from various ethnic groups organize on a panethnic basis to make themselves visible and recognizable to funders and other elites. Walter, a program director at the Chinese Citizens Council, explained how these coordinated efforts helped the organization to compete more effectively for funding and to garner attention from local officials:

> Politically, it allows us to have a much stronger advocacy by having a collection of organizations voicing their concerns over an issue as opposed to us by ourselves, and through that we are able to acquire greater financial resources by working closely together. . . . As individual organizations, it is very difficult to have the political weight to get the attention of policy makers.

For Walter and the ethnic organizations he works with, collaborating across ethnic lines made sense. Organizing as Asian Americans was often a more effective way to gain access to local and state officials than organizing separately as a specific ethnic group.[153] Organizational leaders also worked hard to recognize different needs and strengthen ethnic communities, both of which were viewed as important for the success of the larger collective. Understanding diversity within the Asian American community in regard to ethnicity, generation, and immigrant status is one of the hallmarks of panethnicity. As one leader explained, "We have to continue to think about [how] to promote strong voices for every ethnic community, whether it's Filipino, Korean, or Vietnamese, or any other group." Such an approach reinforces the narrative of diversity and ensures that no one ethnic community dominates.

In the new era, Asians became a *racialized* group: they no longer arrived in successive waves, nor were they viewed as separate "races" by the state. Asian Americans disputed the racial categorization that mainstream institutions used in their everyday practices and in allocating resources because of the diverse needs and histories within the Asian American community, but they still organized on a panethnic basis to garner the attention of funders and other elites. Given these conditions of racialization, we would expect Asian ethnic groups to organize as a panethnic group whenever an issue or problem arose, but this was not the case. Asian Americans did begin to form local and national organizations to serve the needs of the pan-Asian community and engaged in public demonstrations, marches, and boycotts to make claims on behalf of the larger group, but as we will see in the following chapters, panethnic organizing during the post-1968 era was the exception rather than the rule.

SUMMARY

Before 1968, Asian immigrant groups did not form alliances, nor did they view their experiences as similar even though they faced the same discriminatory legislation restricting immigration, naturalization, and civil rights. This is somewhat of a paradox—logic suggests that Asian ethnic groups would band together under such conditions. Instead, it was not until *after* discriminatory legislation had been eliminated and civil rights legislation had introduced new opportunities that activists began building an Asian American movement based on fighting racial oppression and inequality. Asian immigrants had no political rights in the early 1900s, so banding together to increase their political power had not been a realistic strategy for social change. A number of social conditions helped to strengthen ethnic group boundaries during this period, including the hierarchical structure of work, the strained relations between homeland countries, and white dominance of the political economy. Since Asian immigrants were newcomers, they were also learning how to simply survive and adapt to American ways of life. They did not develop cooperative ties with other ethnic communities, but instead found ways to create separate ethnic communities within a society that was largely hostile. Asian immigrants started families, when possible, and formed protective and ethnic organizations.

With the ushering in of a new era in the late 1960s, the experience of Asian Americans shifted. They experienced more freedoms and opportunities with the implementation of civil rights legislation, and large, diverse streams of Asian migrants with different class and educational backgrounds arrived in the United States. In many ways, the formation of a collective Asian American identity seemed less likely in this new environment. But the federal government's implementation and use of racial categories provided the logic and motivation for panethnicity during the post-1968 period. As the dominant group and the larger society came to view and treat Asian Americans as a racial group, flattening distinctions on the basis of nativity, national origin, language, and culture, Asian-origin groups responded by asserting a panethnic strategy.

But not all Asian Americans took up the panethnic label and identity simply because they existed, and their racialization by the state and larger society did not lead all Asian Americans to organize accordingly. In the following chapters, I examine the ways in which Asian Americans expressed panethnicity in the public arena, and I explore the social forces that helped to generate and sustain a panethnic identity over the post-1968 era.

Chapter 3 | The Emergence of Organizational Panethnicity

DURING THE PRE-1968 era, Asian ethnic groups did not view each other as sharing common interests and a unified goal, in part because of their newcomer status, which simply demanded learning how to survive in American society. Local residents, native-born workers, and state officials regarded the different Asian-origin groups as economic competitors, social misfits, and a threat to American culture.[1] As a result, Asian immigrants experienced exclusionary federal immigration policies and anti-immigrant violence. They were also segregated into ethnic enclaves, and extended few social and political rights.[2] Nevertheless, these common experiences of exclusion and segregation did not lead to a shared collective identity among Asian immigrants in this early period. In fact, as elaborated in chapter 2, Asians in the United States formed associations along kin, region, and ethnic lines to address their social and economic needs.

Moving into the post-1968 era, federal policy changes related to citizenship, immigration, and civil rights led to new political opportunities for ethnic and racial groups in the United States, allowing for interethnic cooperation in the face of exclusionary and unfair treatment. The shared experience of membership in a racial minority group in the United States influenced how Asian ethnic groups organized to make public claims or grievances. In particular, the logic for panethnic organizing was clearly provided by racialization—the ways in which the state and the larger society lumped together distinct ethnic and cultural groups and indiscriminately attributed immutable "racial" qualities to them. In the face of this treatment, different Asian ethnic groups were motivated to organize together in pursuit of a common goal.[3]

Immigrant and ethnic groups, in learning how to organize more effectively to address issues that significantly affected their communities, forged potential avenues for social and political change.[4] These ethnic groups broadened their group boundaries and created new organizations to advocate for Asian American communities in major cities such as Los Angeles, Chicago, and New York. Despite the existence of ethnic communities and enclaves, new panethnic organizations formed to serve and bring together ethnic groups that differed by language, culture, religion, and immigration history. Organizations such as the Asian Pacific American Labor Alliance and the Asian Law Caucus challenged racial inequalities and played an important role in securing civil rights for a diverse set of ethnic communities under a unified panethnic framework. These organizations also contributed to the creation of new cultural and political identities, and individuals who had thought of themselves only in ethnic terms were exposed to the broader political and social identity of Asian American.

Panethnicity emerged as a prominent framework that ethnic group members could use to bring attention to the needs of their communities during the contemporary era, but as this chapter will show, the patterns of Asian American panethnicity were not uniform over time or place. This empirical fact suggests that *macro social conditions*, such as changes in immigration and civil rights legislation, can only partially explain the emergence of panethnicity; we also need to consider how *meso-level* or *local conditions*—such as economic and demographic changes—encouraged distinct ethnic groups to organize collectively and assert a new, broader identity in some places but not in others.

Even though "Asian American" is a constructed category—whether a label assigned by the state or a community imagined by group members—it can take shape as a key organizing principle for a formal organization. By examining the patterns of panethnic organizational activity, we can understand how groups assert boundaries and how communities shift and change over time.

This chapter highlights the dynamic nature of group boundaries by identifying patterns of panethnic organizational emergence among Asian Americans in the post-1968 era. It demonstrates that the way in which ethnic groups were structured in local labor markets—as proximate to one another, reflecting racial segregation—was key in encouraging Asian ethnicities to organize as a unified group and take up a panethnic label and identity. This chapter also focuses on the central role of leaders within the Asian American community in forming panethnic organizations during the post-1968 era. It was not simply their distribution in local labor markets that enabled Asian-origin groups to develop the interethnic ties and shared interests necessary to organize as a panethnic group; leaders played a vital role in building a pan-Asian narrative and persuading community members to see themselves as Asian American.

PATTERNS OF PANETHNIC ORGANIZING
The Emergence of Pan-Asian Organizations

Studying organizations provides insights about the ways in which groups display and construct identities and communities.[5] When organizations are formed around specific immigrant, ethnic, or racial populations, this represents the enactment of group boundaries designating who is (and who is not) part of a larger community. Where these group boundaries are drawn has implications for the welfare and social mobility of ethnic and racial groups. Insiders have access to collective goods such as citizenship classes and after-school child care, as well as information about financial aid and affordable housing. Additionally, these institutional structures improve the well-being of communities by consolidating material resources, facilitating communication, and encouraging network ties. They also shape the meanings and definitions that people use to understand their own identities and the world around them.[6]

The pan-Asian organizations that emerged during the post–civil rights era focused on social justice and included ethnic groups that fell under the broad categories of Asian and Asian American. From 1970 to 2000, seventy pan-Asian organizations with national Asian American memberships or constituencies were formed. Although not all ethnic group members participated in the planning, support, and implementation of panethnic organizations, the collective work across ethnic boundaries by a segment of the Asian American population represented a remarkable group effort in light of past animosities and the differences in national origin, language, and culture. These organizations were diverse in goals and strategies, but ultimately all of them served to sustain the idea of an Asian American community and to promote the status of Asian Americans. The emphasis on pan-Asian organizing within a racial framework and on political activism within the public sphere differentiated these new panethnic organizations from traditional Asian and Asian-ethnic organizations.[7]

To provide a broader context in which these organizations were formed, I use data from the *Encyclopedia of Organizations* to compare the numbers of Asian, Latino, and black organizations founded during this period with the total Asian, Latino, and black populations, respectively.[8] The predominance of African American organizations in the data speaks to the influence of the civil rights movement and the dominance of the black racial

Figure 3.1 The Number of Asian, Latino, and Black Panethnic Organizations Formed per 100,000 Asians, Latinos, and Blacks, Respectively, 1970–2000

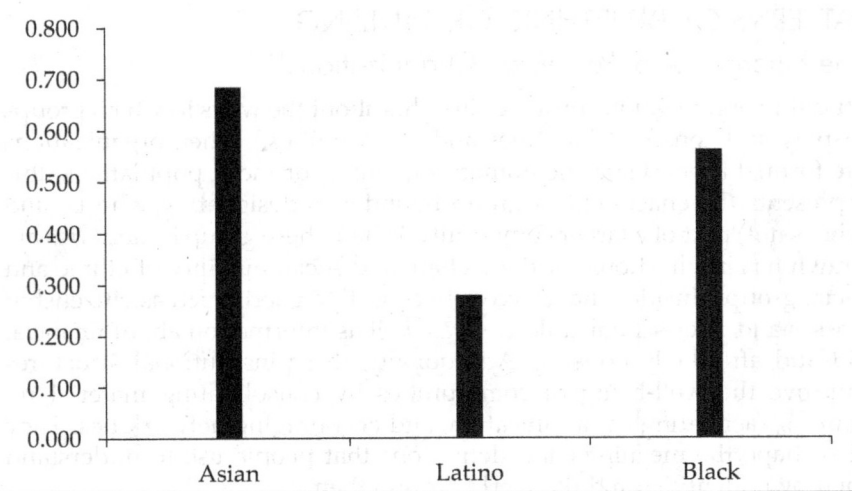

Source: Author's calculation of organization-population ratios, Asian American national organizations data set (Okamoto 2006).

label. From 1970 to 2000, 195 national organizations (such as the Council for African American Progress, the National Black Women's Health Project, and the National Association of Blacks in Government) were formed to serve the black population, which reached over 35.3 million in 2000. For Hispanics, 98 panethnic organizations (for instance, the League of United Latin American Citizens and the National Network of Hispanic Women) were founded during the same period to provide services and advocacy for 34.6 million Latinos. Seventy panethnic organizations were formed to serve the needs of Asian Americans across the United States.

Given the size of the Asian American population in the United States—about 10.2 million in 2000—the total number of national organizations founded during the post-1968 era might seem low. Comparing the number of panethnic organizations to the populations they serve, figure 3.1 shows that 0.68 pan-Asian organizations were formed per 100,000 Asian Americans. These organization-population ratios are even lower, however, for Latinos and blacks, at 0.28 and 0.56, respectively. These ratios suggest that Asian Americans have actually been quite active in the organizational arena during the post–civil rights era, especially compared to

Table 3.1 Types and Examples of Panethnic Organizations in Operation, 1970–2000

Established prior to 1970	
Cross-cultural	Asia Foundation
Research	Asia Institute
Business	U.S. Pan-Asian American Chamber of Commerce
Established after 1970	
Education	Leadership Education for Asian Pacifics
Health	Asian and Pacific Islander Health Forum
Arts/culture	Asian American Arts Alliance
Professional	Asian American Architects and Engineers
Civil rights	Asian American Legal Defense and Educational Fund

Source: Author's calculations based on Gale Research Company (1965–2000).

other racial groups. And if we include ethnic-specific organizations in these total counts, the organization-population ratio for Asians is even higher than the ratios for Hispanics and blacks, given that the number of Asian ethnic organizations (such as Chinese for Affirmative Action, the Japanese American Citizens League, the Korean American Coalition, and the National Association for the Education and Advancement of Cambodian, Laotian, and Vietnamese Americans) is five times that of Latino ethnic organizations (such as the Mexican American Unity Council, the National Puerto Rican Forum, and the Ecuadorian American Association) and over ten times that of black ethnic organizations (for instance, the Caribbean American Intercultural Organization and Friends of Haiti).[9]

The organizations that were formed to serve the Asian American community differed in their approach, their philosophy, and their focus. Table 3.1 displays the types of pan-Asian organizations in operation from 1970 to 2000. Organizations founded before 1970 may have included "Asian" in their names but were not focused on building a multiethnic Asian American community. In 1970 nearly forty Asian national organizations were in operation, half of which were founded in the 1950s, and the most prevalent types of Asian organizations were cross-cultural organizations and research institutes focused on the study of Asia.

Located in San Francisco, New York, and Washington, D.C., organizations such as the Asia Foundation, the Asia Society, and the Asian Cultural Exchange Foundation were founded to promote positive relations between Asia and the United States and to educate the American public about the history, art, and culture of Asia. These organizations did not adopt a pan-Asian ideology focused on political power and social change, nor did they directly incorporate a membership of culturally and linguistically diverse ethnic groups. Most were devoted to the sharing of knowledge between Asia and the United States through educational and cultural exchange programs.[10] A number of institutes promoted the scholarly study of Asia, while other organizations focused on developing networks across the Pacific devoted to trade, business, and policy issues. These early Asian organizations did not focus on the needs of Asian immigrants in the United States, largely because ethnic communities formed separate organizations to address the needs of new immigrants and those who had settled in the United States years earlier. Pan-Asian organizations that emphasized a narrative about the shared history of Asian ethnic groups in the United States and focused on education, health, culture, and professions were virtually nonexistent during this period.

Beginning in the late 1970s, pan-Asian organizations were formed primarily in San Francisco and New York, the two geographic areas that already had a brief history of Asian American activism.[11] Instead of focusing on Asian art, culture, and history, the new organizations addressed the education and health needs of Asians in the United States as a collective group by providing services or advocacy for a diverse Asian-origin population. The National Association for Asian and Pacific American Education (NAAPAE) was one of these organizations. In 1977 a group of Asian American educators attended a conference of the National Association for Bilingual Education (NABE), which mainly focused on Spanish-speaking students and Spanish bilingual teachers. Later that year, to address the language and educational needs of the Asian and Pacific American (APA) population, they founded NAAPAE, a multilingual organization that would advocate on behalf of APA education and promote research on APA educational issues.[12] Three Asian American educators from Seattle wrote up the organization's constitution, which was adopted by its sixteen members during the first conference.[13] Like other pan-Asian organizations formed during this period, NAAPAE was focused on the needs and experiences of Japanese, Chinese, and Korean Americans, who made up the majority of the Asian population in the United States at this time, and thus defined "Asian American" as primarily East Asian.

Ethnic organizations were also forming in the 1970s, and many of them were focused on research and U.S. relations with different countries in Asia (for example, the Japan Institute, the Vietnam Foundation, the U.S.-China Peoples Friendship Association, and the National Association of Japan-America Societies) and on homeland politics (such as the Tibetan Aid Project, Friends of Free China, and Movement for a Free Philippines). A handful of ethnic organizations had adopted a U.S. focus, including the Organization of Chinese American Women, the Taiwanese-American Society, and the Association of Sri Lankans in America. Interestingly, organizations focused on U.S.-Asia relations and research on Asia (the U.S.-Asia Institute, Human Rights Watch/Asia, the Free Asia Foundation) continued to be founded during the post-1968 era, though they were few in number. By the end of the era, twenty Asian organizations, the vast majority of which had focused on cross-cultural relations, had ceased to exist.

The number of pan-Asian organizations continued to increase into the 1980s. In fact, the majority of pan-Asian organizations with a national reach were formed during this decade. Once again, San Francisco was the front-runner in organizational foundings, despite its smaller total Asian population compared to other metropolitan areas such as Los Angeles, Chicago, and New York. Scholars have pinpointed the 1982 Vincent Chin case as the turning point in the Asian American movement that led to the proliferation of pan-Asian organizations. As noted in chapter 1, all Asians felt under threat when Vincent Chin, a Chinese American man, was attacked and killed by two white unemployed autoworkers in Detroit who mistook him for Japanese and blamed him for local job layoffs. But it wasn't until the injustice of the judge's decision for no jail time for Chin's murderers that Asian Americans began to come together as a panethnic group to fight against anti-Asian violence.[14] Interestingly, if we look at figure 3.2, it shows that the high point for organizational formation was in 1980, two years before the Chin case, suggesting that the organizational legitimacy of the pan-Asian model had been established prior to 1982.

So why did so many pan-Asian organizations form in 1980? A number of key events at that time, such as the I-Hotel protests in San Francisco, reinforced an Asian American identity and the effectiveness of the pan-Asian approach (see chapter 2). Even though struggles over the I-Hotel had begun in 1968, protests involving thousands of people culminated in 1977 to prevent the forced eviction of elderly Filipino and Chinese.[15] During and in the aftermath of the protest, new and stronger networks were built between ethnic groups.[16] It was also during this time that the U.S. government introduced the formal category of "Asian or Pacific Islander" for federal agencies to use in collecting and analyzing data.[17] Also, shifts in public funding for welfare services in the 1970s helped to finance a major expansion of the nonprofit sector in the 1980s.[18] Much of the growth in new funding reflected new federal programs or the expansion of existing ones, and a large proportion was channeled toward nonprofit service providers who were mandated to provide services.[19] By the late 1970s, a larger proportion of Asian immigrants had entered the United States through family reunification provisions, resulting in a population of newcomers with a more varied class background. Southeast Asian refugees

Figure 3.2 National Pan-Asian Organizational Foundings, 1970–1988

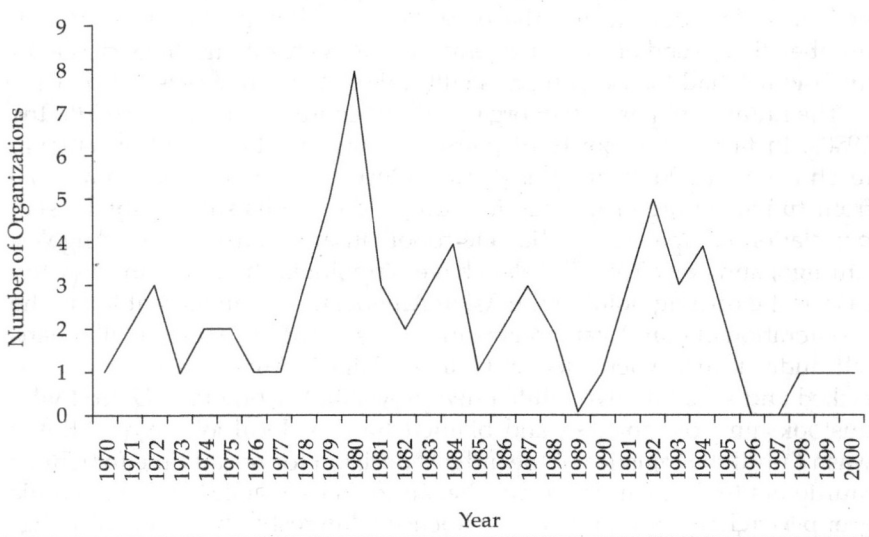

Source: Author's calculation, Asian American national organizations data set (Okamoto 2006).

had also arrived in the United States in larger numbers during this period, further disrupting the notion that Asians as a group were a model minority, since these newcomers' lack of educational and economic resources put them at a marked disadvantage.[20] New pan-Asian organizations were formed to help these new immigrants and refugees adapt to the U.S. context and to empower them politically.

In short, the momentum from key events during which Asian ethnic groups engaged in coordinated group action, coupled with the state's recognition and legitimation of the Asian American label and increased resources from the federal government, encouraged group members to seek collective goods using a panethnic model. Taken together, these social conditions appear to have contributed to the increase in the formation of pan-Asian organizations in the 1980s, but they do not entirely explain why organizations emerged in some metropolitan areas but not others. As we will see later in this chapter, the combination of the state's adoption and use of racial categories, the availability of new funding, and a larger Asian American population did not automatically translate into cooperation and organizing across ethnic lines.

The Evolution of Pan-Asian Organizations

During the 1980s and into the 1990s, Asian Americans founded organizations focused on cultural representation and production, such as the nonprofit National Asian American Telecommunications Association (NAATA) in San Francisco, which addressed issues of diversity in film and on television by funding, producing, and distributing films, television programs, and digital media that conveyed the diversity of Asian American experiences. Recognizing the growing need of Asian Americans to find others in their professional fields for support, networking, and advice, many professionally oriented organizations emerged, including the Asian/Pacific American Librarians Association, the Asian American Manufacturers Association, and the National Network of Asian and Pacific Women. The Asian Pacific American Labor Alliance, an organization with chapters in Los Angeles and New York, was founded to connect Asian American labor union members with the broader labor movement. Additionally, the Committee Against Anti-Asian Violence in New York and American Citizens for Justice in Detroit were created during this period to work for the civil rights of Asian Americans. National organizations were formed during this decade beyond San Francisco and New York—in metropolitan areas like Chicago, Philadelphia, Detroit, Sacramento, and Los Angeles. Many national organizations were also founded with their headquarters in D.C. so as to be close to policymakers.

Into the 1990s, the most typical way of expressing institutional panethnicity at the national level was through civil rights and social justice organizations and professional organizations. As the Asian American population continued to grow and expand, new immigrant destinations, such as Atlanta and Houston, also saw the formation of panethnic organizations. By the end of the 1990s, growth in the pan-Asian organizational field had seemingly stabilized. Figure 3.2 shows that pan-Asian organizational formation flattened out in 2000, but this does not reflect the national organizational activity that proliferated into the 2000s.[21] By 2013 the organizational landscape at the national level had grown to include more professional organizations, reflecting the increasing presence of Asians in particular fields and occupations (the Asian American Convenience Stores Association, the Asian American Real Estate Association, the Asian Health Care Leaders Association, and the National Association of Asian American Law Enforcement Commanders), as well as organizations that deal with community development, politics, and health (the National Coalition for Asian and Pacific American Community Development, Asian Pacific Americans for Progress, and the National Asian American and Pacific Islander Mental Health Association).

Additionally, the trend line shown in figure 3.2 does not take into account the size of these organizations in terms of membership and budget. Clearly, not all organizations are equal: some have larger membership bases and financial resources than others, and some have greater influence in social and political spheres. For instance, the National Coalition for Asian and Pacific American Community Development (National CAPACD) has coordinated the efforts of nonprofits at a national level, engaging in advocacy work to address the housing, community, and economic development needs of diverse and growing Asian American and Pacific Islander communities. National CAPACD works with a budget of over $1 million, and its member network includes more than 100 community-based organizations and individuals. Another major organization, Leadership Education for Asian Pacifics (LEAP), has upwards of 12,000 members and develops leadership among Asian and Pacific Islanders (APIs) through skill building and leadership development programs. To further meet its mission of achieving full equality for APIs, LEAP also provides information to the for-profit and nonprofit worlds and the larger public through diversity training and publications on the API community. The national infrastructure that serves the Asian population in the United States comprises not only these major organizations but also many others, but these are among the most visible and have influence and reach within as well as outside of the Asian American community.

MESO-LEVEL FACTORS, PROCESSES, AND MECHANISMS

By 2000 more than seventy pan-Asian organizations with a national reach were in operation. National pan-Asian organizations had been formed in twelve of the thirty metropolitan areas with the largest Asian American populations, with the largest number of organizations in New York, San Francisco, and Washington, D.C. (see table 3.2).[22] Only a few organizations had been established in Atlanta, Boston, Chicago, Detroit, Houston, Los Angeles, Philadelphia, Seattle, and Denver, and other metropolitan areas had none at all.

The variation in pan-Asian activity by geographic location suggests that panethnic organizing is not constant but can emerge and retreat under certain conditions. According to the racialization framework, the ways in which institutions use race-based policies and practices and individuals come to adopt racialized views and beliefs encourage distinct ethnic groups to organize as part of a larger panethnic group.[23] Although racialization has been the main explanation for panethnicity, it fails to account for the fact that racial policies and categories do not automatically

Table 3.2 Top Thirty Metropolitan Areas with the Largest Asian American Populations in 1990

Anaheim–Santa Ana–Garden Grove, California	Minneapolis–Saint Paul, Minnesota
Atlanta, Georgia[a]	Nassau–Suffolk, New York[a]
Baltimore, Maryland[a]	Newark, New Jersey
Bergen–Passaic, New Jersey[a]	New York, New York[a]
Boston, Massachusetts	Philadelphia, Pennsylvania–New Jersey[a]
Chicago, Illinois[a]	Phoenix, Arizona
Portland, Oregon–Washington	Riverside–San Bernardino, California
Dallas–Ft. Worth, Texas	Sacramento, California[a]
Denver, Colorado	San Diego, California[a]
Detroit, Michigan[a]	San Francisco–Oakland, California[a]
Fresno, California	San Jose, California
Honolulu, Hawaii	Seattle–Everett, Washington[a]
Houston, Texas[a]	Stockton, California
Los Angeles–Long Beach, California[a]	Vallejo–Fairfield–Napa, California
Middlesex–Somerset–Hunterdon, New Jersey	Washington, D.C.–Maryland–Virginia[a]

Source: PUMS (1995).
[a]National panethnic organizations involving Asian-origin groups were formed during the post-1968 era.

translate into panethnic outcomes. Simply because ethnic and immigrant groups are categorized in particular ways by institutions and individuals does not mean that they will act or organize accordingly. The variation in pan-Asian activity by geographic location suggests that racialization emanating from the macro and micro levels alone does not result in panethnic organizational activity uniformly across different locales.

To understand when and where groups take up racial categories and engage in panethnic organizing—in this case, by forming panethnic organizations—a useful approach is to examine local economic and demographic conditions, which can shape how groups view and interact with one another and hinder or encourage their cooperation across ethnic lines. In particular, the ways in which ethnic and racial groups are structured in relation to one another—as proximate, segregated together in neighborhoods and labor markets; or as diffuse, living and working in racially and ethnically diverse and integrated social spaces—may tell us how they develop interests and share commonalities. Competition and segregation frameworks, depicted in figure 3.3, account for variation in group action over time and place by looking to changes in demographic and economic conditions and identifying different mechanisms for the expansion of group boundaries.

Figure 3.3 The Segregation and Competition Models: Local Conditions and Mechanisms for the Emergence of Panethnicity

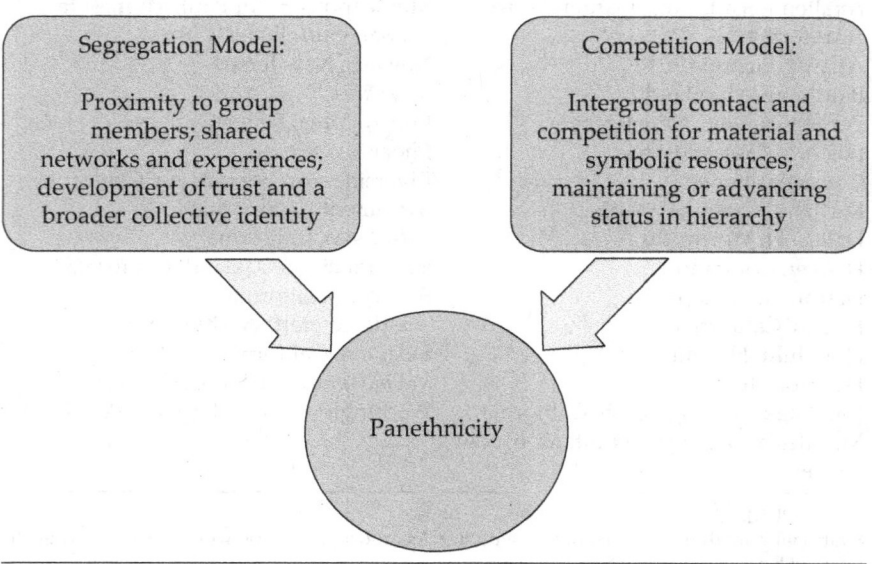

Source: Author's calculations.

According to the competition model, higher levels of panethnicity should emerge when groups are competing with one another for scarce resources.[24] The mechanism of competition links economic and demographic shifts, such as declining economic conditions and increasing contact, to more rigid racial boundaries: as different racial groups interact with one another in local areas and experience declining economic conditions, competition for resources such as jobs, schools, neighborhoods, and even marital partners rises. Ethnic groups that share a racial category cooperate under these conditions so that they can effectively compete—in this case, Asians compete with whites, blacks, or Latinos.[25] In contrast, the segregation model predicts that group boundaries will sharpen when racial groups are segregated from one another, not when they experience increasing contact.[26] Segregation within local labor markets provides a structural location where the distinct ethnic groups in a larger racial grouping can interact as equals, develop trust, and recognize shared interests. Groups may develop an even greater sense of panethnic solidarity if they believe that their concentration in a particular institutional space is due to their racial group membership; they may come to feel like they are part of a community of fate.[27]

When the models are applied to new Asian immigrant groups in the United States, it is not sufficient to simply examine the relations between Asians and other racial groups, whether majority or minority. Relations *within* the category of Asian must be interrogated as well. In other words, whereas researchers who study race and ethnicity might emphasize group cohesion and elaborate on interracial relations, those focused on panethnicity begin by analyzing how the different subgroups making up a broader identity or category view, interact, and relate to one another.[28] Because group boundaries are layered, such that identities can be organized along multiple dimensions, we must pay attention to intergroup as well as intragroup dynamics. To understand how ethnic groups organize upon a new, broader identity, we must recognize that segregation and competition can occur both among and within racial groups, with differing effects on panethnicity. For example, the segregation of Asian ethnic groups from one another in local labor markets hinders the possibility of panethnic activity.[29] If Chinese, Korean, Filipino, Indian, and Vietnamese Americans are concentrated in different industries, jobs, and occupations in Los Angeles and New York to a greater degree than in Chicago and Houston, we would expect lower levels of panethnicity in the former metro areas than in the latter. The labor market distributions of different Asian-origin groups in Los Angeles and New York hinder their ability to interact regularly across ethnic lines and develop common interests around which to organize. Asian-origin groups in Houston and Chicago may not have natural affinities, but they may interact more regularly, come to share common experiences, and develop trust upon which panethnicity can flourish, often at the behest of Asian American community leaders and activists.

Likewise, Asian-origin groups competing with one another in local neighborhoods and labor markets should hinder the possibilities for panethnicity. Although ethnic clustering does occur within labor markets, ethnic groups can challenge the monopoly of particular occupational niches when there are opportunities to do so, generating competitive relations. There also may be a perception of competition if an ethnic group begins to dominate an occupational niche, or even if the size of the ethnic group population rapidly rises. If the Vietnamese population in Houston increases in size and economic status relative to other Asian-origin groups, yet remains stagnant in Chicago, we should see more interethnic contact and competition among Asian-origin groups in Houston. If the competition model is correct, these demographic and economic shifts should result in lower levels of panethnic organizing. In other words, when ethnic groups are competing with one another, panethnicity may be an unlikely outcome.

Separate yet Competing

During the pre-1968 era, Asian-origin groups experienced spatial segregation from labor market competition with one another and the racial majority. Lack of citizenship and property rights, restrictive covenants, and informal discriminatory practices kept Asians segregated into enclaves and ghettos, and separated from the larger society.[30] Within these segregated areas, Asian ethnic groups lived somewhat apart from one another, though Koreans, Filipinos, and Indians settled near or within Chinatowns, and some developed businesses there.[31] Asian ethnic groups also competed with one another within labor markets and industry sectors such as agriculture.[32] As discussed in chapter 2, Japanese tenant farmers and field hands on the West Coast used distancing strategies and espoused a racial ideology to differentiate themselves from Filipino and Indian laborers, whom they viewed as competitors. Asian immigrants also competed with whites and other racial groups in working as strikebreakers in the early twentieth century.[33]

In the post-1968 period, interracial competition has been prevalent in some local and regional areas as Asian immigrants have opened up small businesses in predominantly black neighborhoods, purchased homes near or in white neighborhoods, and entered industries that were once dominated by native-born whites or blacks. For example, Korean grocers and merchants have often functioned as a middleman minority in low-income urban neighborhoods in New York and Los Angeles, a position that has led to interracial tensions and competition for customers, status, and even respect.[34] The influx of Asian immigrants into suburban communities over the past few decades has been accompanied by some interracial conflict as those areas experience the resulting social and demographic changes.[35] A prominent example is the San Gabriel Valley in Southern California, where Chinese, Latinos, and whites have competed for space, political power, and cultural dominance.[36]

Given that Asian ethnic groups have typically settled in immigrant-receiving metropolitan areas, there may be interethnic competition among them for the same resources and occupational niches. Chinese-Vietnamese entrepreneurs tend to dominate Vietnamese ethnic enclaves such as Little Saigon in Southern California, but they still deal with competition from Thai, Taiwanese, and Chinese immigrants who also seek to serve refugee customers.[37] In New York, Korean immigrants have dominated the wholesale businesses in manufactured Asian goods, but many Indian and Chinese immigrants recently entered the scene and have a competitive advantage because they can secure merchandise for cheaper rates from their home countries.[38] The same interethnic dynamics characterize the garment industry in Los Angeles and New York, where Chinese and Korean immigrants are now facing new competition from Vietnamese, Thai, and Indian immigrants.[39]

Asian Americans also experienced segregation in local labor markets during the post-1968 period, an outcome that was shaped by the Immigration and Nationality Act of 1965. The act allowed Asian immigrants to freely enter the United States after over forty years of exclusion. Family reunification provisions were a key part of the new policy, which permitted U.S. citizens to sponsor family members to immigrate to the United States.[40] Because of their history of being excluded and deprived of citizenship rights, Asian immigrants did not arrive in large numbers under the reunification provisions during the first post-1965 wave. Instead, the majority of Asian immigrants entered the United States using the employment-based provisions, which selected for educated and highly skilled immigrants, and resulted in an overrepresentation of Asian immigrants among medical and health care professionals, engineers, computer specialists, and other scientists.[41] Highly skilled immigrants continued to arrive in later waves from different parts of Asia. From 1988 to 1990, more than 150,000 highly skilled immigrants from all over the world were admitted into the United States, and over half of them (77,827, or 51.5 percent) were from Asia.[42] While a significant proportion of professionals originated from China and India, scientists and engineers were overrepresented among Asian immigrants regardless of national origin.[43]

Subsequent waves of Southeast Asian refugees who arrived in the United States under the Refugee Act of 1980, which expanded the definition of a refugee and provided procedures for government resettlement, faced more difficult challenges in the labor market.[44] Cambodian, Laotian, Hmong, and Vietnamese refugees entered the United States with limited English proficiency, low levels of education, and few skills. Their social and cultural adjustment was difficult; they either remained unemployed or found work as assembly-line workers, machine operators, or technicians in labor-intensive industries such as garments and microelectronics.[45] They also found refuge in other segments of the American economy, such as small-scale retail and restaurants, where educational credentials were not required and discrimination against them was less severe, especially within ethnic enclaves.[46]

The changes in federal immigration policy and the restructuring of the American economy in response to globalization contributed to the concentration of Asian Americans in two types of occupations: high-status professional and technical occupations and low-skilled service and manual jobs.[47] Table 3.3 displays the percentage of Asian Americans in selected professional and nonprofessional occupations in 1960 and 2000. In 1960

Table 3.3 Asians in Professional and Nonprofessional Occupations, 1960 and 2000

Occupation	1960	2000
Professional		
Physical scientist	0.7%	15.3
Life scientists	3.6	14.7
Computer specialists	1.2	13.2
Mathematicians	0.6	11.1
Engineers	0.9	9.9
Nonprofessional		
Machine, transportation, and other operators	1.7	16.4
Personal service workers and barbers	0.5	5.1
Cleaning and food service workers	1.1	4.7
Craftsmen	0.3	4.7
Total percentage Asians in occupations	0.5	4.1

Source: Xie and Goyette (2004).

Asians made up 0.5 percent of the labor force and were overrepresented in occupations where they comprised more than 0.5 percent, such as life scientists (3.6 percent), computer specialists (1.2 percent), machine and transportation operators (1.7 percent), and cleaning and food service workers (1.1 percent). By 2000 Asian Americans were over 4 percent of the labor force and continued to be overrepresented in many of the same professional and nonprofessional occupations.[48] For example, of all machine and transportation workers in the United States, over 16 percent were Asian American, even though Asians were 4.1 percent of the total national workforce.

Although Asian Americans experienced labor market segregation and competition during the post-1968 era, it is not clear whether these processes affected the expansion of group boundaries among Asian Americans. Table 3.4 shows that metropolitan areas with higher levels of panethnic organization formation (such as Los Angeles, New York, and San Francisco) experienced higher levels of segregation—measured here as occupational hierarchy (the extent to which Asians were concentrated in low-skill occupations relative to other racial groups)—than metropolitan areas with lower levels of panethnic organization formation (such as Atlanta, Baltimore, and Sacramento). Being segregated from other racial groups could have led to higher levels of group solidarity among Asian ethnic groups, resulting in pan-Asian activity. These same "high-panethnicity" areas also experienced higher average unemployment ratios between Asians and other racial groups compared to "low-panethnicity" areas. An

Table 3.4 Labor Market Segregation and Competition in Metropolitan Areas, by Levels of Panethnic Organizational Formation, 2000

Metropolitan Area	Segregation	Competition
High panethnicity		
New York	0.095	1.17
San Francisco	0.089	1.15
Los Angeles	0.082	0.85
Low panethnicity		
Sacramento	−0.030	1.03
Atlanta	−0.006	1.05
Baltimore	−0.007	1.76

Source: Author's calculation from 2000 U.S. census public-use microdata samples (PUMS).
Notes: "Segregation" refers to the extent to which Asians are concentrated in the lower part of the occupational structure relative to other racial groups in the metropolitan area. Higher values are associated with higher levels of segregation. Competition is captured with an unemployment ratio, which measures the ratio of the percentage of unemployed Asians to the percentage of unemployed in other racial groups in a metropolitan area. A value greater than one indicates that Asians are doing better relative to whites and other racial groups in regard to employment.

unemployment ratio compares the percentage of unemployed Asians and the percentage of unemployed members of all other racial groups. A value of one indicates racial parity, whereas a value greater than one indicates that Asians are better off economically (that is, a lower percentage are unemployed) relative to other racial groups, which could spur intergroup competition because Asians are making gains relative to other groups. In turn, competition could encourage Asians to organize as a larger political unit to make claims, gain access to resources, and solidify their group position above others.

Which, if any, of these factors encouraged Asian-origin groups to take up the label of "Asian American" and build new institutions? In the next section, I discuss my focus on panethnic organizations and test these theoretical ideas about the underlying meso-level conditions shaping the assertion of panethnic group boundaries.

FORMING PANETHNIC ORGANIZATIONS

Understanding the formation of organizations with a national reach is important for gaining insights about the strength of the pan-Asian organizational field. Given my interest in examining how economic and demographic shifts in local areas have shaped panethnic organizing in the post-1968 era, one might wonder why I focus on the emergence of *national* rather than local organizations. In other words, why not examine the formation of local organizations over time and place?[49]

As I looked more closely at the histories of national Asian American organizations, I became convinced that they are an appropriate object of analysis if the goal is to understand the local dynamics of group boundaries. It became clear that pan-Asian national organizations did not start as large entities with mission statements, full-time paid staff, organizational space, and boards of directors. The vast majority of these organizations began locally, with an idea and a need in the community they sought to address. Their first efforts were characterized by a core group of Asian Americans who volunteered to provide services or advocacy for the Asian immigrant community. Eventually, these organizations developed formal programs and services and applied for grants from public and private funders. Over time they evolved to oversee other chapters and build larger constituencies spanning local areas. Today these organizations play an important role in claims-making and advocacy because they consistently work to ensure that immigrant, ethnic, and racial group concerns and issues are met by local and national authorities. These pan-Asian organizations often serve as the main liaison between the Asian American community and political officials and policymakers, and often establilsh the key issues, strategies, and networks. For example, in the 1990s and again in the 2000s, national panethnic organizations requested that the U.S. Commission on Civil Rights conduct public hearings on the widespread bias and worsening social and political climate for immigrants and Asian Americans. Furthermore, I note that building a panethnic organization with a national reach is no easy task.

Given this history and evolution, local conditions should play an important role in the formation of these organizations. To find out if and how economic and demographic shifts have been associated with pan-Asian organizational formation during the post–civil rights era, I estimated the effects of competition and segregation on the emergence of panethnic organizations each year within thirty metropolitan areas with the highest Asian American populations. Methodologically, it was important to select locations where Asians resided, and not only those places where pan-Asian activity had occurred.[50] Even though the thirty metropolitan areas have large Asian American populations, they vary on a number of dimensions, including population size, racial and ethnic diversity, size of the Asian population, financial and human capital resources, political opportunities, and organizational dynamics. Because many of these factors have been important in predicting the founding of voluntary and social movement organizations, I created variables to capture these

Table 3.5 The Effects of Racial Competition and Segregation on the Formation of Pan-Asian Organizations, 1970–1998

Independent Variable	Regression Coefficient	Standard Error
Competition		
In-migration rate	6.82	(4.23)
Asian-white unemployment ratio	6.47	(9.24)
Poverty rate	−0.11	(0.09)
Labor market segregation		
Racial segregation	0.24	(0.18)
Racial hierarchy	3.63***	(0.76)
Intercept	10.30	(9.25)
−2 log likelihood	223.37	
McFadden's R-squared	0.45	

Source: Author's analysis of Asian American national organizations data set (Okamoto, 2006).
***p < .001 (two-tailed tests)
Note: N = 870. Results are generated from a zero-inflated Poisson regression model. Robust standard errors are presented in parentheses. Racial segregation measures the degree to which Asians as a group are occupationally specialized relative to all other racial groups. Racial hierarchy refers to the degree to which Asians as a group are concentrated in low-status occupations relative to all other racial groups. All variables are measured at the metropolitan-area level. These models also include the percentage Asian, the size of the metropolitan area, ethnic diversity, prior organizational foundings, and a host of other control variables (see table A.2 and appendix A for further details).

constructs and included them in the models presented here.[51] I estimated a zero-inflated count model that allowed me to find out whether competition and segregation encouraged the emergence of panethnic organizations above and beyond the impact of other factors, such as the percentage of Asians and resources available in the local area.

The results for the main variables of interest are displayed in table 3.5. A key finding is that the occupational segregation of Asian Americans encouraged the formation of national pan-Asian organizations. Specifically, when Asians found themselves segregated in lower levels of the occupational structure—reflecting racial hierarchy—racial group boundaries tightened, leading Asians to form their own institutions along panethnic lines.[52] Figure 3.4 demonstrates that higher levels of racial hierarchy are associated with higher predicted probabilities for the formation of panethnic organizations. This result may be surprising, given that the model minority stereotype would suggest that Asian Americans are assimilating and doing well occupationally.[53] However, even though Asian Americans are concentrated in professional occupations in the fields of medicine, sci-

Figure 3.4 Predicted Probabilities for the Formation of Panethnic Organizations, by Level of Racial Segregation in the Labor Market

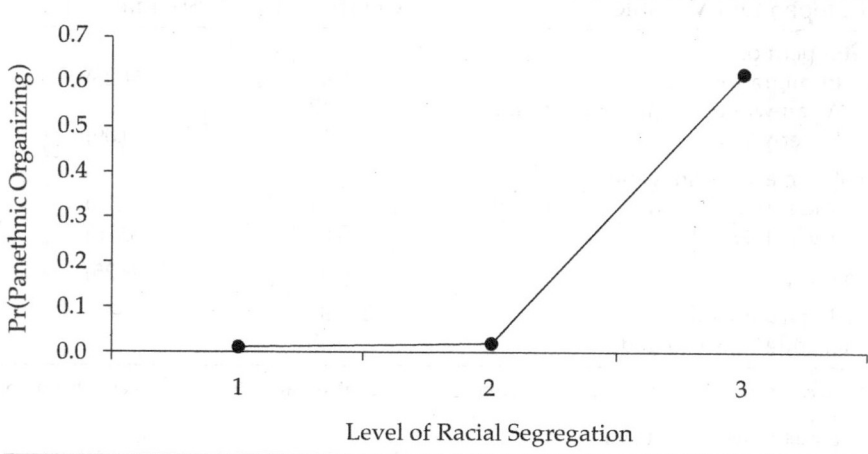

Source: Asian American national organizations data set (Okamoto 2006).
Note: Racial segregation refers to occupational segregation between Asians and all other racial groups.

ence, and technology, they are also concentrated in low-skilled jobs in the service and manufacturing sectors.[54] In fact, as we can see in table 3.3, from 1960 to 2000 there was an increase in the number of Asians employed in low-skilled manual work, such as textile operators, craftsmen, other operators, and cleaning and food service workers. This bimodal occupational distribution of Asian Americans is due to the fact that many Asian immigrants and refugees who settled in the United States had little education, little to no English-language fluency, and skills that did not translate well into the American context, while others arrived here with technical skills, education, and ties to capital in the homeland.[55]

This result showing the key role of racial segregation in generating panethnic organizational activity is not consistent with a competition framework, which suggests that the conditions associated with higher levels of intergroup contact in neighborhoods, workplaces, schools, and public spaces (less racially segregated labor markets and increases in the proportion of newcomers in local areas) result in competition for scarce resources and the sharpening of group boundaries. Under such conditions, and in the face of threat from whites and other racial groups, Asian ethnic groups

Figure 3.5 Predicted Probabilities for the Formation of Panethnic Organizations, by Ethnic Segregation in the Labor Market

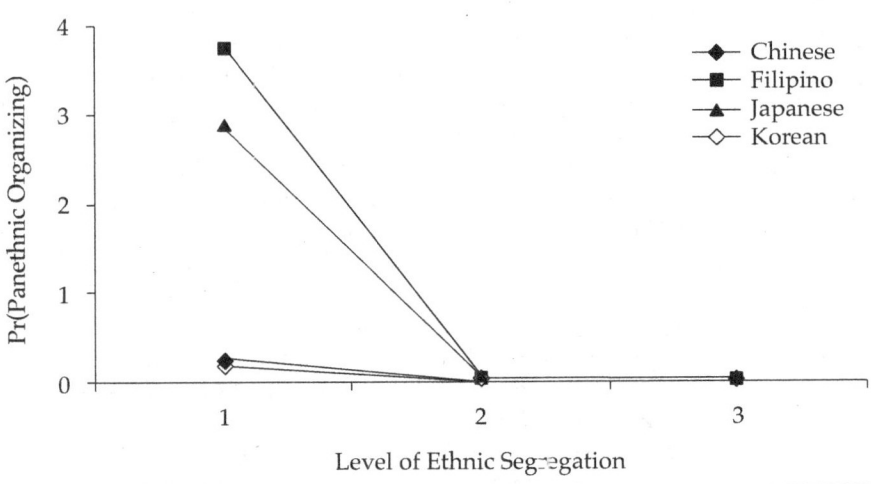

Source: Asian American national organizations data set (Okamoto 2006).
Note: Ethnic segregation refers to occupational segregation between each Asian ethnic group and all other Asian ethnic groups (that is, Chinese and all other Asian ethnic groups combined; Filipinos and all other Asian ethnic groups combined, and so on).

should cooperate with one another and engage in panethnic activity—an effective way to signify or enact group boundaries. Additionally, the results reported in table 3.5 do not support another major tenet of competition theory: economic downturns in local areas (captured by relatively high levels of poverty and unemployment rates) increase intergroup competition for jobs, housing, and social status.[56]

When examining the relations among Asian ethnic groups, we find that when Asian ethnic groups are segregated from one another in local labor markets, this discourages panethnicity. Under these conditions, it is more difficult for distinct groups to create interethnic networks and form a common identity upon which to organize. Figure 3.5 illustrates the predicted probabilities of panethnic organizational emergence for four Asian-origin groups. The pattern shown here indicates that panethnic organizations are more likely to arise when the ethnic groups are less segregated.

Competition between Asian ethnic groups also does not discourage panethnicity (see table A.3 in appendix A). Instead, the entry of different

Asian ethnic groups into local areas actually facilitates new panethnic organizational activity. Even though new immigrants may not initially identify as Asian American, immigration from different countries throughout Asia contributes to a population that can be served by new organizations with a diverse Asian American constituency. A growing Asian American population has been vital in the institutionalization of a panethnic community, as the vast majority of national pan-Asian organizations that were formed to provide direct services and advocacy for their local Asian American population have evolved into organizations with a national reach. Therefore, it makes sense that organizations are forming where there are visible Asian American communities.

It is also important to note that the already established presence of panethnic organizations in a metropolitan area encourages the formation of yet more organizations; thus, panethnic organizational density may promote the institutional acceptability and legitimation of the panethnic form, increasing the rate of new foundings.[57] Additionally, attacks against Asians increased the formation of pan-Asian organizations, which supports work by Yen Le Espiritu, which has suggested that anti-Asian sentiment and violence are key factors in generating panethnicity.[58] Espiritu notes that attackers often do not differentiate between Asian-origin groups, mistaking one Asian ethnic group for another, and the chilling result is that all Asians are under threat. This dynamic creates a "reactive (pan)ethnicity" as Asians recognize their shared status and organize together to combat anti-Asian violence.[59]

In general, these findings demonstrate that both intergroup and intragroup dynamics are key in understanding the emergence of panethnic organizing: racial segregation in local labor markets encourages Asian-origin ethnic groups to organize as a larger panethnic collective and form pan-Asian organizations, while segregation among Asian ethnic groups comprising a racial category complicates their ability to interact and build new identities, dampening the possibilities for panethnicity.

Although both ethnic and racial segregation shape panethnicity—in opposing ways, as shown in figure 3.6—I wanted to find out which is more central to understanding boundary expansion. Does ethnic segregation have such large effects that racial segregation plays only a small role in explaining panethnicity? Or does racial segregation play a more significant role? In additional analyses, I included both Asian ethnic and racial segregation variables in the same model and found that racial segregation is key for understanding boundary change. When controlling for the extent of segregation among Asian ethnic groups, Asian occupational segregation still increased the odds of panethnic organizational emergence,

The Emergence of Organizational Panethnicity   75

Figure 3.6 Opposing Effects of Ethnic and Racial Occupational Segregation on Panethnicity

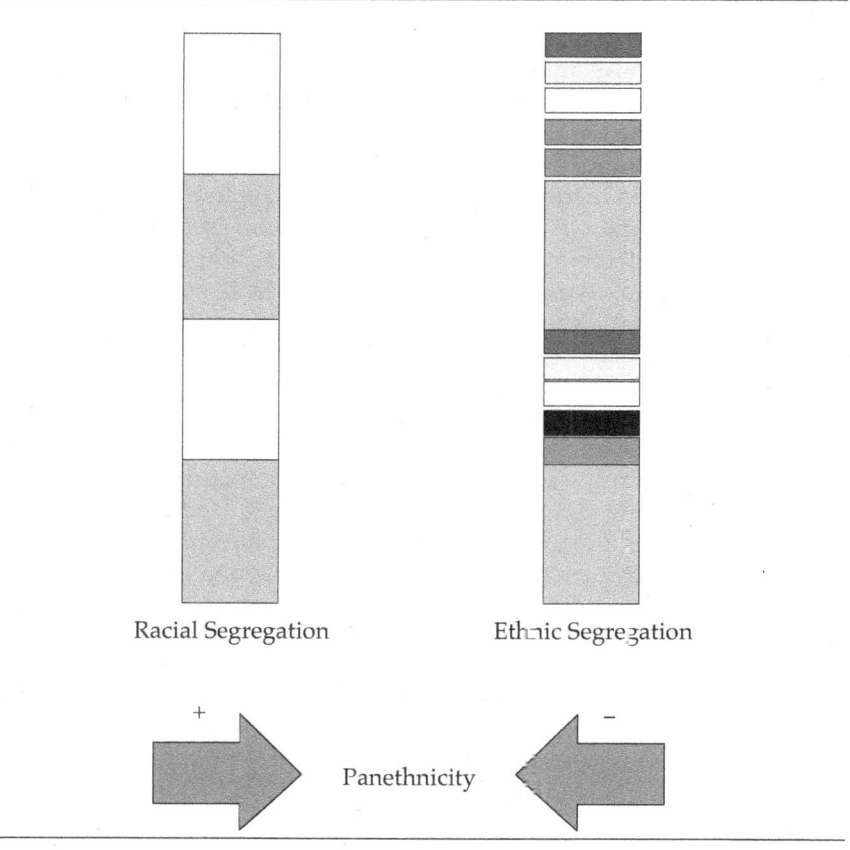

Source: Author's calculations.
Note: Column 1 represents racial segregation in the labor market where white blocks refer to Asians and shaded blocks refer to non-Asians. In column 2, the different smaller corresponding blocks with various shading represent Asian national-origin groups and their segregation in the labor market from one another. The arrows indicate the direction of the effects of racial and ethnic segregation on panethnicity.

and its positive effect was larger than the effects of ethnic segregation. Clearly, how groups are organized and structured in regard to race and racial categories—whether by discrimination, preference, or inertia—heightens group boundaries and fosters in-group interests and networks. In this case, it also produces pan-Asian activity.

ESTABLISHING GROUP BOUNDARIES

Broader social conditions such as changes in immigration policy, new social and political opportunities, and social movements encouraged the formation of a pan-Asian ideology and label. Nevertheless, it was racially segregated occupational structures in local contexts that encouraged the development of trust and solidarity across ethnic lines after 1968 and led Asian Americans to take up and use the panethnic label when building new institutions. In metropolitan areas that had higher average levels of organizational foundings—New York and San Francisco, for instance, as opposed to Philadelphia and Boston—it was not simply the size of the Asian American population that led to organizational emergence, but the way in which Asians were distributed and structured in local labor markets. These labor market conditions were critical to the ability of Asian-origin groups to develop interethnic ties and shared interests and engage in pan-Asian organizational activity.

Finding support for the segregation model is particularly interesting given that in past research the mechanism of competition has been successful in explaining ethnic collective action.[60] Such studies have demonstrated that competition by newcomers and racial minorities has motivated dominant groups across different historical contexts to engage in exclusion activities and protests and form new organizations. For example, whites fought to maintain their social and economic status when new immigrants entered the United States at the turn of the century, when students were bused between urban and suburban areas to integrate public schools in the 1960s, and when local economies experienced declines in multiracial cities in the contemporary era.[61]

The majority of the research, which has tested and refined the competition model, has focused on majority group collective action, and this has hidden the fact that the structural location and placement of groups in the racial hierarchy plays an important role in shaping collective organizing. Whites remain at the top of the racial hierarchy in the United States, and historically their engagement in protests and attacks against other groups symbolized the *defense* of group boundaries, access to privilege, and a monopoly over resources.[62] In contrast, Asian ethnic groups are located below whites in the racial hierarchy, and as a group Asians are not defending their place in the stratification system; they are considered an immigrant and racial minority group and only recently asserted their shared interests across ethnic lines. Instead of *defending* group boundaries, Asians are *establishing* new group boundaries around which to organize and build communities and identities. Although competition has transpired between Asians and other racial groups over the post-1968 era, it is not a driving force for pan-Asian organizing. Competition in the standard sense—interracial competition stemming from demographic and economic changes—does not encourage the expansion of ethnic boundaries. This is consistent with the narratives of some Asian American organizational and community leaders who are veterans of the nonprofit world: they view Latinos and African Americans, not as competitors, but as collaborators and even in-group members in the larger project of social justice.[63]

The Role of Leaders and Panethnic Narratives

It was not simply segregation and the mechanisms of intergroup interaction and the development of shared interests and trust among Asian-origin groups that drove panethnic organizational emergence. I argue that *leaders* also played a key role in the panethnic process. Although segregated occupational structures facilitated interaction among ethnic groups and broke down cultural barriers, they also represented a visible inequality that advocates and organizers could draw upon to form organizations to serve the needs of low-wage workers and to address the underrepresentation of Asian Americans in certain sectors of the economy (such as journalism, social sciences) and society (such as arts and the media) and their lack of access to networks and power structures within these sectors. These organizations addressed the economic, social, and political inequalities faced by Asian Americans, whether focused on labor, education, arts and culture, or politics and citizenship.

While Asian immigrants experienced residential segregation along with occupational segregation, it was more difficult for activists and community leaders to construct a narrative around the residential segregation of Asian Americans. One reason was that many Asians in the post-1968 era were no longer confined to ethnic enclaves. In fact, a large proportion of the Asian American population moved to suburban areas, though this did not necessarily mean that Asians had assimilated into predominantly white neighborhoods.[54] Some Asians remained within ethnic enclaves, but many of these areas were now considered desirable social locations where immigrants can access community organizations, churches, restaurants, and other businesses that cater to their needs.[65] Ethnic enclaves were no longer associated with filth and second-class citizenship, but with opportunities for employment and ethnic entrepreneurship.[66] A racially segregated occupational structure, on the other hand, was associated with clear economic inequalities and unfair treatment upon which leaders could capitalize.

A significant number of pan-Asian organizations founded during the post-1968 era—both nationally and locally in the San Francisco–Oakland metropolitan area—provided underserved, low-income Asian American populations with information and resources about their rights. Often founded by a small group of community members, these organizations provided services and advocated for immigrants who were segmented in the secondary labor market, where jobs were associated with low wages, instability, poor working conditions, and few health benefits. Over time, professionals joined the ranks of these nonprofits, providing an important link between the primary and secondary occupational sectors and often enabling organizations to form, grow, and reach a broader Asian American population.[67]

Organizations such as the Asian Pacific American Labor Alliance (APALA) and Asian Immigrant Women's Advocates (AIWA) were founded to educate Asian American workers, promote political organizing, and provide training and leadership.[68] Located in Oakland, AIWA opened its doors to serve the needs of low-income Asian immigrant women and help them address shared issues related to labor discrimination and exploitation.[69] The women who have used AIWA's services and attended their workshops are primarily of Chinese, Vietnamese-Chinese, and Korean descent and are employed as seamstresses, hotel cleaners, janitors, and electronics assemblers. Serving a national membership of union workers, APALA advocates for similar issues, but on a broader scale.[70] Both organizations sponsor community education workshops to raise awareness among workers and employers in different industries and to help organize Asian American workers to advocate for their rights. By participating in these APALA and AIWA programs and similar ones in other organizations, different ethnic groups have the opportunity to work together on campaigns, advocate for their rights under one banner, and benefit from the political advances made by Asians as a group—and to build a broader and stronger panethnic community in the process.

Community activists and leaders not only founded organizations to help Asian ethnic groups concentrated in low-wage jobs to coordinate their shared interests but also created and reproduced a larger pan-Asian narrative to combat the stereotype of Asians as model minorities and make the lives and experiences of Asian laborers more visible. The pan-Asian framework often articulated by leaders, referenced that Asian Americans make up a political community with shared interests, experiences, and histories. For example, APALA leaders have drawn upon the past histories of Asian laborers in the United States—Chinese railroad workers, striking Hawaii plantation workers, Filipino farmworkers—and highlighted their shared experiences of legalized exclusion to bolster a pan-Asian framework. They also intersperse this narrative with contemporary examples of Asian Americans—a Burmese steel worker, an Indian shipyard worker, a Chinese casino dealer, a Vietnamese civil engineer—who have experienced employer intimidation, health and safety violations, wage theft, and union suppression.[71] For example, an APALA report likened a Filipino teacher's experience of worker exploitation—having to share one room with eighteen other workers and being charged different amounts by Philippine and U.S. recruitment agencies—to "a form of indentured servitude that recalls memories of the conditions that the first 'coolies' faced while working on the railroads."[72]

Organizational leaders also emphasize the diverse experiences of the different Asian ethnic groups: not all, for instance, are as high-achieving as the model minority stereotype would purport. The leaders of Asian Americans and Pacific Islanders in Philanthropy (AAPIP) and Asian Pacific Environmental Network (APEN) are representative of many leaders of pan-Asian advocacy organizations: although they use different approaches to create social change—philanthropy and grassroots organizing, respectively—the leaders of both organizations use a pan-Asian narrative about the social inequalities that Asian Americans face, and they do so within what they refer to as Asian American "marginalized" communities. These organizations push back against the model minority stereotype by noting that Asian Americans are disadvantaged by their immigrant, refugee, racial minority, or low-income status when it comes to environmental justice, access to health care, affordable housing, and workers' rights. Leaders at both organizations also work to educate the larger public about why Asian Americans are organizing their communities. A leader at APEN explained: "One of the questions that we get so often at APEN is, 'Why is there a need to organize the API community?' And so there are a couple of different levels there. One is that people think of the model minority rep, or they just don't know about the problems that exist and the whole diversity of the Asian community." He went on to talk about the dire needs of Laotian and Cambodian communities in the Bay Area and the high rates of poverty and unemployment, exposure to environmental toxins, and lack of adequate access to health care among the Southeast Asian, Filipino, and Chinese populations—facts that are often invisible to outsiders who subscribe to the stereotype and view Asians as a monolithic group with high rates of achievement and occupational success.

For AAPIP, a lack of support from organized philanthropy and public resources—because of misperceptions and stereotypes about the Asian American community in the United States—gives rise to the same issues. AAPIP's annual reports and organizational documents articulate a narrative about the diversity of the Asian American community and its lack of visibility in mainstream America. Its 2001 annual report noted, for example, that

> new AAPI [Asian American and Pacific Islander] communities are springing up, others exist quietly hidden from mainstream's view, while established communities are themselves in transition. Each struggles for voice and visibility, hoping to retain the richness of their culture while participating in the richness of America. They are the older communities whose roots harken to China or Japan, the invisible communities from Laos or the islands in the South Pacific, and the recently-established pockets of residents from India and Thailand. The nuances of their cultures as well as their needs are often overlooked or misunderstood by mainstream America.

AAPIP presented a similar narrative in organizational materials twelve years later, in 2013, suggesting that the Asian American community has still not been fully incorporated into and recognized by the larger society; indeed, in 2013 AAPIP cited the 2012 Pew report on Asian Americans and its retreat to the use of broad stereotypes in the face of an increasingly complex Asian American community.[73] AAPIP and its leaders see the lack of support for the Asian American community from organized philanthropy and public resources as an opportunity "to make visible that which organized philanthropy—and society, at large—has tried with intention or in effect to render invisible."[74] In its work over the past decade, AAPIP has prioritized programs that reflect the nuances and needs of the groups often underrepresented in the panethnic community, such as a funding collaboration among Arab, Middle Eastern, Muslim, and South Asian community-based organizations (CBOs) to build collective power; a leadership program for young Vietnamese Americans to improve their communities; and a program to engage Cambodian women in philanthropy. AAPIP and AAPN both continue to use the pan-Asian framework and reproduce it by developing programs and funding streams that support different Asian-origin groups.

When forming organizations and creating narratives, leaders drew upon the fact that Asian Americans have been overrepresented in low-income jobs. These leaders and activists also formed pan-Asian organizations in response to Asian Americans' underrepresentation and the lack of diversity in other sectors of the economy. They have also constructed panethnic narratives about Asian Americans' shared experiences in U.S. society. Media and arts organizations, such as the Center for Asian American Media and the National Asian American Theatre Company, support Asian American artists and advocate for accurate portrayals of Asian Americans in the media. By funding individual artists and collaborative projects, featuring performances, and distributing media that reflect the experiences of Asian Americans, these organizations aim to counter stereotypes and the invisibility of Asians and Asian Americans in film, art, and television. A second-generation leader from a pan-Asian arts organization elaborated on the need for such organizations:

> Our idea about arts is about fostering leadership of Asian American arts. There are a lot of Asian Americans acting in films that don't necessarily know that there is a growing number of Asian American filmmakers, but at a certain level there's not that much support. Rather than it be about the music or the making of an art or film, it's really about the opportunity for Asian Americans to be leaders in a creative process.

This leader, like many others, sought to create a safe and productive space for Asian Americans in the arts, where there is often little support and few role models. One way to do so is under a panethnic umbrella that reinforces shared experiences and interests while providing encouragement and resources to pursue artistic freedom.

Asian Americans also formed professional organizations such as Asian American Architects and Engineers (AAAE), the Asian American Manufacturers Association (AAMA), and the National Association for Asian American Professionals (NAAAP), which share the goals of developing networks, encouraging equal employment opportunities, and exchanging knowledge in the field. These organizations seek out members from different Asian ethnic groups and offer regular meetings, professional development seminars, national conferences, and opportunities for community work. Even though Asian Americans are concentrated in the upper part of the occupational structure, this does not mean that they are well represented in all occupations or that their labor market experiences are free from racial discrimination or bias. In fact, research has documented that Asian American professionals have experienced being shut out of powerful networks and passed over for promotions because they are not viewed as "manager material" and are even rendered invisible as their accomplishments and efforts are downplayed or ignored.[75] Studies also have shown that despite their socioeconomic achievements, Asian Americans still do not achieve full parity with whites in regard to earnings.[76]

Members of panethnic professional organizations share not only an occupation or profession but also a common social position and experience due to their racial status as Asian Americans in the United States, and this is often reflected in how organizations and their leaders frame organizational missions, goals, priorities, and programs. For example, the Asian

American Journalists Association (AAJA), which was founded by a small group of Asian American journalists to provide encouragement and support for one another, also works to increase their employment opportunities as news managers and media executives. AAJA and its leaders place high priorities on providing the Asian American community with an understanding of how to gain fair access to the media; the organization also works to encourage fair and accurate news coverage of Asian and Asian Pacific American issues. AAJA has moved toward achieving these goals by developing mentoring and leadership programs, organizing conferences for networking and education opportunities, and fostering career development. In their efforts to improve the opportunities and experiences of both immigrant and native-born Asian Americans by providing the knowledge, tools, and narratives to help them break through glass ceilings, develop network ties, and compete in the job market, AAJA and many other professional organizations founded during the post-1968 era have constructed and fortified a pan-Asian identity and narrative.

While there is considerable variation among these organizations in terms of practice, approach, and activity, gaining insights into how leaders formed pan-Asian organizations to serve the diverse needs of Asian Americans helps us to understand that Asians, in searching for their piece of the pie, have not formed organizations because they felt threatened by whites, blacks, or Latinos who were making social, economic, or political gains. There is no evidence that Asian Americans have engaged in panethnic organizational activity as an attempt to exclude other racial groups from attaining the resources necessary to move up in the social hierarchy. In fact, a number of Asian American organizations have been affiliated with coalitions of color to provide a stronger voice for all racial minorities in the United States. Instead, it is the structural context of occupational segregation—which derives from historical exclusion, immigrants' recent settlement patterns, and group preferences—that has facilitated interethnic networks and the construction of a social reality that community leaders and activists can draw upon when creating pan-Asian narratives that encourage distinct ethnic groups to view one another as having interests in common.

In short, upon finding themselves without representation, resources, opportunities, and at times fair treatment in the post-1968 era, Asian Americans proceeded to form pan-Asian organizations to attain these collective goods.

SUMMARY

Organizations founded by Asian Americans during the post-1968 era differed from their predecessors. The new organizations were no longer simply protective in function, nor did they serve to maintain ties to the homeland; their goal was to provide social services and advocacy for a broad range of Asian ethnic groups. They had panethnic names to reflect their constituency and membership and adopted a pan-Asian ideology as part of their mission to work across ethnic lines to address the continuing needs of the Asian American community through education, advocacy, legal action, and protest. Although pan-Asian organizations did not replace ethnic organizations as systems of social and economic support, they supplemented the work of ethnic organizations, and in seeking to provide for the needs of all Asian Americans, they brought a new approach to advocacy and service.

Broad social conditions—such as changes in federal legislation regarding immigration and civil rights—set the stage for panethnic organizational emergence (see chapter 2), but as highlighted in this chapter, local conditions shaped the ways in which groups enacted and expanded boundaries. Although ethnic groups experienced racialization by the state and the larger society and faced a political climate that was open to claims by minority groups, panethnicity was not an automatic outcome. Panethnic group formation was more likely when ethnic groups were positioned to develop shared interests, relations, and ties. In particular, the segregation of Asian-origin groups—rather than competition between them—encouraged panethnicity during the post-1968 era. The mechanisms of intergroup interaction, shared interests, and membership in a community of fate were more important than competition in shifting group boundaries. The concentration of Asians in the lower part of the occupational structure not only delineated a panethnic boundary, leading Asian Americans to found their own institutions, but also signaled that Asian Americans were not completely integrated into mainstream society despite their access to citizenship and civil rights. Community leaders and organizers were able to draw on the visible inequality in labor markets to form organizations to serve the needs of low-wage immigrant workers and Asian Americans who were underrepresented in certain sectors of the economy and lacked access to power structures within these sectors. These pan-Asian organizations were key in helping Asian Americans navigate within the larger society on an equal basis.

Furthermore, leaders and advocates crafted and reinforced a pan-Asian narrative based upon the idea that Asian Americans have shared experiences of historic and contemporary discrimination, yet also represent diversity and complexity due to the specific needs and issues of each national-origin group. By using this narrative to combat the embedded stereotype of Asians as model minorities, leaders made the lives and experiences of Asian Americans more visible and helped to improve access to social and civil rights for all Asian Americans, especially those concentrated at the bottom of the occupational structure. But even educated and highly skilled Asian Americans in the professions faced unequal wages, lack of access to key networks, and slower promotion rates, because Asians were not viewed as equal to whites. Community leaders organized around these social facts, formed new organizations, and created narratives about the shared interests of Asian Americans as well as their struggles and inequalities, which countered the model minority image. It is important to note that professional, advocacy, and labor organizations could not have been effective if Asians had been racially integrated into the occupational structure; in that event, they likely would have ceased to exist. Organizing as a broader entity brought attention to the issues that affected the diverse Asian communities—workplace inequalities related to labor, immigration, and language rights, as well as unequal access to legal services and health care—and leaders of these organizations played an important role in generating and reproducing pan-Asian narratives that emphasized common experiences and histories as well as a diversity of needs.

As we have seen in this chapter, it is important to interrogate and explore the processes and conditions under which panethnic group boundaries are formed or activated; we cannot make assumptions about how ethnic, language, and cultural groups will organize, as there are no natural affinities. "Asian American" is a socially constructed panethnic category that we now take for granted, but the structural conditions that have encouraged group formation and the narratives used and reproduced by leaders and organizations have been key to that process. Building on these insights, chapter 4 examines the emergence of pan-Asian protest and civic action in the post-1968 era and illuminates the interplay between ethnicity and panethnicity, thus helping us further understand how, when, and to what extent group boundaries shift and change.

Chapter 4 | The Ethnic-Panethnic Dynamics of Collective Action

IN STUDYING PANETHNICITY, we look at how groups draw boundaries largely in relation to others—defining who they are and who they are not—but we must also pay attention to the layered nature of group boundaries, especially in the case of new immigrant groups in the United States, where they can create identities and organize along multiple dimensions. Upon arrival, new immigrants hold national-origin identities, yet are often assigned to one of the racial groups upon which panethnic identities are formed. Chinese, Japanese, Korean, and Vietnamese Americans can organize along not only ethnic or national-origin lines but also the larger, panethnic boundary of "Asian American"; these two levels of organizing are often complicated, however, by differences in language, culture, and immigration history.

In the post-1968 era, ethnically and generationally diverse Asian Americans organized in the public arena across the United States—in Los Angeles, New York, Chicago, Detroit, Sacramento, and elsewhere—in response to police brutality and racial profiling, unfair political redistricting, and negative media representation.[1] Often with the help of panethnic organizations, Asian ethnic groups participated in rallies on the steps of city hall, voter registration drives in their neighborhoods, and letter-writing campaigns in the halls of local community centers in the hopes of influencing policymakers, the larger public, and their own ethnic communities. Organizing as Asian Americans, the different ethnic groups raised their voices in the political arena, and many of their collective efforts were successful. Yet during this same period *ethnicity* continued to be a salient boundary upon which to coordinate group action. Asian ethnic groups organized their own communities in response to urban redevelopment efforts, labor issues, and unfair treatment by local authorities.[2] They also engaged in collective action to bring visibility to important issues unfolding in their homelands.[3]

In further exploring the ways in which Asian Americans organized themselves in the public arena during the post-1968 era, this chapter traces patterns of collective action and demonstrates that ethnic and panethnic organizing can operate as complementary forms. The finding that ethnic organizing helped to build up and support panethnicity during this period is consistent with the idea that group boundaries are layered: organizing along ethnic lines neither attenuates nor diminishes panethnic collective action. Both types of organizing can flourish in a local environment, and often do. In fact, ethnic organizations and events are necessary building blocks for successful pan-Asian collective action across ethnic lines because of the support, resources, and networks they bring to the table. Moreover, the importance of ethnic-panethnic dynamics complicates the threat and racialization explanations of panethnicity: threats by the state or the larger society are not enough to generate panethnicity in the absence of local structures, such as ethnic organizing, which bridge different ethnic communities and serve as an infrastructure for collective organizing.

Besides ethnic organizing, segregation in local labor markets and the leaders within the Asian American community were also central factors in the emergence of panethnic collective action after 1968. As with the formation of pan-Asian organizations (see chapter 3), Asian-origin groups were more likely to organize across ethnic lines as a panethnic group when segregation situated them closer to one another than to other racial groups. Panethnic solidarity and cooperation were facilitated with this structural context, which encouraged interethnic ties, trust, and shared interests to develop. Group leaders contributed as well: they encouraged community members to see themselves as Asian American and to recognize the common position in the labor market and in U.S. society that they shared with other Asian-origin groups. Asian American leaders also built and reinforced the pan-Asian narrative that was used in protest and civic actions in the public arena.

PROTEST AND CIVIC ACTION IN ASIAN AMERICAN COMMUNITIES
The Struggle of Panethnic Organizing

When individuals work together in the pursuit of a common goal and make claims on behalf of an ethnic or racial group, a broader process of collective identity and group formation is at work.⁴ Engaging in public collective events such as protests, demonstrations, festivals, and celebrations on behalf of Asian Americans represents the grassroots efforts of community members to make broader statements about the needs and achievements of their communities.⁵ Community leaders play a role in the process by organizing group members, disseminating information, using organizational networks and resources, framing issues, building bridges between communities, calling on donors, and even setting the larger agenda for mobilization efforts.⁶ These collective efforts by group leaders and members required something that did not come naturally for Asian-origin groups: communication and coordination as well as shared interests across ethnic lines.

Sam, a veteran leader of a Japanese American organization in San Francisco, explained why coalitions and other organizing efforts within the Asian American community are not easy: "As a community activist both in Los Angeles and here, I couldn't do anything effective with the Chinese and Korean groups because of my ethnicity. I had to go through friends I had and work through them to work their own community." For Sam and other leaders of Asian American nonprofit organizations who had been in the nonprofit world for over two decades, developing links with other East Asian groups had been challenging because of ethnic prejudices and interests, and it continued to be difficult. In talking about interethnic group relations today, Sam plainly stated, "If you get into the heart of a community, especially in the immigrant community, you don't see that spirit of cooperation, it's much more protective, guarded." Even for this veteran leader, building ties and partnerships was a delicate task, and it was further complicated by the cultural, language, and ethnic differences that arise from the fact that Asians as a group are nearly 60 percent foreign-born. Many immigrant groups are unaccustomed to participating in collective action events, let alone organizing across ethnic lines, creating yet another barrier to involving community members in panethnic efforts.

Given such challenges, what did patterns of collective organizing among Asian Americans look like from the late 1960s to the early 2000s—the period after the rise of the Asian American identity and label? During this time, the national press covered 374 collective action events in which participants articulated an ethnic or panethnic claim on behalf of Asian ethnic groups or Asian Americans. I counted the total number of these events in metropolitan areas with the thirty largest Asian American populations.⁷ The vast majority of the events were ethnic in nature; only 59 were panethnic—two or more ethnic groups organizing collectively as Asian Americans—and as such these 59 events represent a lower bound estimate of panethnic activity, since the mainstream press typically reports on large, publicly visible events and tends to miss smaller, peaceful activities.[8] Nevertheless, this pattern of activity illustrates that even when panethnic mobilization could leverage Asians Americans as a group to compete for more economic and political resources, it does not often materialize. Ethnic groups have developed their separate interests, owing to their different immigration histories, cultures, languages, and religions, and they can more easily coordinate their interests; they may also prioritize issues differently from other groups in the Asian American category. For example, Chinese Americans may be more willing to engage in collective action behavior when the economic base of Chinatown is at stake than to protest a hate crime in another city or state. Protest issues often are more locally based for ethnic groups, while the issues for panethnic groups are likely to be larger and national in scope, requiring more resources and organization. This may explain why panethnic events have not occurred as often as ethnic events in the contemporary era.

How does the total number of pan-Asian events compare to the collective action efforts of other racial minority groups? African Americans also engaged in rallies and protests during the post-1968 era, but the height of their collective action occurred during the civil rights movement from 1955 to 1970. In 1965 alone, African Americans participated in over 200 events across the United States.[9] Between 1970 and 1998, African Americans engaged in a total of 268 collective action events, and Asian Americans participated in 59 pan-Asian events to bring visibility to issues of unfair treatment and racial discrimination and assert a collective identity.

To provide a context for understanding the extent and prevalence of panethnic activity among Asian Americans, figure 4.1 compares population-event ratios for blacks and Asians—the number of collective action events organized by and for African Americans and the number of events organized by and for Asian Americans in each decade between 1970 and 1998, divided by the size of the African American and Asian American populations, respectively. We can see that the population-event ratio increases for Asians and declines for African Americans over the nearly 30-year period. From 1970 to 1979, the ratio of protest events per 100,000 African Americans was nearly 0.6, and for Asian Americans the ratio was just above 0.1. By the 1990–1998 period, the ratios had shifted: for African Americans the ratio of protest events per 100,000 was 0.1, and for Asian Americans it was above 0.3. This pattern suggests that panethnic activity among Asian Americans can be understood as comparable to and even surpassing such activity among blacks, given their differing population sizes, in the latter part of the post-1968 era. And if we include ethnic events involving Asian Americans, the differences in the population-event ratios for blacks and Asians over the post-1968 era would be even more striking, as the ratio for

Figure 4.1 African American and Pan-Asian Protest Events in the Post–Civil Rights Era, per 100,000, by Decade

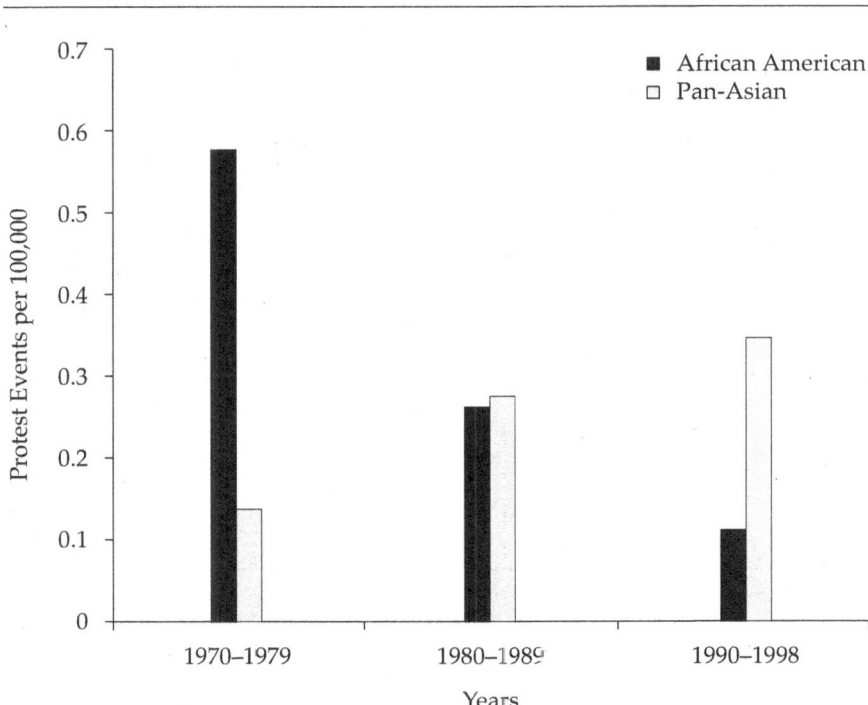

Source: The author's calculations using the data set on Asian American events from Okamoto (2003) and data on African American events from Jenkins, Jacobs, and Agnone (2003).

Asian Americans would be even higher. That said, a better comparison for Asian Americans may be Latinos, who are a new immigrant group rather than an established racial minority, but comparable data on Latino collective action are currently unavailable. Nevertheless, the comparison between Asian Americans and African Americans provides a useful context for understanding Asian American collective organizing from 1970 to 2000 in the United States.

Early Activism Among Asian Americans

In the first decade of the post-1968 era, there were few pan-Asian collective action events, as shown in figure 4.2. News reports about Asians during this period were focused on U.S. officials traveling to different parts of

Figure 4.2 Ethnic and Panethnic Collective Action Events Involving Asian Americans, 1970–1998

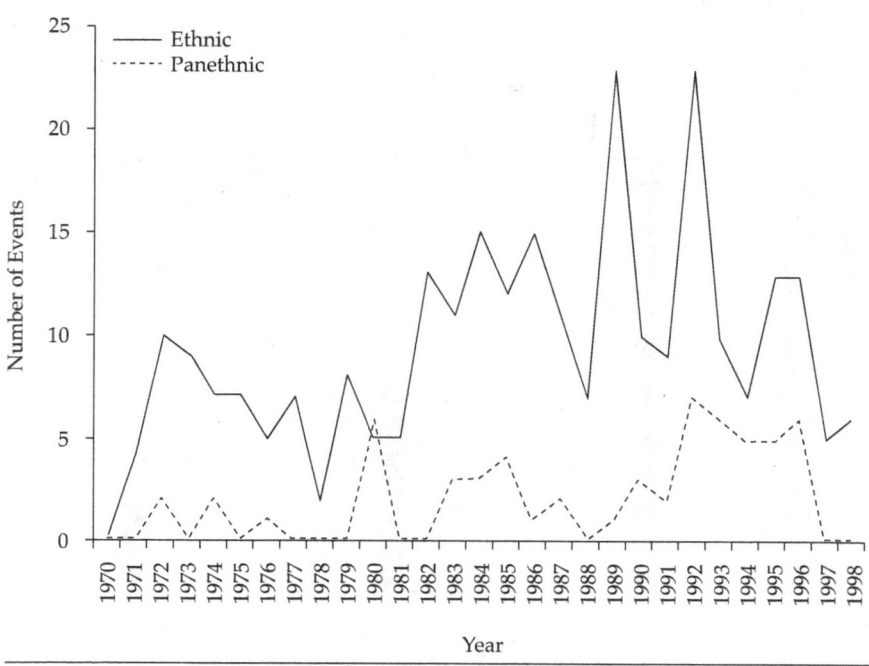

Source: Asian American event data collected by the author from the *New York Times*, the *Los Angeles Times*, and the *Chicago Tribune*.

Asia, the rising economic power of East Asian countries, turmoil in Southeast Asian countries, the U.S. secret war in Laos, and U.S.-Asian relations more broadly. Asian Americans themselves were organizing along ethnic lines about issues related to homeland politics and community revitalization efforts. They also participated in marches and demonstrations to challenge unfair treatment on the basis of ethnicity or national origin. For example, in the mid-1970s Chinese Americans organized a number of public marches and demonstrations in New York City—some of which were so large that they obstructed traffic in major thoroughfares—in response to police brutality, discrimination, and incidents of Chinese Americans being racially profiled as gangsters, drug dealers, or illegal aliens. The incident that particularly incensed the Chinatown community was the beating of Peter Yew, a young engineer from Brooklyn. The police attacked Yew in the street, and allegedly took him into custody and beat him again.[10] The marches and demonstrations were organized by Chinese community leaders, but people from all walks of life within the Chinese community participated—students, mothers with their children, businessmen, and merchants. These protest events were also clearly linked to claims based on ethnicity—how the police treated individuals because they were Chinese. The ethnic nature of the event was confirmed by the statement of an eighty-year-old woman who participated in one of the rallies: she explained through a translator, "I'm joining the demonstration because I'm Chinese."[11]

Ethnic groups also organized in the public arena to bring attention to ethnic issues such as redevelopment efforts that threatened ethnic enclaves.[12] Chinese, Japanese, and Filipino Americans protested the razing of ethnic neighborhoods and cultural institutions.[13] Chinatowns, Japantowns and Little Tokyos, Koreatowns, and Manilatowns in Los Angeles, San Francisco, Seattle, Philadelphia, and New York experienced redevelopment pressures that involved plans to destroy key institutions within ethnic enclaves to make way for high-rise buildings and commercial developments.[14] For example, in the 1970s the Little Tokyo community in Los Angeles protested the city's redevelopment plan that would have displaced the Japanese American community. In 1976 the Little Tokyo People's Rights Organization (LTPRO) held marches and demonstrations against the demolition of the Sun Hotel, sixty-two rooms of low-income housing, and the Sun Building, which housed Japanese American community and cultural organizations.[15] Japanese American activists stressed the symbolic and historical significance of Little Tokyo as an "indigenous base of Japanese American ethnicity," which would be destroyed by building an expensive hotel for tourists on the site of the Sun Hotel and Building.[16]

In the 1970s, Asian Americans participated in protests that were specific to the different ethnic communities where the Asian population resided in the United States, and there was very little interethnic cooperation. Many Asian-origin groups had settled and remained in immigrant and ethnic enclaves, further solidifying ethnic boundaries. Jonathan, a leader of a Chinese American organization, addressed the social and geographic distance between East Asian ethnic groups during this period when he explained, "The lines were drawn very clearly. Chinatown was Chinatown, J-town was J-town. You didn't come into each other's territory." During the early part of the post-1968 era, leaders and community members understood that the events and happenings in Chinatown and Japantown were unrelated to one another or to what was happening in other ethnic enclaves for that matter.

The Continuing Rise of Panethnic Organizing

The period from the mid-1970s through the administrations of Ronald Reagan and George H. W. Bush became known as "a winter of civil rights": increasing class polarization and an erosion of hard-won rights combined during this time with an economic recession.[17] Yet it was also during this period that panethnic organizing among Asian Americans reached its height and the number of panethnic events nationwide quadrupled. The dramatic expansion of ethnic group boundaries was due in part to the Vincent Chin case, which marked a new point in Asian American political organizing. When the economic recession in the United States coincided with the rise of the Pacific Rim economies in the 1980s, Asian Americans were viewed as economic competitors.[18] Plagued by layoffs and downsizing, many Americans attributed the decline in the U.S. auto and manufacturing industries to the rise of Japanese cars and electronics sold in the United States and directed their anger toward Asian Americans. Even though they had nothing to do with the rise and fall of international competition, Asian Americans became targets of anti-Asian sentiment and violence.[19] It was in this context that Vincent Chin, a Chinese American man, was mistaken for a Japanese national and attacked and killed by two white unemployed autoworkers in Detroit. When the judge ordered the perpetrators to pay a $3,000 fine each and serve no jail time, this injustice galvanized the Asian American community.[20]

Charles, a leader of a national Chinese American organization who had worked in the nonprofit sector for over twenty-five years, explained the importance of the Chin case in generating Asian American cooperation:

> At first we were out there on our own, really trying to anticipate core problems. . . . It wasn't until Vincent Chin was killed in Detroit that all the segments of the Asian population realized, we're in this together. That for white America there was no difference between Chinese, Japanese, Korean, and most of the groups. It was the first time I had seen coalition work. Before that we were really unable to create effective coalitions.

When Asian ethnic groups realized their shared racialized status, they began to work across ethnic lines to organize protests and create civil rights organizations, such as American Citizens for Justice in Detroit and the Asian American Justice Center in Washington, D.C., to contest racial prejudice and hate crimes against Asian Americans.

Into the 1980s, pan-Asian demonstrations and marches addressed the use of damaging racial stereotypes in the media (films, plays, radio stations, newspapers) and by political officials and united the Asian American community in Los Angeles, San Francisco, Chicago, Detroit, and New York.[21] Protesters organized in public spaces and fought against simplistic portrayals and understandings of the Asian American community as foreigners, illegal aliens, unfair competitors, gang members, and model minorities—all stereotypes that reflected the ways in which Asians were treated as less than full Americans.[22] Other major protests addressed the low visibility of Asian Americans in formal politics by encouraging group members to be more active in the civic and political arena; these events were held on college campuses, at cultural and ethnic centers, and in front of government institutions such as consulate buildings and police departments. The panethnic label used at all of these events was expansive, as panethnic organizing typically represented the efforts of several Asian-origin groups, not just two or three.[23]

Although the number of panethnic events dramatically increased in 1980, the majority of panethnic events reported by the national press took place during the 1990s. Coverage increased in part because Asian Americans were continuing to participate in protests and demonstrations to fight against anti-Asian sentiment and violence in locations such as Chicago, Philadelphia, and San Diego.[24] Asians were also forming coalitions with other immigrant and ethnic groups to address broader issues related to immigration reform, language rights, and legislation that threatened the Asian American community.[25]

In addition to protests, Asian ethnic groups organized and participated in forums, conferences, festivals, commemorations, and celebrations that contributed to building community across ethnic and cultural lines.[26] About 30 percent of the events in the sample were considered civic collective action, and nearly all of these events occurred in the 1990s, suggesting that protest activities may have been a necessary precursor to public expressions of collective civic action across ethnic lines. Asian Americans first engaged in protests, marches, and campaigns to extend their rights as U.S. residents and citizens outside of the formal political process; then they organized public events that showcased the traditions of the Asian American community, celebrating and educating the public about the panethnic group's history and generating stronger panethnic ties.[27] These civic events were planned activities that often required the collaboration of many individuals and organizations, including government officials, nonprofit and private sponsors, volunteers, local entrepreneurs, and members of the panethnic community.[28]

Pan-Asian civic events were primarily community building in nature, but some also incorporated political elements. For example, a pan-Asian festival organized by the Vietnamese, Cambodian, Hmong, Asian Indian, Korean, Pakistani, and Thai communities in Orange County, California, featured ethnic foods and cultural traditions. The purpose of the festival, according to the organizers, was to take a step toward political and cultural unity: "We would like to unify the Asian community. It's a time to learn from each other, to share the heritage we brought with us from our various countries."[29] Khoa Van Le from the Vietnamese community explained that another key purpose of the festival was to bring Asians into the American democratic process. Festival-goers could find information about the political process and register to vote at booths that were set up at the park where the festival was held.

Many cultural celebrations and public festivals have been viewed as a symbolic way for ethnic groups to express panethnicity, but some have also facilitated interaction between the Asian ethnic groups and generated new knowledge, understanding, and interethnic ties. The planning process, which often starts a year in advance, can provide a context in which groups make decisions, coordinate interests, and develop a plan. The organizing committee of the Asian Pacific Dance Festival in Los Angeles, for example, was comprised of members from different Asian-origin groups, and their charge was to come to a consensus about which participants to feature at the festival. To do so, they had to gain a solid understanding of the traditional and contemporary dance forms associated with the different ethnic groups. One of the organizing committee members explained that choosing and coordinating participants for the event was a learning process. It forced people to check their assumptions and be open to new ways of thinking about dance and performance because of the diversity of the groups involved: "Even if the festival never happened, the communities, the artists, and the committee have already gotten something that did not exist before."[30] After months of discussions and meetings, the committee members had learned about one another's cultures, traditions, and experiences. This example shows that, at least for organizers, the result was a deeper understanding of ethnic and cultural differences.

During this period, hate crimes, racial stereotyping, and other threats to Asian Americans provided a clear incentive for Asian ethnic groups to organize, but collective action events did not occur uniformly in areas with sizable Asian-origin populations; Asian ethnic groups did not automatically respond to all incidents related to racial discrimination or bias by cooperating and organizing. As we will see later in this chapter, within the context of a growing Asian American population and the social reality of the inequalities they faced in the labor market and the larger society, community leaders and activists created and deployed pan-Asian narratives at collective action events that countered the model minority stereotype of Asians as high-achieving individuals with few problems in U.S. society. We must remember that socially constructed categories, such as

"Asian American," need to be propped up by structural conditions that encourage group formation and by narratives that are used and reproduced by leaders and organizations.

The Continued Salience of Ethnic Ties

Throughout the post-1968 era, ethnic organizing remained highly visible.[31] Among the most prominent campaigns was the redress and reparations movement for Japanese Americans to remedy ethnic discrimination by the federal government.[32] With the leadership of the Japanese American Citizens League (JACL), the Japanese American community pushed for the creation of a U.S. Commission on Wartime Relocation and Internment of Civilians to investigate the government's wartime actions.[33] Organizations such as the National Coalition for Redress and Reparations (NCRR) and the National Council for Japanese American Redress (NCJAR) were also formed during this period to consolidate efforts to bring public attention and awareness to the violation of the civil liberties of the Japanese Americans who were interned during World War II.[34] Throughout the 1970s and 1980s, Japanese Americans also organized several marches and demonstrations, but most of the collective action took the form of press conferences, public hearings, and workshops to bring visibility to the cause and push for a formal governmental response.[35] Finally, in 1988, the Japanese American community achieved its objective with the signing of the Civil Liberties Act, which recognized that the constitutional rights of Japanese Americans had been violated when they were forcibly taken from their homes and placed in internment camps without due process.[36]

Panethnic activity had decreased in the late 1980s, and this hard-won victory for Japanese Americans, like the work of other Asian ethnic groups organizing around their own issues during this decade, could have detracted from other pressing issues that the panethnic community was facing. There were two key efforts at this time: Filipino Americans' fight against the U.S. government to fulfill its promise to grant U.S. war veteran benefits to the Filipino men who fought under the American flag during World War II; and the struggle of Vietnamese, Hmong, and Mien Americans with the U.S. government over their role in the Secret War in Southeast Asia.[37] Both of these campaigns were the direct result of U.S. military interventions in Japan and Southeast Asia. The U.S. government had requested aid in fighting its enemies in exchange for rights and recognition. These interventions resulted in immigration and refugee flows to the United States, and when Filipino and Southeast Asian Americans discovered that their agreements with the U.S. government had been violated, they learned how to engage in collective efforts to educate the larger public and make their claims visible to policymakers and the press.

Filipino Americans had protested for years and even decades about the fact that the U.S. government had not made good on its promise to Filipino men who fought in World War II. They should have received full veterans' benefits, which would have given them access to higher education, health care, and housing.[38] Many of these veterans lived in poverty and were not recognized for their service until 2009, when Congress, with the backing of President Barack Obama, passed a bill to grant a onetime payment for "suffering endured" to Filipino war veterans. Every year since 1993 a version of the bill had been introduced in Congress, only to die in committee. Using a similar strategy, the Southeast Asian community protested about the invisibility of the Secret War, which was omitted from the history books used in public schools. Community members and leaders eventually encouraged their representatives to draft and introduce AB 78, a California State Assembly bill that would require California public schools to introduce the Secret War in Laos (1961–1973) to the social sciences or history curriculum.[39] The proponents' main concern was that the curriculum accurately portray the critical role of Hmong and other Southeast Asians in the Secret War, which they argued is a part of American history. The bill was passed by the California State Assembly and Senate and approved by the governor's office in 2003.

Other collective efforts that dealt with homeland issues included: Chinese Americans participating in nonviolent protests to support the demonstrators in China who had occupied Tiananmen Square to demand government reforms; Korean Americans encouraging democratic reforms in South Korea; Sikh American protests and marches against the attack on the Golden Temple in the Punjab state of India by Indian troops; and Tibetan American demonstrations to bring attention to Chinese repression in Tibet.[40] Organizations such as the Chinese Alliance for Democracy, Young Koreans United, and the Tibet Fund helped to coordinate these homeland efforts to bring awareness to issues abroad, which contributed to ethnic solidarity within ethnic communities. These struggles were clearly ethnic in nature, but received support from other ethnic communities as well as the larger public among those who were sympathetic to causes invoking broad issues such as freedom of expression and democracy.

It is important to note that some Asian ethnic groups organized against one another on a few occasions, thus revealing the potential for interethnic conflict and challenging the notion that ethnic and panethnic interests are usually complementary. For example, Chinese and Chinese Americans have long campaigned for acknowledgment by the Japanese government of its role in the atrocities of World War II. In Los Angeles in the early 1980s, over 500 Chinese Americans marched from City Hall to the Japanese consulate to decry the textbooks used in Japan that did not accurately portray Japan's invasion and occupation of China in the 1930s. The protest was directed at the Japanese government, but the participants marched through Little Tokyo, the heart of the Japanese American community, and carried signs that encouraged people not to eat Japanese food or buy Japanese cars. The organizers of the event threatened to boycott Japanese goods if changes to these textbooks were not made.[41] Similar events erupted again in the early 2000s, but this time the protesters were of Chinese, Korean, Filipino, and Okinawan ancestry. More than 200 protesters at the Japanese consulate in Los Angeles demanded that the Japanese government pull back new history textbooks that did not provide accurate information about wartime atrocities—a reversal from earlier efforts by the Japanese government, starting in 1996, to acknowledge the existence of comfort women and other brutal aspects of Japanese colonialism.[42]

Nevertheless, ethnic and panethnic organizing continued to coexist through the 1990s and 2000s. Japanese Americans participated in annual pilgrimages to Manzanar and other internment cites to keep the collective memory of the internment alive; Chinese Americans celebrated Chinese New Year and participated in marches to commemorate the return of Hong Kong to China; Korean Americans engaged in protests over legislation to provide funds for rebuilding businesses in Koreatown after the 1992 Los Angeles uprising. These ongoing collective actions required considerable time, effort, and focus on the part of participants and could have detracted from panethnic efforts.

ETHNIC AND PANETHNIC ORGANIZING

On the face of it, ethnic and panethnic events seem to have simply coexisted, with some ethnic activities possibly even overshadowing panethnic efforts. I argue, however, that ethnic and panethnic organizing were deeply intertwined during the post-1968 era, although these relationships and what they produced were not always visible. Ethnic groups organized in the public arena to bring attention to ethnic issues, but those efforts were not entirely removed from panethnicity. In fact, many of the ethnic events were informed by panethnic efforts. Likewise, many of the panethnic events were heavily shaped by effective ethnic organizing and strong leadership from ethnic organizations. Taking a closer look in this section at these collective action efforts, we will soon see that ethnic and panethnic organizing were mutually supporting.

In the 1970s, some of those who participated in ethnic organizing to fight redevelopment and the displacement of ethnic communities were key players in the Asian American movement, and their activism crossed ethnic lines. Organizations such as the J-Town Collective in San Francisco's Japantown, the Free Chinatown Committee in Boston, Yellow Seeds in Philadelphia's Chinatown, and later the Little Tokyo People's Rights Organization in Los Angeles, as well as other ethnic organizations, engaged in anti-gentrification struggles. These organizations saw themselves as part of a larger Asian American collective working to preserve ethnic communities while adopting democratic values and engaging in grassroots organizing.[43]

The redress and reparations movement among Japanese Americans in the 1980s provides another example of how ethnic activism was linked with a broader ideology about the shared history and oppression of all Asian ethnicities. The entire redress movement centered on the experience of Japanese Americans as the sole Asian ethnic group that was interned during World War II. Other Asian ethnic groups were not sent to the camps, and some of their members even wore buttons during the internment period to distinguish themselves as Chinese or Korean.[44] Nonetheless, the National Coalition for Redress and Reparations (NCRR), a key organization in the development of the redress campaign, emerged from the Asian American movement.[45] NCRR was formed by members of the League of Revolutionary Struggle, a multiracial radical organization made up of former members of Eastwind and I Wor Kuen that joined with Japanese American community activists from LTPRO and other progressive ethnic organizations. The organization was vital in shaping the redress movement because it pressured the JACL to support community reparations and include monetary compensation as one of its demands on policymakers. NCRR also worked to mobilize the larger community and unite various coalitions to coordinate efforts for redress. Activist Merilynne Hamano Quon explained: "We launched a massive community education campaign to get people to testify and to attend. Packed hearings didn't 'just happen.' It took mass mailings, phone calls, and presentations to churches and community organizations."[46] She added that the campaign on behalf of an ethnic group could not have succeeded without the support of the broad-based coalition that had been forged during the Asian American movement.

The pan-Asian events documented over the post-1968 era were supported and sponsored by multiple organizations and did not take place apart from ethnic efforts. While panethnic organizations were present at more than one-third of these pan-Asian events—playing a key role in generating participants and support—ethnic organizations also were important players in pan-Asian protest and solidarity events, participating in one-third of these events during the post-1968 era. Ethnic organizations were both supporting the issues of each other's ethnic groups and collaborating on larger projects that served all Asian Americans, while still maintaining their distinct ethnic identities.[47]

A protest in New York City exemplifies how ethnic organizations fortified panethnic efforts during this period. After a city councilwoman from Queens referred to new Chinese immigrants as criminals, rude merchants, and illegal aliens when speaking with a major media outlet, thousands of Asian Americans gathered at City Hall to demand an apology.[48] Despite the fact that the disparaging comments were made about the Chinese immigrant community, a broad pan-Asian response quickly emerged. The Asian American Alliance, comprising more than forty social, political, and religious organizations representing different Asian ethnic groups, was formed by local leaders and organized the rally at City Hall. The Korean American Association of Mid-Queens, the New York Chinatown Senior Citizens Center, and a host of other Asian ethnic community-based organizations were part of the alliance. Asian Americans succeeded in gaining the attention of political elites and the press and eventually received a formal apology from the councilwoman. This panethnic event was heavily shaped by the strength and leadership of ethnic organizations, supporting the idea that ethnic efforts are key to their success.

Ethnic organizing can also transform into panethnic experiences in the civic realm. Asian ethnic communities showcase their culture, traditions, and foods through cultural celebrations, festivals, parades, and commemorations such as Nisei Week, India Day, Philippine Independence Day, and the Tet Festival, and today some of these public festivals and celebrations have become panethnic events. Chinese New Year celebrations have been known to include the cultural traditions of other Asian ethnic groups and to feature pan-Asian activities alongside traditional Chinese festivities. While Chinese, Koreans, Vietnamese, and other Asian ethnic groups tend to celebrate the Lunar New Year separately, enjoying their own special foods and music and spending time with their families, some metropolitan areas have created multiethnic celebrations. For example, thousands of Asians in Chicago participate in the Lunar New Year Celebration, an annual event organized to celebrate the common heritage of Asian Americans and hosted by a different Asian ethnic community each year. In 2011, when the Indian community was in charge of the celebration, one of the organizers explained the importance of the event for Asian Americans: "Our culture, family life and the unique experiences and challenges that we bring to the table continually redefine American society. This year's theme, 'One Vision, Many Voices,' embodies our journey leading to the next level of impact—we must come together as a community to embrace, support and lift up all Asian Americans."[49] Panethnic celebrations like this one, organized across ethnic lines, are particularly interesting because they embody both a melting pot metaphor (an Asian American culture and ideology) and a cultural pluralist metaphor (all ethnic cultures celebrating their own traditions and customs in order to educate each other). Such events also demonstrate that ethnicity and panethnicity can coexist and that one orientation does not have to preclude the other.

Throughout the post-1968 era, ethnic groups were able to make claims on their own when their interests were underrepresented or challenged, and they were proud to publicly display and celebrate their ethnic identities and traditions. Mobilization among Asian Americans was both ethnic and panethnic during this era, and the events that emerged had several goals in common, such as attempting to restore rights, bringing visibility to claims and causes, and showcasing community traditions. Some of the same players and organizations were involved in both ethnic and panethnic efforts, but what the data do not show is whether these two distinct types of organizing have affected each other more broadly. Do they compete with or reinforce each other? Beyond the handful of events discussed here, to what extent does ethnic organizing affect panethnicity? These questions are important because they can provide insights into the flexibility and layered nature of group boundaries.

ETHNIC-PANETHNIC DYNAMICS: MUTUALISTIC OR COMPETITIVE?

Ethnic organizing can certainly benefit broader panethnic efforts in some ways. Ethnic groups that already have experience with organizing understand how to coordinate participants and local organizations, generate community interest and involvement, organize the main event, contact the media, and work with the local police. This experience also makes it easier for them to organize together in the future.[50] Ethnic organizers working together gain a better understanding of the rules of the game and may gain access to more resources, which enable them to coordinate their efforts when needed, either in response to an emerging crisis or as a long-term planning strategy.

But experience with ethnic collective action may not translate easily into protest or civic activity that incorporates all Asian ethnicities. Such work involves developing and activating networks among different Asian-origin groups, and leaders who can direct diverse interests toward a unified collective goal.[51] Even if Asian ethnic communities are well organized in a particular metropolitan area, this does not necessarily mean that eth-

Table 4.1 The Effects of Ethnic Organizations on Rate of Pan-Asian Collective Action Events, 1970–1998

Independent Variable	Model 1	Model 2
Ethnic organizations	0.40* (0.25)	1.41* (0.65)
Panethnic organizations	−0.11 (0.54)	1.29* (0.68)
Panethnic organizations × ethnic organizations	—	0.06* (0.00)

Source: Asian American event data set (Okamoto 2003).
Note: Results are generated from an event history model. Numbers in parentheses are estimated standard errors. N (uncensored spells) = 59. Control variables are included in the models but not shown here.
*$p \leq .05$ (one-tailed tests)

nic groups can successfully manage and coordinate their efforts. In fact, ethnic and panethnic organizing may essentially be incompatible sometimes, with the predominance of one kind of organizing working to the detriment of the other.[52] Consistent with this logic, the two forms of organizing can affect each other negatively when they are competing for time, energy, and finances. When resources are finite, investing in one kind of activity can detract from the resources available for the other.

We can examine the relationship between ethnic and panethnic organizing by using larger samples of events and organizations that span the post-1968 era—from 1970 to 1998—as well as different metropolitan areas across the United States. I employ an event history model and hold constant a host of variables for each metropolitan area, including percentage Asian, total population, and economic conditions, in order to isolate and evaluate how ethnic organizing in local areas is associated with panethnicity, if at all (see appendix A for full models).

As shown in table 4.1, this analysis reveals that the relationship between ethnic organizations and panethnic collective action is mutualistic, not competitive. As the number of ethnic organizations increases in a metropolitan area, the rate of panethnic collective action in the same locale increases and ethnic organizations work in broader coalitions to coordinate, support, and facilitate panethnic protests and civic activity. This relationship holds even when we include a count of panethnic organizations and prior panethnic collective action events, both of which promote public group action across ethnic lines. And as the number of pan-Asian organizations in a metropolitan area increases, the facilitating effect of ethnic organizations diminishes. In other words, ethnic organizations provide a foundation for pan-Asian efforts, and as more pan-Asian organizations are formed, there is less need for ethnic organizations to advance panethnic collective action.

Table 4.2 The Effects of Ethnic Events on the Rate of Pan-Asian Collective Action Events, 1970–1998

Independent Variable	Model 1	Model 2
Ethnic events^{t-1}	−0.01* (0.01)	−0.04** (0.02)
Panethnic events^{t-1}	0.59** (0.20)	0.49** (0.20)
Panethnic events^{t-1} × ethnic event^{t-1}	—	0.00* (0.00)

Source: Asian American event data set (Okamoto 2003).
Note: Results are generated from an event history model. Numbers in parentheses are estimated standard errors. N (uncensored spells) = 59. Control variables are included, but not shown here. Ethnic and panethnic events are measured as occurring in prior month.
*$p \le .05$; **$p \le .01$ (one-tailed tests)

Do ethnic *events* have the same facilitating effect on panethnic organizing as ethnic *organizations* do? The answer is yes and no. Table 4.2 shows that ethnic events initially competed with panethnic events: metropolitan areas with higher rates of ethnic events experienced lower rates of pan-Asian activity. But as pan-Asian organizing increased, this competing effect declined. We see less competition between the two types of organizing in metropolitan areas with a history of panethnic events because the ideology and form of pan-Asian events are recognizable in these areas and an infrastructure of organizations, networks, and resources to support pan-Asian collective action has developed. These organizing efforts and infrastructure help to maintain and reproduce the form and narrative of a pan-Asian label and identity.

We can see these dynamics play out in the aftermath of the Vincent Chin case. Before this event, Asian Americans in Detroit and other U.S. cities typically organized along ethnic lines. When Asian Americans realized that the murder of Vincent Chin affected all Asian communities, protests and demonstrations erupted.[53] Ethnic organizations reacted by linking different immigrant communities to one another and promoting pan-Asian activities; in doing so, they used resources that could have been directed toward ethnic activities. But over time, as more pan-Asian events transpired, this form of organizing became more accepted and an infrastructure to deal with panethnic claims and activities developed. Ethnic organizations, networks, and resources were no longer alone in encouraging both ethnic and panethnic collective action as panethnic organizations emerged to help shepherd these efforts. Evolving together, ethnic and panethnic organizations learned how to effectively bridge ties and organize side by side when needed, sometimes filling different niches and other times working toward a shared solution to a collective problem.

Ethnic and panethnic organizations are an important part of the collective action process. An area's past history of panethnic organizing is often associated with access to bridging networks, a culture of organizing, and an infrastructure that makes collective organizing more likely than in areas where there has been no visible panethnic activity. Organizations and their leaders also play a key role in generating support from different ethnic communities and garnering funds, but perhaps even more importantly, they help to activate and reproduce a pan-Asian ideology, which gives it lasting power.

In sum, racialization alone will not generate panethnic collective action; local structures conducive to the development of shared experiences and the construction of collective identities, such as ethnic and panethnic organizations, must be in place.

WHY PANETHNIC ORGANIZING EMERGES

As paradoxical as it might appear, ethnic organizing is a structural condition that encourages interethnic cooperation. Organizing along ethnic lines does not simply benefit the ethnic community but also builds an infrastructure that enables ethnic groups to collaborate and support one another. In addition, the structural condition of segregation plays a role in generating panethnic organizing. The spatial distribution of ethnic groups in local areas shapes their ability and motivation to engage in pan-Asian collective action. Intragroup interaction and the development of shared networks and trust are encouraged when Asian ethnic groups are closer to one another than to other racial groups; it is more difficult to build interethnic ties and common interests when Asian-origin groups are spatially separated from one another. This is borne out in the event history analysis shown in tables 4.3 and 4.4.

When different Asian ethnic groups were diffused throughout the occupational structure rather than concentrated in certain areas, pan-Asian collective action declined because ethnic group members were less likely to interact with one another and develop common ties and shared outlooks (table 4.3). Additionally, the racial segregation of Asians as a group in local labor markets (table 4.4) allowed Asian ethnic groups to develop interethnic ties more readily than interracial ties and to recognize their shared interests and identities as Asian Americans. Whether Asian ethnic groups were segregated in labor markets owing to preferences, networks, or discrimination, their position reflected broader social conditions of inequality at worst, and lack of social integration at best.

Competition between Asians and other racial groups did not encourage panethnic organizing. Indicators of intergroup contact (declines in occupational segregation, the entrance of new immigrants into local areas),

Table 4.3 The Effects of Interethnic Labor Market Segregation on the Rate of Pan-Asian Collective Action Events, 1970–1998

Independent variable	Model 1: Chinese	Model 2: Filipinos	Model 3: Japanese	Model 4: Koreans
Ethnic segregation	−4.08 (3.37)	−3.71* (1.92)	−7.17** (2.94)	−8.09 (13.70)
Change in ethnic segregation	−8.91** (3.90)	−5.05 (4.35)	3.06 (2.46)	−2.57 (1.79)
−2 log-likelihood	308.14	325.21	311.88	317.51

Source: Asian American event data set (Okamoto 2003).
Note: Results are generated from an event history model. Number of uncensored spells = 59. Numbers in parentheses are estimated standard errors. The four models test the effects of labor market segregation for each national-origin group on the rate of pan-Asian collective action. Unemployment ratios and immigration rates are also included in the models and are shown in table A.4. All models include group-specific variables for Chinese, Filipinos, Japanese, and Koreans, respectively. Ethnic labor market segregation measures the degree to which a specific Asian ethnic subgroup is concentrated in low-status occupations relative to all other Asian ethnic subgroups combined.
*$p \leq .05$; **$p \leq .01$ (one-tailed tests)

worsening economic conditions (poverty and employment rates), and direct competition (employment and income ratios) were predicted to increase interracial competition and result in pan-Asian collective action as a strategy to maintain group position in the racial hierarchy, but these effects did not consistently bear out in the analysis. For the most part, con-

Table 4.4 The Effects of Interracial Labor Market Segregation on the Rate of Pan-Asian Collective Action Events, 1970–1998

Independent Variable	Regression Coefficient	Standard Error
Racial segregation	−1.63	(1.01)
Change in racial segregation	2.27**	(0.99)
Anti-Asian attacks	0.18	(1.54)
Degrees of freedom	14	
−2 log-likelihood	316.37	

Source: Asian American event data set (Okamoto 2003).
Note: Number of uncensored spells = 59. Results are generated from an event history model. Numbers in parentheses are estimated standard errors. Racial segregation refers to the degree to which Asians as a group are concentrated in low-status occupations. Other variables such as poverty rate, unemployment ratios, size of metropolitan area, percentage Asian, and ethnic heterogeneity are included in the model but not shown here. The full model is shown in table A.5.
**$p \leq .01$ (one-tailed tests)

ditions that should have increased intergroup competition had no influence on the rate or occurrence of pan-Asian events (see table A.5). In fact, direct competition, as measured by income and employment ratios, was associated with less frequent pan-Asian collective action. In general, examination of the competitive relations between Asians and other racial groups turned up no evidence to support these relationships.

I also note that attacks against Asians—a manifestation of the racialization process that many scholars deem central to the emergence of panethnicity—did not figure as a key factor in understanding panethnic collective action. On average, racialized threats to the group did not generate protest and solidarity events across different metropolitan areas. When groups were faced with racist or xenophobic attacks, it may have been difficult to respond in kind through protest activity. Group leaders may have prioritized other types of collective action as a long-term solution to counter threats, such as forming organizations (see chapter 3). Instead of addressing individual attacks, community leaders and members appear to have engaged in protest and civic action to address issues related to local and state initiatives—an arena in which political representation and agitation are readily rewarded by state officials.

That said, Asian Americans have organized events that were far from the "source." Only a handful of very large and visible pan-Asian events in the sample addressed issues that were linked to key events that set off protesting across the country, such as the Vincent Chin case. Although acts of anti-Asian violence and racial profiling may galvanize the Asian American community, the key factors that translate such threats and inequalities into panethnic action are the spatial structuring of ethnic and racial groups and the leaders who draw on pan-Asian narratives and prioritize panethnic work.

Organizing Around the Pan-Asian Narrative

The racial segregation of Asians as a group from whites and other racial groups in local labor markets (table 4.4) not only allowed Asian ethnic groups to develop shared interests and identities but also produced a social reality about the inequalities that Asian Americans face. Community leaders and activists could draw on this social reality when building narratives, and in fact it was necessary to do so for collective action to be viable. Asian American leaders constructed pan-Asian narratives that emphasized a unified political community comprising diverse groups, and these narratives helped to mobilize the Asian American population. Some community leaders, in working to bring visibility to the issues faced by Asian immigrants concentrated at the bottom of the economic structure, fought against the model minority stereotype of all Asian Americans as high-achieving and located at the top of the occupational structure. Other leaders crafted narratives that emphasized the needs of the entire Asian American community and its untapped political strength. Some leaders also organized Asian ethnic communities panethnically by arguing that the educational and occupational success of some Asian Americans had led to neither the political incorporation of all Asians nor their full acceptance as Americans.[54] But more often, leaders challenged racial stereotypes about the status of Asian Americans as "forever foreigners" with divided loyalties. They put forth panethnic narratives based in Asian Americans' shared history of being racialized as a "foreign other," and they mobilized Asian ethnic groups to make their collective voices heard in the public arena. Thus, it was not simply structural conditions, such as segregation, that generated the understanding, trust, and common interests across ethnic lines that contributed to the emergence of panethnicity; leaders were key in helping to frame, direct, and organize panethnic group interests.

One of the first large-scale pan-Asian rallies in Los Angeles provides a useful example of how Asian American leaders deployed panethnic narratives when organizing protests to improve the lives of working Asian Americans and mobilize the Asian American population. In 1996, more than twenty-four Asian ethnic groups participated in a public demonstration, coordinated by leaders from the Asian Pacific Policy and Planning Council, to address the economic and political issues affecting the Asian American community in Los Angeles; such a demonstration was unprecedented at the time. The president of the Council explained that Asian Americans needed to have their voices heard by elected officials, especially during a time when the federal government had restricted immigrants' access to welfare and made cuts to other resources for low-income Asian communities. Noting that Asian Americans had low visibility in formal politics yet were the fastest-growing minority group in the United States, he told the crowd of hundreds, "We are here to stake a claim on the political landscape." He encouraged community members to participate in a letter-writing campaign to address citizenship and immigration issues, a voter registration drive to get more Asian Americans involved in the formal political process, and an all-day conference on the impact of welfare reform on Asian Americans.[55] During the rally, speaker after speaker called on the diverse Asian ethnic communities to use these issues to unite. One leader stated, "People united will never be defeated," invoking the pan-Asian narrative that Asian ethnic groups shared common experiences and interests and organizing as a larger collective would bring political power and attention to issues that affected the larger Asian

American community.⁵⁶ In turn, hundreds of Asian Americans at the rally were energized and vowed to engage in local politics, reinforcing the idea that a unified panethnic community could make a difference and ultimately shape public policy. Leaders highlighted the fact that the Asian American population included low-wage workers who needed access to governmental and community resources. They also forged commonalities across ethnic lines through the narratives they expressed at the rally, and they encouraged different Asian-origin groups to work together to achieve a desired outcome—political participation and visibility.

Asian American leaders continued to organize around issues affecting low-income populations and used narratives about the diversity of needs when targeting mainstream institutions. For example, a U.S. census post-enumeration plan in Los Angeles was met with a pan-Asian protest. After the 1990 U.S. census was administered, federal officials planned to conduct a survey to improve the accuracy of population counts for the next decennial census in 2000.⁵⁷ Because the allocation of federal and state funding to nonprofits serving needy populations is based on census numbers, the undercounting of minority communities is of great importance. The post-enumeration survey in Los Angeles thus should have been a welcome exercise in the city's racial minority and low-income communities, but the problem was that the survey would not have distinguished between Asian and white respondents. The two groups' responses would have been lumped together, making it difficult for officials to make informed decisions about the Asian American population.⁵⁸ The Asian American community protested against the post-enumeration plan and publicly denounced it for ignoring the long-fought battles since the 1980s to use ethnic categories to enumerate the Asian population in the United States.⁵⁹ One of the protest leaders explained: "In the last decade, Asian-Americans have fought two presidential administrations to ensure a correct count. Now the Asian community is back at ground zero."⁶⁰ Community leaders and activists emphasized that simply lumping all Asian Americans into one racial category was consistent with the model minority stereotype, which masks the differences in needs, cultures, and languages among the different Asian-origin groups. Categorizing Asian Americans' responses with whites' responses would have done further damage, making it impossible to make accurate counts of Asian Americans, let alone the population sizes and economic needs of each Asian ethnic group.

Similarly, in the late 1990s and into the 2000s, Asian American college students protested the lack of services, programs, and curricula for Asian American populations. They used a diversity and model minority narrative when engaging both university administrators and the larger public, emphasizing that Asian Americans were a heterogeneous grouping that did not fit the model minority stereotype. When Asian Americans entered higher education in larger numbers in the late 1980s and 1990s—they would come to represent 20 to 40 percent of the undergraduate population at some universities[61]—they soon recognized the lack of programs and curricula that represented their backgrounds and experiences.[62] At a rally that drew over 300 students at the University of California–Davis, an undergraduate student talked about the need for expanded programs and services on campus: "We shouldn't have to wait for some of these things. Our numbers are increasing, and these are things that should be provided for the students." She noted that the common perception of Asian Americans as "model" minorities often masked the particular hardships, pressures, and needs of diverse Asian American students in the university setting.[63]

Asian American campus leaders at Stanford, Columbia, Harvard, Yale, Northwestern, City University of New York–Hunter College, Tufts, the University of Illinois–Chicago and elsewhere also drew on a panethnic narrative about a cultural and political community to mobilize students to demand the establishment or expansion of Asian American studies programs and services for Asian American students. Reminiscent of the protests at San Francisco State and UC Berkeley during the early 1970s, students at UC Irvine wore yellow armbands to symbolize pan-Asian unity as they marched into the administration building and chanted into megaphones demanding new programs.[64] Asian American students at Northwestern organized a rally and hunger strike, which sparked a resurgence of pan-Asian student activism. Hundreds of students participated in the rally, and over 1,000 students signed a petition demanding an Asian American studies program, reinforcing the panethnic narrative that the active participation of diverse Asian ethnic groups sharing a common position, experiences, and interests in American society could bring about political change.[65]

Finally, Asian American leaders also organized communities across ethnic lines to protest against instances that clearly indicated Asians were not being fully incorporated into the mainstream as equal citizens, such as when public officials or media personalities made questionable claims about Asians as forever foreigners. In these instances, leaders would use panethnic narratives to counter the erroneous belief that because many Asian Americans were foreign-born, they could never be fully American and hold allegiance to the United States.[66] A key event in Asian American activism was the case of Wen Ho Lee, which garnered national attention. Lee was a Taiwanese-born nuclear scientist who had worked at Los Alamos National Laboratories for twenty years, and government officials had racialized him as a foreign spy. Suspected of stealing nuclear secrets for China, he was suddenly fired in 1999 and placed in solitary confinement in New Mexico for ten months—an unusually harsh restriction. Lee was eventually charged with mishandling classified information, a misdemeanor. His supporters contended that he was targeted because of his ethnicity. Press reports highlighted his Taiwanese background and promoted the idea that Asian Americans have divided loyalties. The *New York Times*, along with other major media outlets, did not initially report that Lee had been an American citizen for twenty-five years.[67] Lee's advocates also emphasized the fact that the former head of the CIA, John Deutch, had also mishandled data but was not charged with a crime or jailed.

The next year, in 2000, the Coalition Against Racial and Ethnic Scapegoating (CARES) organized a "National Day of Protest," and Asian Americans in San Francisco, Los Angeles, New York, Albuquerque, Detroit, Miami, Seattle, Salt Lake City, and several other U.S. cities engaged in rallies and demonstrations, demanding due process and fair treatment for Lee. "The goal of our campaign is to ensure that no more Asian Americans will be treated like Dr. Lee," said Daphne Kwok of the Organization of Chinese Americans in Washington, D.C. "We want to stop this discrimination, stop the stereotyping that Asian Americans and other people of color are somehow suspect simply because of how we look."[68] Karen Narasaki, president of the National Asian Pacific American Legal Consortium, stated that for much of their history in the United States, Asian Americans had been viewed as "the foreigner, not necessarily being trusted." She explained: "No matter how hard you work and how much you've contributed to the community, how well you raise your children, your loyalty is still going to be questioned just because of what you look like."[69] Other leaders talked about the presumption of Asian Americans' disloyalty that led to the prosecution of Lee and characterized the portrayal of Asian Americans as potential security risks as dangerous and unethical.

The Lee case is reminiscent of the experiences of Asian immigrants who are viewed as loyal to their country of origin, not the United States.[70] It also clearly illustrates why Asian Americans protested about racial stereotypes during this era: powerful institutions and individuals can make decisions about the lives of racial group members based on inaccurate and distorted images, often with harmful or even deadly consequences. Community and organizational leaders countered with a panethnic narrative about how Asian Americans are racialized as foreigners and share this common experience, which must be challenged in order for Asian Americans to be fully incorporated into American society.

Panethnicity emerged not only where ethnic and panethnic organizations existed to help facilitate organizing efforts but also where Asian American leaders drew upon and deployed a pan-Asian narrative about a cultural and political community with shared interests yet diverse needs—a narrative that countered the model minority stereotype of Asian Americans as facing few challenges in American society. Additionally, panethnic events organized around key issues helped to reinforce panethnic identities and reinvigorate pan-Asian activism.

SUMMARY

Despite the efforts of Asian American activists in the 1970s to form an enduring Asian American movement, panethnic organizing was not a uniform strategy during the rest of the post–civil rights era. When Asian ethnic communities sought recognition and rights from the larger society, they continued to organize along *ethnic* lines. Asian-origin groups were able to make claims when their interests were underrepresented or challenged, and they were proud to publicly display and celebrate their ethnic identities and traditions. Clearly, the contemporary experience of race and the availability of a pan-Asian ideology were not enough to disrupt ethnic organizing, as ethnicity continued to be salient in the lives of Asian Americans.

This chapter has argued that ethnic and panethnic organizing during the post-1968 era did not simply coexist but were intertwined. Taking a closer look at the details of key panethnic events, such as the Japanese American campaign for redress and reparations and protests over the Vincent Chin case, reveals the relationships between ethnic organizations and what those relationships produced—resources, networks, leaders, infrastructure, and access to elites. The interplay between ethnicity and panethnicity is complex and multidimensional, but the data and analyses demonstrate that ethnic and panethnic organizing were complementary and mutually supportive rather than competitive. Although ethnic mobilization efforts could have attenuated or detracted from pan-Asian activities, instead they were a key part of the pan-Asian collective action process. Under the direction of leaders and with the participation of community members, ethnic organizations were central in providing the necessary foundation and infrastructure to generate the support of different Asian-origin communities, and ethnic events reinforced the ethnic solidarity that would prove important for building a strong pan-Asian community. This is consistent with the idea that group boundaries are layered: that is, the assertion of one group boundary (ethnic) does not preclude the assertion of another (panethnic).

In addition to ethnic organizing, segregation played an important role in generating shared interests across differences, in that the segregation of ethnic groups in the labor market shaped the ability and motivation of Asian ethnic groups to engage in pan-Asian organizing. Finally, panethnic organizations and leaders were also important in generating pan-Asian collective action because they constructed and reinforced narratives about shared needs and interests, and used to frame and motivate protests and civic action, while still recognizing and valuing ethnic differences.

To further unpack the interplay between ethnicity and panethnicity, chapter 5 will take a closer look at the role of ethnic leaders and organizations in the San Francisco–Oakland area and show how they invoke ethnicity as an important and salient way to organize group members and maintain ethnic ties, culture, and traditions while also expanding ethnic boundaries to include others. Examining the ways in which some ethnic organizations are able to engage in panethnic practices, blurring and complicating group boundaries while providing resources and services to a broader population, while others have more difficulty negotiating panethnicity, the chapter will highlight the complicated and layered nature of ethnic boundaries.

Chapter 5 | Ethnic Organizations and the Flexibility of Group Boundaries

IN THE EARLY 1970s, ethnicity was the traditional way in which immigrants organized themselves in defense of threats and to provide social and economic support for ethnic group members. By the 2000s, panethnicity was a key organizing principle and approach to building a broader community and bringing national attention to issues such as racial profiling, hate crimes, and discrimination against Asian Americans. The panethnic model had become an established organizational form recognized by funders, foundations, policymakers, government officials, and the larger public.[1] Ethnic organizations and leaders serving the Asian American population had to operate within this new environment and faced institutional pressures to adopt panethnic practices.

In chapter 4, I argued that ethnic organizations were a central part of the panethnic collective action process: they fostered solidarity among ethnic communities that was later harnessed into panethnic activity, and ethnic leaders helped generate support for panethnic efforts. But the challenges and realities faced by ethnic organizations and their leaders when coordinating political action might differ considerably when providing advocacy and services. In other words, ethnic organizations may respond differently to institutional pressures to shift their practices and priorities and expand their boundaries to include other Asian ethnic groups as members, constituents, and clients than they do to challenges to join collective action efforts. This chapter elaborates upon the interplay between ethnicity and panethnicity by investigating if and how the panethnic model shaped Asian ethnic-specific organizations in the San Francisco–Oakland area.

As we will see, even in a place with a deep history of progressive activism in the Asian American community, panethnicity was not always a smooth or uncontested process on the ground. Ethnic organizations did not automatically embrace panethnic practices, and when they did, the transition was not easy and their adoption of expansive practices did not necessarily translate into a shared panethnic identity. For half of the twenty-seven ethnic organizations representing the Chinese, Filipino, Japanese, Korean, Vietnamese, Laotian, Cambodian, and South Asian populations from which I drew observations and interviews, participating in programs or developing partnerships across ethnic lines became a regular aspect of their organizational work.[2] Group boundaries were flexible for these organizations as they expanded to include other Asian-origin groups as members of the larger community while still engaging in programs and practices that served ethnic needs and maintained ethnic identities.

The daily work of these community-based nonprofit organizations often included the input of the local community, but ultimately the leaders—some of whom were elite, but many of whom grew up in low-income immigrant neighborhoods—made the decisions and choices, prioritizing certain programs and initiatives over others. They also shaped how group members perceived their own interests and the interests of others, and they pushed toward or away from cooperation with other ethnic organizations and the promotion of common cultural, social, and political linkages.[3] Under the direction of leaders, ethnic organizations learned to adapt to the panethnic model and played a key role in the panethnicity project by providing support for other ethnic groups' causes and expanding organizational resources. Interestingly, organizational leaders managed the activation of panethnicity by using the language of assimilation even as they emphasized ethnic boundaries to appease group members.

Group boundaries became visible not only through routine organizational practices such as programming and partnerships but also in the ways certain identities were managed and sometimes privileged by leaders. Examining organizational practices and how leaders frame and manage those practices helps us to understand how ethnic group boundaries can be both *permeable* and *durable*. In contrast to the assumptions of traditional assimilation theories, ethnicity or national origin can still be invoked by an Asian-origin group as a salient and important marker when group boundaries expand to include other Asian-origin groups. Furthermore, by comparing the ways in which Asian American leaders and organizations work to expand group boundaries to include other Asian-origin groups and racial minorities such as blacks and Latinos, we gain insights into the durability of racial boundaries and the importance of leaders in promoting commonalities across racial lines, reinventing community boundaries, and carrying out work on behalf of expanded group affiliations.[4]

ORGANIZATIONS IN SAN FRANCISCO: A CONTEXT FOR ORGANIZATIONAL CHANGE

Immigrant and ethnic groups have needs and interests that are unique to their communities and are often expressed and projected in ethnic organizations.[5] Community and cultural centers, after-school programs, professional associations, and low-income advocacy organizations serving specific ethnic populations provide a social space where group members can interact, share resources, and work collaboratively. As a result, these community organizations often function as institutions that reinforce ethnic boundaries, especially when they are located within ethnic enclaves.[6]

From the more than 250 Asian ethnic organizations currently in operation in the San Francisco Bay Area, this chapter draws on a sample of 27 ethnic organizations and 33 ethnic leaders in San Francisco and Oakland (see appendix B). East Asian organizations (Chinese, Japanese, Korean) appear in the sample in larger numbers than Southeast Asian (Cambodian, Hmong, Laotian, Filipino) and South Asian organizations, owing to the larger number of ethnic organizations serving the Chinese, Japanese, and Korean populations in this area as well as the established nature of these organizations, many which were founded in the early 1970s and 1980s (see table A.6 for a breakdown by ethnic category). Table 5.1 provides descriptive information about the leaders interviewed. The sample is more or less evenly split along the dimensions of gender, generation, veteran (versus newcomer) status in the nonprofit world, and age, but it was more common for leaders to be male, 1.5 generation or later, age thirty-five or older, and to have worked in the nonprofit sector for more than fifteen years.

The San Francisco Bay Area has a long history of Asian American activism involving interethnic and interracial coalitions to combat racial inequality. An organized Asian American movement developed at San Francisco State and UC Berkeley in the late 1960s when Asian American students from different ethnic backgrounds organized together with African American, Chicano, and Native American students as part of the Third World Liberation Front.[7] Asian activists embraced the radical ideology of power and self-determination with the aim of serving the people and enacting social change through political means in Chinatown and Japantown (see chapter 2).[8]

In addition to this history of progressive politics, the majority-minority cities of San Francisco and Oakland are racially diverse and home to a

Table 5.1 Characteristics of Leaders of San Francisco Bay Area Ethnic Organizations

Characteristics	Number of Leaders
Nonprofit experience	
Veteran	18
Newcomer	15
Gender	
Female	14
Male	19
Generation	
First	14
1.5 or later	19
Age	
Twenty-five to thirty-five	15
Thirty-six or older	18

Source: Asian American community-based organization sample (Okamoto 2004).
Note: N = 33.

large Asian American population (see table 5.2). Early immigrants to the United States from China, Japan, and Korea created ethnic communities in San Francisco, and later waves arrived from Southeast Asia as refugees in the 1970s; the region has since seen continuing immigration from China, Cambodia, India, Laos, Pakistan, Vietnam, and the Philippines.[9] In 2010 nearly 1 million Asian Americans resided in the area, comprising just under one-fourth of the population in Oakland (17.7 percent) and over one-third (34.6 percent) in San Francisco, representing the highest concentration of Asians in the United States outside of Hawaii.[10] In 2000 San Francisco was deemed the most residentially segregated metropolitan area for Asian Americans, owing in part to the immigrant replenishment of Southeast Asian, Filipino, and Chinese ethnic enclaves in the Tenderloin, South of Market, Daly City, Chinatown, Visitacion Valley, and the Richmond District.[11]

The San Francisco Bay Area also boasts a vibrant nonprofit sector.[12] Moreover, local government has a strong commitment to contracting with and funding local nonprofits that are well positioned to address the growing and diverse social, health, and economic needs of low-income, immigrant, and ethnic communities through family resource centers, afterschool and summer programs, youth employment, community empowerment, and violence prevention programs.[13] Additionally, there are many small organizations that serve needy populations and have not yet incorporated as nonprofits but have fiscal sponsors that provide support, direction, and mentorship.

Table 5.2 Racial and Ethnic Population of San Francisco and Oakland, California, 2010

	Oakland		San Francisco	
	Number	Percentage	Number	Percentage
Non-Hispanic white	101,308	27.2%	337,451	43.6%
Non-Hispanic black	106,637	28.6	46,781	6.0
Hispanic	99,068	26.6	121,774	15.7
Asian	65,811	17.7	267,915	34.6
Total	372,824	100.0	773,921	100.0
Asian Indian	2,114	0.5	9,747	1.3
Chinese	34,083	9.1	172,181	22.2
Filipino	6,070	1.6	36,347	4.7
Japanese	2,031	0.5	10,121	1.2
Korean	2,446	0.7	9,670	1.2
Vietnamese	8,766	2.4	12,871	1.7
Other Asian	10,301	2.8	16,978	2.2

Source: FactFinder, Census 2010.

Despite the region's supportive context for nonprofit work within ethnic communities, organizations must respond to their environments if they want to survive and grow.[14] They must secure a regular stream of funding, increase their visibility among elites, build their reputations in the nonprofit world, and effectively serve target populations. Organizations must also be flexible enough to adopt new practices and organizational forms.[15] For ethnic organizations originally founded to serve the needs of a specific ethnic population, the panethnic model can shape organizational practices because it has become the established organizational form (see chapter 3). Foundations and government agencies more readily recognize an "Asian American" organization than an ethnic-specific one when distributing grants and other financial resources.[16] Organizational leaders understand that broader panethnic partnerships are essential to secure funding opportunities. Submitting grant proposals for programs serving "the Asian community" rather than just the Chinese, Filipino, or Vietnamese community gives nonprofit organizations a distinct advantage.[17] Collaborating across ethnic lines when creating a new program often enhances organizational effectiveness because, at the very least, the legitimacy associated with the panethnic model facilitates transactions with other organizations.[18] In organizational theory terms, a shift toward a panethnic approach confers survival advantages as organizations conform more closely to institutional rules and expectations about appropriate models.[19] It is in this way that panethnicity influences established ethnic organizations.

But even with the predominance and legitimacy of the panethnic organizational model, the need for funding, and the San Francisco Bay Area's history of Asian American activism, ethnic organizations did not automatically adopt panethnic practices. Instead, the process of panethnicity had to be negotiated and constructed. The broader institutional environment shaped how ethnic organizations operated and survived, but not all ethnic organizations expanded their group boundaries in the same ways, and some did not expand their group boundaries at all. For some ethnic organizations, crossing ethnic lines to carry out service or advocacy work was not a priority. These organizations focused their efforts on building up their ethnic community and did not seek out collaborations with other ethnic groups. When community-based ethnic organizations did widen their boundaries, they were able to serve and support a greater diversity of new immigrants along with established ethnic communities.

Thus, funding incentives, racialized categories, and the legitimacy of the panethnic model did not produce uniform organizational outcomes. Instead, how and to what extent ethnic organizations moved toward a panethnic model primarily depended on their leaders, some of whom created inclusive narratives, prioritized certain programs over others, and adopted policy stances that benefited groups beyond ethnic lines. Before turning to these organizational panethnic practices and the meanings that organizational leaders constructed to articulate them and ease their organizations' transition, I provide a brief history of ethnic organizations in the San Francisco Bay Area in the next section.

THE EVOLUTION OF ETHNIC ORGANIZATIONS IN SAN FRANCISCO

Immigrants from Asia had originally formed associations based on kin, province, and dialect lines soon after their arrival in the United States. Beginning in the 1920s and continuing through to the 1970s, there was a marked increase in the formation of organizations along national-origin lines to serve the needs of immigrant communities (see chapter 2). Ethnic organizations developed in the United States in part because of increasing hostility toward groups on the basis of ethnicity.[20] For example, a small group of Chinese Americans in San Francisco formed the Native Sons of the Golden State in 1895 to fight increasing anti-Chinese sentiment. By 1913 local chapters had been established in Oakland, San Francisco, Los Angeles, Fresno, and San Diego, and in 1915 the organization changed its name to Chinese American Citizens Alliance (CACA) and altered its charter to better reflect the needs and concerns of the Chinese community. The organization's main purpose was to attain civil and naturalization rights while promoting the welfare of the Chinese community. Among the main principles upon which CACA was founded, one in particular signaled change within the Chinese community: "No members are permitted to use provincial, clannish, Tong or political pressure against one another."[21] In many ways, this statement symbolized the transition of the Chinese community from traditional associations based on kin and region to associations based on ethnicity, which were started by the second generation.

The Japanese Association of America (JAA), founded in 1909 to keep track of all Japanese in the United States, was considered an Issei (first-generation) organization. In 1929 the Japanese American Citizens League (JACL), a Nisei (second-generation) organization, was founded in San Francisco to address discrimination against persons of Japanese descent in the United States. At the time, over 100 statutes in California restricted the rights of the Japanese. The JACL was determined to organize its members and challenge policies at the state and federal levels.[22] With limited resources, it was one of only a few organizations in the 1920s and 1930s willing to address the exclusionary policies of the state.

Ethnic organizations serving Asian immigrants were transformed by the Asian American movement of the late 1960s. San Francisco–based organizations such as Chinese for Affirmative Action, the Chinese Progressive Association, and Filipinos for Affirmative Action/Filipino Advocates for Justice were born from the movement to organize and empower local communities. Additionally, the passage of civil rights legislation ushered in a new era with the expansion of advocacy and social welfare programs directed at racial minorities.[23] Voluntary associations and government-funded agencies emerged to provide aid and services to the Asian population.[24] Mainstream agencies, however, lacked the language and cultural competency to effectively serve the different Asian ethnic groups. Instead of creating protective organizations, immigrant leaders and communities found that they had to form their own organizations in San Francisco, such as the Southeast Asian Community Center, the Korean Center, and the Vietnamese Youth Development Center, to gain access to health and social services. Jan, a first-generation leader at a community-based health organization, remembered what it was like for immigrant communities during that period:

> These [immigrant] communities were not going to these mainstream organizations to get services, and that is why many of us saw that void and saw what the problem was. It wasn't because the services weren't there, it's that they weren't being provided in the language people could listen to and un-

derstand the cultural sensitivity. Most of us who have been involved with nonprofit communities for over thirty years, we started and founded different organizations to fill that void. That's the bigger picture in terms of why these organizations came about and they were very ethnic-specific.

The ethnic organizations that developed in the 1970s followed the traditional mission of earlier organizations by providing aid, support, and knowledge to ethnic communities. These service- and advocacy-based organizations were aimed at helping immigrants adapt and assimilate. Many prominent Asian ethnic organizations were formed in San Francisco and Oakland, including the Chinatown Community Development Center, the Japanese American Citizens League, the Japanese Cultural and Community Center of Northern California, the Korean Center, the Korean Community Center of the East Bay, the Southeast Asian Community Center, and the Vietnamese Community Center. The establishment and maintenance of ethnic organizations generated strength in numbers and networks of information that could be used to coordinate ethnic group members and facilitate their participation in collective actions such as strikes, demonstrations, and protests. Ethnic organizations were also a vehicle for keeping alive and reproducing language, culture, and traditions in the face of assimilation demands.

PANETHNIC PRACTICES WITHIN THE ORGANIZATIONAL FIELD

Given the predominance of the panethnic model in the nonprofit organizational field in the 2000s (see chapter 3), how did ethnic organizations shift their practices, if at all? Figure 5.1 displays the organizational practices of ethnic organizations in San Francisco and Oakland, according to their greater or lesser openness to other Asian ethnic groups. On one end of the continuum, ethnic organizations simply maintain their boundaries and do not look to other ethnic organizations when planning events, applying for grants, or building communities. The opposite end of the continuum signals greater commitment to other Asian ethnic groups and long-term, inclusive practices such as changing the organizational name, broadening public mission statement and goals to include all Asian-origin groups, and developing programs and activities that highlight shared interests among the Asian population. Less extensive panethnic collaborations that fall somewhere in the middle of the spectrum are cosponsored activities and events and joint applications for foundation grants and government funding for panethnic programs and projects. Collaborating with other Asian ethnic groups to apply for funding can be seen as strategic

Figure 5.1 Organizational Practices of San Francisco and Oakland Ethnic Organizations Related to Expanding Boundaries

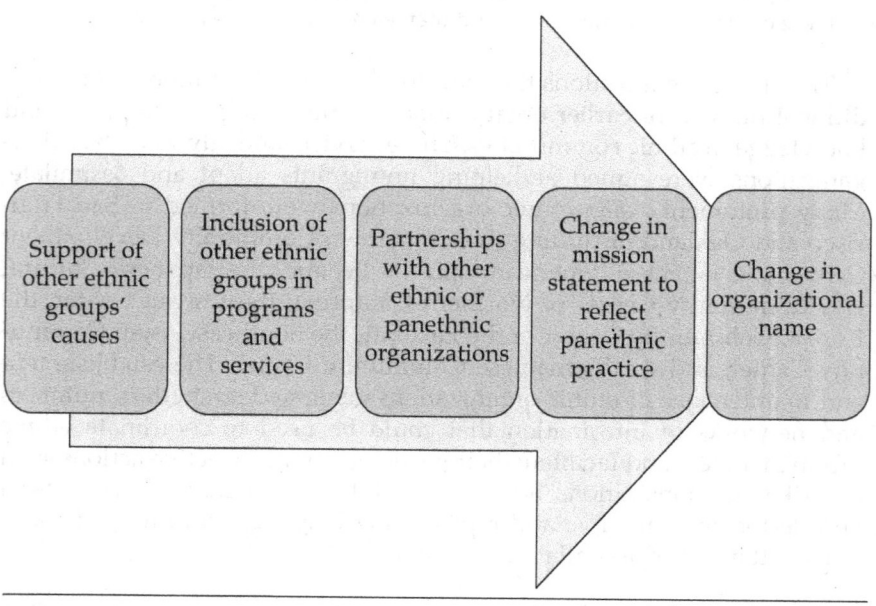

Source: Author's calculations.
Note: The figure shows a continuum of panethnic organizational practices enacted by Asian ethnic organizations. These practices are not presented sequentially but in increasing degree of panethnicity, moving from left to right.

and instrumental, and alone as a practice, this could be the case. But ethnic organizations engaged in multiple panethnic practices are expressing a more inclusive panethnicity, with implications for building interethnic trust and cooperation. I elaborate on these patterns of boundary-related organizational practices in the next sections.

REMAINING ETHNIC

Some ethnic organizations in the Bay Area distanced themselves from the panethnic model and chose not to foster panethnic ties or practices. In fact, half of the ethnic organizations in the sample focused entirely on developing programs to serve newcomers and addressing problems within their ethnic communities (see table A.6 for characteristics of ethnic organizations). Rather than generating ties and networks across ethnic lines to build broader coalitions, their main priorities were to help ethnic group members become a part of the mainstream through employment programs and citizenship classes, to educate the public about the ethnic group, and to provide a community space for ethnic group members. These ethnic organizations took up the charge of ensuring that immigrant and ethnic populations had the skills, knowledge, and information to navigate American norms, values, and institutions.

Josh, a 1.5 generation leader of Korean Americans for Social Change (KASC), was among several of the interviewees whose priority was to create a well-functioning space for the ethnic community. He explained why KASC had not reached out to other ethnic groups: "You have to make sure your house is in order first, and I never feel that our house is ever in order. So I don't feel like this organization is ready to open our doors yet [to other groups]. We can't get it right in our own community, so how do we go out and work on voter registration with the entire Asian American community?" This idea of "not getting it right" referred to the difficulties that many leaders face when trying to organize an ethnic community, provide services, and effectively advocate for ethnic group members. Ethnic organizations like KASC had been formed within the last decade, but their leaders voiced concern that they had not achieved organizational success and stability—that is, they had not established the programs, services, and funding streams needed to support their own communities. These organizational leaders also noted that closing the generational gap in their communities was a challenge they needed to address before working with other ethnic groups. The tendency of older generations to focus on the past and hold conservative values and of more assimilated newer generations to hold more progressive political views can generate conflict and make it difficult to build a cohesive ethnic community.[25]

Another difficulty that Bay Area ethnic groups faced in generating an organized ethnic community was the geographic dispersion of the region's ethnic populations. As these populations moved to areas outside of the central cities and to suburban areas in the larger Bay Area, ethnic communities were no longer located only in the central parts of San Francisco and Oakland. The movement of some ethnic groups into predominantly white neighborhoods was reflective of spatial assimilation process.[26] Other ethnic populations settled in suburban ethnoburbs characterized by coethnic populations and businesses.[27] These demographic shifts made it more challenging for ethnic organizations to reach their communities and maintain a membership base and constituency. Because younger generations tend to be more assimilated, it was also harder to involve them in the organizations. Working to find ways to incorporate and involve the newer generations has been key in preserving ethnic organizations as well as ethnic communities.

Other organizations did not expand their group boundaries because they simply did not have enough funding to serve more than one ethnic group, often because they were newly formed and had not yet established a track record of funding. Kiri, the twenty-five-year-old executive director of the Cambodian Family Association (CFA), explained, "We try to limit ourselves, because sometimes it's hard. We don't want to expand yet to serve other languages because we will not have enough staff to serve our community." CFA was a relatively small organization founded within the last ten years and was continuing to expand and develop programs for the Cambodian community related to employment, citizenship, education, health care, and seniors. With a budget of less than $25,000 a year, CFA needed to build up its own infrastructure and programming before expanding services to other ethnic communities. The newness of some ethnic organizations and their lack of resources constrained their ability to include others.[28]

While some ethnic leaders aspired to have their organizations participate in pan-Asian activities, they claimed that doing so at this point in time would detract from the larger goal of building up the ethnic community. Despite the possibility of discovering commonalities across ethnic lines because of shared local experiences, organizational leaders prioritized the development of programs to bridge the generational gap within ethnic communities and worked to establish an ethnic legacy, ensuring that their ethnic histories, culture, and traditions would remain for generations to come. For example, the Filipino Community Development League (FCDL) recently completed the construction of a new community center. Jocelyn, a second-generation Filipino American leader, clarified why one of FCDL's main organizational goals was to draw multiple generations to the new Filipino community center:

> Building communities . . . it is intergenerational. So you have children teaching their children and children teaching their parents, so it's really something. That's what we call connected consciousness, connected memory . . . because if communities do not have a working-together experience, the future is uncertain. But if they have a working-together experience and then there are challenges, it's easier to keep them together.

She went on to explain that by accomplishing community tasks—from participating in parol-making (lantern-making) workshops to organizing "ethno-tours" that highlight Filipino history and landmarks in San Francisco—ethnic group members share ideas, coordinate efforts, and develop strategies and the experience generally creates a stronger bond between the generations.

While information and communication flowed back and forth between the generations at FCDL, other organizations differed in how they built intergenerational relations. Joanie, a second-generation Korean American, explained how the organization she led, Koreans for Community Action (KCA), coordinated a number of events designed to teach the first generation how the second generation did things. She talked about the very different approaches of the generations, even in something as simple as holding a meeting: "It has been challenging working with the first-generation organizations. They obviously have a different mind-set." She went on to describe one of the events sponsored by KCA: "We just invited them to come and watch. And it kind of opened a lot of people's eyes, and they said, This is how you guys do things. This is how the new generation does things.' ... It's teaching our parents." For KCA and many other ethnic organizations, bridging the differences between the generations took a considerable amount of work and left little energy or resources to devote to other ethnic groups and organizations.

Other organizations continued to maintain ethnic practices and did not expand their efforts to other Asian-origin groups because their leaders wanted to develop culturally relevant and appropriate strategies to serve ethnic-specific immigrant communities. Mainstream organizations as well as many Japanese, Chinese, and Korean organizations did not have the cultural or language capacities to address the needs of Cambodian, Hmong, Filipino, Vietnamese, and South Asian immigrant populations. Ethnic leaders who formed new organizations often did so to address the social problems and needs of their communities that could be met only by a coethnic organization with culturally competent leaders and staff. For example, South Asian Women United (SAWU) was founded by six women in the South Asian community who recognized that South Asian women needed domestic violence services and had nowhere to turn because of cultural and linguistic barriers. Similarly, the Filipino American Community Foundation (FACF) was formed to reach the local Filipino population and develop appropriate ways to address its needs. Other service providers with sophisticated infrastructures were located in the area, but they did not have the cultural competency to serve South Asians or Filipinos, respectively. The providers were not coethnic, did not have translation services, and did not understand South Asian or Filipino culture, which many community members and leaders viewed as problematic for any attempt to reach a needy population. While creating ties across ethnic lines to generate a more powerful network for addressing immigrants' rights and needs would have been a useful strategy, these ethnic organizations were primarily focused on outreach to their own communities, developing effective programs to address ethnic-specific needs, and staying financially afloat.

A few of the ethnic organizations were limited in their ability to expand group boundaries because of their need to work with organizations that had the same goals. Almost all of the organizations claimed to be constrained in this way, but when pressed further, Luoc, a leader of the Vietnamese Community Center, talked about the importance of working with other organizations that understood the history, politics, and experiences of Vietnamese refugees. Given the unique situation of the Vietnamese population in the United States, Luoc believed that it was crucial to work with other organizations and communities that understood why Vietnamese refugees were in the United States, the circumstances that had pushed them out of their country of origin, and their political stance against communism. A partnership with an ethnic organization that lacked knowledge of Vietnamese American history and culture was unlikely to be fruitful. Like mainstream organizations that did not have the cultural capacity to serve Asian immigrant populations, not all Asian ethnic organizations had the cultural competency to serve the same populations.

But for others, remaining ethnic also reflected a conflict within the Asian American community regarding the lack of representation of some groups in panethnic coalitions. Historically, pan-Asian collaborations and partnerships have been between Japanese and Chinese organizations and other ethnic groups have been marginalized.[29] Shawna, one of the founders of South Asian Women United, confirmed this. For a very long time, she noted, the South Asian community was not considered part of the Asian American community, but over time it had become much more inclusive. South Asians were being asked to join pan-Asian partnerships and collaborations, but progress had still been somewhat slow. Similarly, Tran, the leader of a Vietnamese organization, told me that he had sent out invitations for the Tet Festival, an annual New Year's festival for the Vietnamese community, to several ethnic organizations but received no responses. He had tried to reach out to other ethnic communities, but had seen little progress. When talking about the different ethnic groups and organizations in the Bay Area, a leader of a Laotian organization explained in simple terms why some groups did not work with one another: "Different politics, different faces, different histories."

Figure 5.2 summarizes the narratives used by these leaders to explain why panethnic work was not their priority. Many organizational leaders found it difficult to think about reaching beyond ethnic boundaries because there were many unmet needs within their own ethnic community. In fact, these leaders tended to welcome and appreciate new ethnic organizations that could fill a particular niche and further strengthen their community.

Figure 5.2 Ethnic Leaders' Narratives to Explain Why They Maintained Ethnic Boundaries

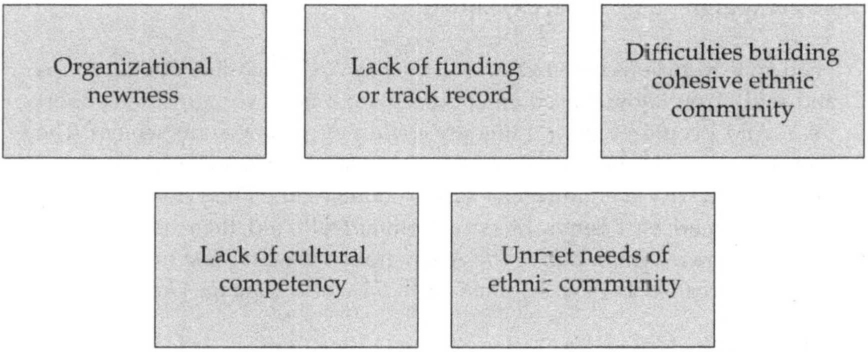

- Organizational newness
- Lack of funding or track record
- Difficulties building cohesive ethnic community
- Lack of cultural competency
- Unmet needs of ethnic community

Source: Author's calculations.

NEGOTIATING PANETHNICITY

In contrast to the organizations that maintained their ethnic boundaries, other organizations that were originally formed to serve ethnic-specific populations had adopted panethnic practices. These organizations did not claim to have shared interests across ethnic lines from their inception. Such interests had to be negotiated and constructed over time, and leaders were an essential part of this process; how they framed issues for their members and supporters was key in expanding organizational practices outside of ethnic group boundaries.

Endorsing a campaign or joining a coalition to provide symbolic support for another Asian ethnic group was considered "low risk" because the effort was short-term and did not require the sharing of material resources. However, the panethnic practice of providing symbolic support for another ethnic group's grievances, issues, or campaigns, though taken for granted today, was not always a given; such support reflected hard work and negotiation. Even though this panethnic practice typically did not require a high level of commitment, in the past it had often been difficult to gain support from other groups because Asian ethnic groups did not trust one another, nor did they see themselves as sharing a collective identity, history, and culture.

An example from the earlier part of the era provides some insights. In the late 1970s and through the 1980s, the Japanese American Citizens League sought redress for the internment of Japanese Americans during

World War II. Given the nature of the issue, JACL reached out to civil rights, religious, and ethnic organizations, but initially could not get support from any Asian ethnic organizations. Stephen, the director of the redress campaign at the time, explained:

> I had gone to various organizations in the Bay Area and other ethnic groups and said, "You know, I need an endorsement, I need you guys to support this." And I couldn't get it. I literally could not get one endorsement. The group that gave us a personal endorsement was the American Jewish Committee. Then we got endorsements from churches, the Presbyterian Church and the American Friends [Service Committee]. And then other groups started following in place. . . . The Asian groups were the last ones to come on board because there was still enough old world baggage between all of the groups.

Chinese and Korean American groups were reluctant to get on board and publicly state their support for the Japanese American campaign for redress and reparations, Stephen said, because of mistrust and bad feelings. Japan's occupation of both countries in the early 1900s was still having a negative impact on how the different Asian-origin groups related to one another.[30] While Chinese, Korean, and Japanese Americans had participated together in the Asian American movement, the ethnic organizations operating during the late 1970s tended to prioritize the issues of the first generation who still carried "old world baggage." Eventually, Asian ethnic groups signed on and supported the campaign, but it was not yet customary during that time for an ethnic group to take on another group's issues or concerns.

Over time, ethnic organizations engaged in panethnic practices beyond simply supporting one another's interests or causes, and expanded membership, services, programs, and mission statements to include other Asian ethnic populations. These boundary shifts had to be negotiated as well. While funding and government agencies and the larger society may have viewed Asians as a unified group, established ethnic organizations did not have the cultural competency, language proficiency, and, at times, access to other ethnic and immigrant communities to expand their services or advocacy work to all Asian ethnicities. Mark, a second-generation leader from a Japanese American organization, put it this way: "We certainly are not experts in serving the Southeast Asian communities or the Korean community. So I think having culturally competent groups to work with is much more effective than us doing it by ourselves."

As a result, smaller ethnic organizations often found themselves serving as cultural brokers or authorities, working to provide expertise to other Asian ethnic groups about their communities. Organizational leaders spoke on behalf of their own group at panethnic events and gave input on their group for panethnic project or grants; they also provided access to their ethnic community. Hun, a second-generation Korean American leader of a community center, explained:

> Our approach has been to work with larger API-based organizations that have the administrative and the technical capabilities to coordinate very different communities and work with them to develop new areas of focus, and our approach has been to be the organization that has the access and expertise, cultural expertise, with the Korean community, to then address larger API issues within this community.

Ethnic organizations such as this Korean American one thus acquired a seat at the table and gained symbolic and material benefits from working with larger organizations that typically had established relationships with funders. These organizations also were able to bring attention to their own community's needs and have a voice in shaping the larger Asian American agenda. Without collaboration across ethnic boundaries, other organizations would not have access to different Asian-origin communities, nor would they have the cultural competency to reach those communities. Additionally, by playing the role of cultural expert, ethnic organizations were able to engage in panethnic work while maintaining their commitment to their own ethnic group; this is one example of ethnic group boundaries being permeable yet durable.

Another key part of negotiating panethnicity was respecting the cultural authority of other ethnic communities, and organizational leaders were key in this delicate process. Michael, a leader at the Japanese American Center for Civil Rights (JACCR), talked about how he needed to keep his distance yet also provide support for other ethnic groups' issues. He elaborated on the balancing act he had to manage—working with other Asian ethnic groups for a successful collective outcome and supporting their issues, while preserving group boundaries: "I can talk to the Chinese American leadership and work with all of them. That's not a problem once the coalition starts to build. But I can't go to Chinatown and walk in there and say, 'I think this is what we should be doing.' I would get thrown out, and I ought to get thrown out. That's not my community." He added, "That's why we want a coalition—because you do the work in your community, you get that message across to the folks in your community, just as we do in ours."

By respecting the authority of other ethnic groups and working within their own communities to generate support for issues, ethnic organizations can serve as effective bridging institutions while still focusing on their own ethnic communities and maintaining distinctive ethnic boundaries.

ASSIMILATION NARRATIVES AND EXPANSIVE BOUNDARIES

Leaders of ethnic organizations that adopted panethnic practices often claimed that they expanded their group boundaries to include other Asian-origin groups in response to assimilation within the ethnic community; this illuminated how they understood and justified organizational change to their members and supporters. Figure 5.3 displays the different assimilation narratives that leaders used and referred to when talking about organizational change, as well as the new types of inclusive programming they prioritized.

Leaders of organizations serving Vietnamese, Cambodian, and Laotian populations often referred to "the changing needs of the first generation" as an impetus for adopting panethnic practices. The Southeast Asian population first arrived in the United States as refugees during the 1970s and 1980s, and over time its needs shifted beyond newcomer services such as language translation and help with citizenship. Leaders serving this population talked about how they wanted to maintain their refugee and newcomer services, but needed new constituents to advocate for and new clients to serve.

Duong, the leader of Vietnam Outreach (VO), continued to put time and effort into the refugee forum, a weekly meeting where local organizational leaders came together to share information and solve problems, even though Vietnamese refugees were no longer arriving in the United States:

> Vietnamese refugees, not many are coming, right? So why should we spend a lot of time with the forum? But keep it going to help the needy people. Before I was a refugee, lots of people [were] helping me. And now a new kind of refugee, why should I run away? If we can afford it, then we afford it. I'm going to get the resources to help those guys. If I can help, then yes, but if cannot, I gotta help my group.

Vietnam Outreach began to serve Afghan refugees because of a need in the local community, and Duong stated that if he was able to continue to secure funding for the current VO refugee programs, he would help the newcomers. If additional funding was scarce, however, he would need to put all of his efforts into new programs to serve the assimilating Vietnamese first generation. But given the relationships with funding agencies he had developed over the past twenty years, it was likely that he would be able to secure funding to support the refugee and newcomer programs. Expanding group boundaries to include other Asian-origin groups in long-standing programs had allowed ethnic organizations like VO to sur-

Figure 5.3 Assimilation Narratives and Program Activities Used by Ethnic Organization Leaders to Manage Organizational Shifts Toward Panethnicity

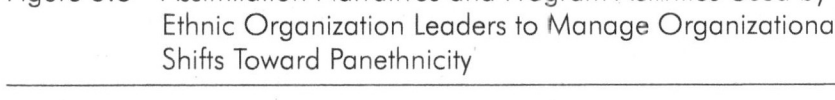

- **Assimilation of First Generation**
  - Fewer newcomer services needed
  - Long-term residence in the United States
  - Programs on asset development, homeownership assistance, business loans

- **Assimilation of Ethnic Group**
  - No longer need services or advocacy
  - Use resources to help other groups
  - Outreach to other communities through conferences, workshops, educational sessions

- **Assimilation of Second Generation**
  - Panethnic identity needs of second generation
  - Multicultural outlooks
  - Programs on domestic violence, youth, and community organizing to attract younger generation

Source: Author's calculations.

vive as they made the transition to develop new programs and update their services for increasingly established Vietnamese, Cambodian, and Laotian immigrant communities.

This was also the case for the Lao Mutual Association (LMA), an organization founded in the 1970s that established a strong reputation and funding track record over decades while providing newcomer services for Laotian refugees. Even though Laotian refugees were no longer coming to the United States in large numbers, the established partnerships with governmental agencies and private funders kept LMA's newcomer programs in place, and the organization now regularly serves Cambodian, Vietnamese, and other refugee groups through citizenship and immigrant programs as well as English language and family literacy classes. Elizabeth, an LMA leader, explained that because of their long-term residence in the United States (some for more than twenty years), the Laotian first generation was in need of programs related to homeownership assistance, asset development, and financial education, not simply emergency and translation services. LMA adapted to the changing needs of the assimilating Lao population and, while developing new programs, continued to support its old programs by serving new ethnic and refugee populations.[31] Elizabeth further supported this idea when she stated that the organization had "become much more diverse, but our mission is still, our primary focus is on Southeast Asian communities, because that's where our ties and history are the strongest."

But the fact that an ethnic organization was engaged in panethnic practices does not tell us anything about how expansive or committed they were to other Asian-origin groups. In fact, even leaders whose organizations included other Asian-origin groups in their programs or services often articulated the ethnic and cultural differences among these ethnic groups and the challenges they faced in forging interethnic ties. Organizations that responded to the changing needs of the first generation by incorporating other Asian ethnic groups into their programs and services were often practicing *accommodation*—including other groups to take advantage of funding opportunities, but not adopting inclusive mission statements, goals, and staff to signal a broader commitment to other Asian groups.[32] Additionally, the panethnic work of these organizations was usually short-term and represented a small part of their overall programming, and some of these organizations did not acknowledge a shared sense of status with other minority or immigrant groups, even though they often had common experiences due to the fact that the larger society lumped them all together as newcomers. This was the case for most ethnic social service organizations, and more inclusive organizational change was difficult to achieve.[33]

But LMA was an unusual case: because its leaders made decisions about expanding services to other groups in a deliberate way, it was considered a *transformative* organization. Elizabeth talked about LMA's development over the years and its focus on access to health care, employment, and housing for low-income refugees and immigrants through the provision of multilingual services:

> We're actually one of the few mutual assistance organizations that has grown beyond its ethnic identity. . . . One of our goals is to make sure that these communities have access, and then beyond that our real goal is to help people to be more self-sufficient, and we help them meet their basic needs, maybe through learning English and gaining skills of their own, or it can be through something like asset development, just being more financially stable.

LMA's leadership focused on developing broader commonalities among local populations related to low-income, refugee, or newcomer status by hiring multilingual staff and changing its mission statement to serve a broader population. LMA and other ethnic organizations like it undertook these programming changes not simply because of a funding incentive, but out of a shared sense of status with immigrant and refugee groups in need—as articulated by the organizational leaders who set the organizational agendas and made key decisions about programming.³⁴

Some ethnic organizations—mostly Southeast Asian—expanded their boundaries to solve organizational problems that arose due to the assimilation of the first generation. A handful of Japanese and Chinese American leaders talked about needing to find new constituents to advocate for, but they described the expansion of group boundaries as related to the assimilation of *the ethnic group as a whole,* not just one generation. The Japanese American Center for Civil Rights (JACCR) provides an example. JACCR was founded to advocate for the rights of Japanese immigrants in the United States. Over time, Japanese Americans successfully assimilated to the American mainstream, as evidenced by the patterns of their geographic dispersion, their educational and occupational attainment, and their high rates of intermarriage.³⁵ These assimilation patterns—which were also due in part to the lack of recent immigration from Japan to replenish Japanese immigrant communities—shaped the direction taken by JACCR and facilitated its pan-Asian work. JACCR leaders said that the Japanese community no longer needed a civil rights organization solely for its own benefit. While the organization still provided a multitude of advocacy and cultural programs specifically for Japanese Americans, one of the results of assimilation was that other ethnic groups could benefit from JACCR's efforts.³⁶

Given the infrastructure, knowledge, and reputation of well-established ethnic organizations such as JACCR, helping other ethnic groups with civil rights and advocacy work keeps these organizations alive and builds community when their own ethnic populations are declining in numbers or cannot be effectively reached. As a Japanese American leader at JACCR explained, "Japanese Americans have reached the point in our evolution in this country through assimilation. We understand how to avoid all of these problems. . . . What happens is that the newer or younger groups, you have immigrants who don't yet understand potential problems they're walking into, they walk straight into it. . . . I rarely ever get a call from a Japanese American. It's usually someone who's Chinese, Vietnamese, Korean, South Asian." JACCR was able to use its resources, networks, and members to bring an issue to the larger public through news conferences and organizing efforts, advocate for policies supporting the expansion of civil rights, and create inclusive programs that benefited the groups that came to them in need. Interestingly, JACCR leaders did not think it was viable to change their name to reflect the services they provided to new constituents, a subject that I discuss in the next section. Nevertheless, developing panethnic programs and partnerships was a key way for these leaders to keep the Japanese ethnic legacy alive as they tied their work with other Asian ethnic groups to their own experience as an ethnic community.

A specific example of this panethnic work was JACCR's outreach to South Asian communities after the terrorist attacks of September 11, 2001. The JACCR leadership recognized that Arab Americans, Muslims, and South Asian Americans would be targeted in ways similar to how Japanese Americans had been targeted after Japan's attack on Pearl Harbor in 1942, and they moved swiftly with media and organizational resources to ensure that these communities remained safe. Stanley, a JACCR leader, talked about his reaction to the events of 9/11 when he was watching the news reports come in that morning:

> I heard Peter Jennings say this is only the second time in the history of this country that this has happened. My immediate reaction was "Oh God, I know exactly what's going to happen." I sent an action memorandum, and I basically told the chapters, "I want you to anticipate what's going to happen, if you have Arab, Muslim, or South Asian communities in the area, there's going to be a backlash and [don't] wait until it happens. So get out there and be pro-active and send the packet out, things like resolutions to give to the city council to do press conferences, just to meet them and get to know them, shake their hand, and let them know that we're here to help."

Leaders have been able to preserve and highlight the Japanese American history and experience by making linkages to other populations facing similar experiences of discrimination and injustice. These linkages are made visible through conferences, workshops, educational sessions, and websites that provide a shared narrative among different Asian-origin groups (also shared, in JACCR's case, with Arab Americans and Muslims) and highlight the Japanese American experience, which is a key way of reinforcing ethnic boundaries and solidarity. For JACCR and other ethnic organizations serving Japanese or Chinese Americans, the assimilation of the ethnic group as a whole has encouraged leaders to expand group boundaries and utilize their resources to advocate for other Asian ethnic communities, while at the same time keeping the ethnic legacy of ethnic communities alive.

Yet another way in which leaders of Japanese, Chinese, and Korean American organizations have framed the expansion of group boundaries and the shifting of organizational practices is as a response to the interests and needs of the second generation. In the past, recent immigrants made up the Asian population in the United States and organizations provided newcomer services such as English language training, employment assistance, and citizenship programs. Today, however, as organizational leaders explained, in many ethnic communities the second and even third generations are coming of age, and their experiences, ideas, and approaches differ from those of the first generation, complicating the work of ethnic organizations. Many second-generation youth—those born and raised in the United States during the post–civil rights era with one or more foreign-born parents—would like to learn more about their panethnic identities, which they see as relevant in today's multicultural world. As a leader of a Japanese American organization put it

> Younger people these days are looking to join pan-Asian organizations, so we already know that we are going to have to start changing with the time. Over half the young people are going to be in intermarriages, and that's going to become an issue for this organization, which actually will be healthy, because it'll take the [organization] in an area where it's inevitable anyway. If you change a lot of the thinking within the organization, you become much more diverse, you become more like a pan-Asian group rather than to maintain the status quo.

Similarly, a leader of a Korean American organization explained, "Our community is growing, just generally a lot of second-generation activity is beginning to adopt its own cultural norms and beliefs as well as risks and problems. So some of our programming is geared towards taking more of a multicultural approach." Because many ethnic organizations are membership-based, they must shift their practices to address the interests and demands of their constituencies—in this case, the growing second generation—or risk becoming obsolete.

To deal with the changing needs of the second generation, leaders of many Chinese, Japanese, and Korean American organizations began to collaborate with other Asian ethnic groups to develop programs focused on domestic violence, youth, and community organizing. These programs involved Asians from different ethnic groups and often addressed issues related to education, empowerment, culture, and identity. For example, Japanese American Advocates (JAA) now has a thriving and inclusive pan-Asian youth program that addresses issues of cultural awareness, identity, and diversity through workshops and special events. The organization hosts conferences that provide opportunities for youth to develop leadership skills and meet other Asian Americans from different parts of the region and country. Interestingly, one of the recent conferences featured finalists for a public speaking contest who were asked how they would approach the challenge of meeting the needs of a community that had become increasingly diverse in regard to ethnicity and generation. Another JAA conference focused on the role of public policy in generating social change in the Asian American community and drew on a pan-Asian narrative about the shared experiences and histories of Asian-origin groups in the United States. Even though the conference was coordinated by an ethnic-specific organization, the attendees were of different Asian-origin backgrounds, and their experiences typically extended beyond group boundaries. One of the attendees explained: "Everyone came from different backgrounds, but at the conference I felt as if we were working together as one to find ways to promote and advocate for Asian American awareness and look at the issues."

Generally, when leaders talked about panethnic work in response to the assimilation of the second generation and the ethnic group as a whole—whether the subject was incorporating Asian-origin groups in individual campaigns, organizational goals, or long-term partnerships—they adopted a narrative about the distinct culture and history of Asian Americans. The commonalities developed among the different groups were not framed as a shared status among immigrants and newcomers, but as a social and political community with shared experiences of being racialized as foreigners and model minorities. Many leaders also talked about serving their own ethnic group and Asian Americans more broadly, often not making distinctions between the two when they discussed their organizational work. That said, most of the ethnic organizations that had adopted panethnic practices did so to accommodate other groups while maintaining a focus on their own ethnic group; leaders lamented the difficulty of developing a "real pan-Asian organization." Considering that these organizations were originally founded to serve specific ethnic groups, however, it is not surprising that expanding their programs, resources, and missions to include the needs and voices of a diverse Asian American community would be a challenge. Only a handful of ethnic organizations were transformative, taking active steps to include other Asian-origin groups as part of their broader community through long-term inclusive programming and regular collaborations. Taken together, these steps provided the foundation for panethnic coalitions and collective action and also had important implications for adaptation because when organizations work together, they often are able to provide a broader array of resources and information for group members.

But what led some ethnic organizations, like LMA and JAA, to be more transformative? Their leaders played key roles in reinventing community boundaries and carrying out work on behalf of expanded group affiliations by prioritizing programs that incorporated multiple Asian-origin groups, developing ties between different ethnic communities, and reproducing the pan-Asian narrative.[37] Yet at the same time, other factors, such as an organization's reputation, access to funding, and history, not only shaped organizational change but also the extent of its inclusiveness.

Not surprisingly, transformative ethnic organizations often originated with missions and goals related to civil rights and social justice. Ethnic boundaries were more permeable for these organizations, since progress toward equality for one ethnic group was linked to the progress of the larger Asian American collective group. These organizations were founded by Asian American activists who wanted to improve their ethnic communities and often brought progressive ideologies and strategies to the task. Civil rights organizations also tended to be inclusive because they often dealt with issues affecting other ethnic communities and embraced a social justice ideology, which was conducive to helping groups outside of ethnic boundaries. In addition, these organizations did not have to decide how to divide funds for housing development or health care within different ethnic neighborhoods or among different ethnic groups. They often advocated for policy that directly affected various immigrant, ethnic, and racial groups. Furthermore, transformative ethnic organizations often had access to resources such as large organizational and staff capacity, funding streams, established programs, and strong reputations in the field that helped them maintain services and programs for their own ethnic community in conjunction with extensive panethnic work. Although a handful of accommodating organizations also shared these characteristics in terms of capacity and reputation, their leaders did not typically connect a progressive ideology with panethnic work.

Ethnic organizations shifted their practices and broadened group boundaries as a response to assimilation within and across generations. As ethnic groups became more integrated into the American mainstream, leaders and their organizations responded by becoming more inclusive to reflect the needs and interests of their constituents and members. These organizational changes represented an opportunity to create programming and partnerships across ethnic boundaries, but they were also necessary for survival. Although the adoption of panethnic practices may have reflected different forms of assimilation—for the first and second generations and for the ethnic group as a whole—panethnicity was not equated with the dissolution of ethnic boundaries. As the next section aptly shows, even though ethnic organizations began to practice panethnicity and some changed their mission statements to reflect the new populations included in their services and programs, very few, if any, changed their organizational name.[38] In other words, ethnic organizations adopted panethnic practices while maintaining ethnic boundaries, providing further support for the notion that ethnicity and panethnicity can coexist and the presence of one does not preclude the other.

WHAT'S IN A NAME? ETHNIC LEGACIES AND SYMBOLIC BOUNDARIES

The issue of name change is highly controversial in ethnic communities. In most cases, the older generation who founded and initially supported an organization do not want the boundaries of the organization expanded. A name change clearly indicates that other groups will benefit from the organization. This perspective on the importance of maintaining ethnic boundaries tends to conflict with the views of the newer generation, who are more likely to recognize the changes within ethnic communities and to take a progressive stance toward social change. From this perspective, a name change may be desirable because it would reflect what the organization is doing and which communities it is actually serving.

Some of the most established Chinese and Japanese organizations have gone through periods when the leadership initiated discussion of a name change. For example, in the early 2000s, after the Asian Cultural Center (ACC) in Oakland decided to change its name to the Asian Pacific Cultural Center, controversy ensued. The ACC was founded by Chinese Americans in 1984 to preserve the Chinatown culture, but over time its cultural and arts programming shifted to represent many different ethnic groups, including Koreans, Japanese, Laotians, South Asians, Cambodians, and Vietnamese. Despite this shift in programming, some Chinese members feared that the name change would overrun their legacy and culture. According to Jeff Chan, an ACC program developer, the name change did not mean that "we're turning our back on Chinese culture." Referring to the addition of Pacific Islanders to the name of the center, he said, "One doesn't block out the other."[39] Nevertheless, the addition of Pacific Islanders, a group that is often seen as part of the larger Asian American community, sparked enough tension and controversy that the original name of the center was restored. Clearly, it is much easier for organizations to change their practices than their name—to this day ACC's documentary materials still state that its mission is "to promote Asian Pacific American arts, culture, and heritage to help build and sustain vibrant, healthy communities"—and the tensions that arose at ACC over the name change attest to the strength of ethnic group boundaries.

Similarly, a Chinese advocacy and direct services organization founded in the early 1970s was mired in controversy when its board of directors voted to change the name of the organization to reflect its panethnic work. The board of directors claimed that a name change would increase the organization's effectiveness in advocating for the entire Asian American community. But Chinese community members were concerned that the change would affect their access to the organization and jeopardize the history and reputation of the organization. Kevin, a senior program director for the organization who had been working in nonprofits for the last fifteen years, explained:

> The people who felt the strongest about opposing the name change were people who really do want to see this organization still rooted in the Chinese American community. It's definitely generational. Ultimately we did not go forward with the name change because it's one of those things where you need the support of all members. . . . It would have really left a part of our longtime supporters behind had we done that.

For the well-established Japanese American organizations, group members had similar concerns about a name change. Jane, the executive director of Japanese Americans for Justice (JAJ), explained that even though the organization worked on behalf of Asian Americans as well as other racial and ethnic groups, she believed that keeping the name of the organization was important because it came with a reputation that had value in political circles and among community members. She put it this way: "It's the same thing as the NAACP [National Association for the Advancement of Colored People]. They've gone through some issues and kept their name. They kept it mainly because the name has value to them, it has cachet. If you go anywhere and talk to politicians and you mention NAACP, they know exactly what you're talking about." Even though JAJ's work has expanded to include advocacy for non-Japanese groups, keeping the founding name was important to maintain organizational stability and legitimacy. Since the organization had been around for over twenty years and had created a strong reputation, changing the name would have decreased the value and recognizability of the organization.

The issue of name change came up for other organizations besides East Asian organizations. The Vietnamese Community Association (VCA), founded in 1975, had expanded its services over the past several years and considered a name change to reflect the Cambodian population it served and wanted to serve more effectively. Cynthia, the executive director of VCA and a second-generation Vietnamese American in her thirties, explained:

> There is a long history of conflict between Cambodian and Vietnamese people due to war, and many Cambodian people do not feel comfortable coming to a Vietnamese agency because once again you're selling out or they came and destroyed our country. Why are you coming to VCA? A lot of our young Cambodian staff has to deal with that with their parents. So if our staff is already dealing with that, you can imagine what the young students

are dealing with. They are coming here to use these services, even as mundane as receiving an employment service, but it's still coming to a Vietnamese center.

Some of the VCA leaders supported the name change to more accurately reflect the population the organization served. Such a change would also have alleviated the discomfort of the Cambodian clients and might even have attracted more clients of different ethnic backgrounds who lived in the area. To date, however, no concrete plans had been made to implement an organizational name change.

Ethnic leaders from newer organizations serving the Southeast Asian population made similar arguments about recognizability and name change, even though a long-standing reputation associated with a particular name was not an issue for them. Because there are very few ethnic organizations serving Cambodians or Vietnamese compared to other Southeast Asians or Asian Americans, leaders viewed the names of ethnic organizations as unique markers that might help them stand out when applying for funding.[40]

Ethnic organizations may have participated in collaborations across ethnic boundaries and served other ethnic communities besides their own, yet they still encountered intergroup tensions related to organizational name changes. Ethnic group members, especially those of earlier generations, wanted to keep their legacy intact. A name change threatened this legacy. Because the newer generation adopted more of a pan-Asian identity and a progressive stance toward social change, they were more likely to be in favor of a name change. At the same time, some leaders felt that it was important to maintain an ethnic name as a symbolic boundary marker, especially if the organization had built a strong reputation over decades. Identity branding was key for such an organization's continued success in maintaining a loyal constituency and funding streams and collaborating with other organizational partners.[41]

To avoid strife and controversy in trying to meet the conflicting demands of their constituencies, organizational leaders found creative ways to participate in and seek out panethnic projects while maintaining effective programs and services for the single-ethnic community. The Chinese American Citizens Council (CACC) launched a new major project with a panethnic name that highlighted its advocacy work for all Asian Americans and showcased the organization's participation in statewide policy work. Using this strategy, CACC was able to avoid the controversy of a name change and satisfy the different interests of its constituents while signaling its panethnic work to funders, community members, and the larger public. Instead of changing its name to reach a broader clientele, the Vietnamese Community Association developed a strategy similar to the one adopted by CACC. The VCA set up off-site programs in city recreation and community centers and public schools—neutral territory where Cambodian youth could be reached without fear of being ostracized or ridiculed by their parents or coethnic peers. If Cambodians and other ethnic group members in need were not coming to their doors, the VCA leaders were determined to provide services and information to them in a nonthreatening environment, even if doing so required moving outside of the organization's home base.[42]

BEYOND RACIAL BOUNDARIES: WHAT'S IN IT FOR US?

Virtually all organizational leaders and group members acknowledged the Asian American construct, but not all saw their communities as tied to other racial groups. Some leaders viewed building relations with Latinos and African Americans as more difficult to manage than developing ties with other Asian-origin communities. These leaders often constructed an Asian American community that was distinct from other racial groups, and while this facilitated panethnic work, at times it hindered their ability to expand group boundaries further, across racial lines.

Stephen, the leader of Japanese Americans Creating Action (JACA), provided a useful example. Even though JACA partnered with Latino and black organizations, Stephen viewed such work as a way to effectively serve Asian communities rather than as a way to work on behalf of broader group affiliations. He described a number of campaigns and programs that he helped to forge with other racial groups to fight against hate crimes and discrimination that affected all racial minorities. In Stephen's eyes, the unique and separate circumstances of Asian Americans made it difficult for interracial coalitions and partnerships with blacks and Latinos to endure after a campaign or issue ended. He gave his thoughts on the matter:

> I don't know if partnerships really work quite honestly. . . . [Foundations will] tell us that we should go work with some black or Latino organization and do these joint projects, [but] they have their problems and we have our problems. We want to work on what we want to work on. We know what our issues are, and our issues are not Latino or black issues.

Despite recognizing that shared interests with other minority groups helped to build interracial coalitions, Stephen's focus on "our issues" signified a clear boundary between JACA's community of interest—Japanese and Asian Americans—and other racial groups.

Some ethnic organizations did adopt panracial practices because their leaders viewed relations with other racial groups as key to social justice and change. These leaders also adopted a narrative that emphasized the bond that Asian Americans shared with other racial minorities and the importance of mobilizing in a larger struggle against racial oppression. This narrative enabled these ethnic organization leaders to regularly create partnerships across racial lines and support other racial groups because they viewed their own interests as tied to other communities of color. For these organizations, the strength of the Asian American community was important, but the main goal was social justice for all groups.

The tensions of panracial work were felt by these organizations. While Asian ethnic group members seemed to understand that engaging in panethnic work brought the larger collective more resources, visibility, and political power, the immediate advantages of panracial work were often less apparent. Leaders of these organizations had to work harder to explain why they made certain decisions and supported certain campaigns; Asian ethnic group members had a more difficult time understanding what was in it for them.

Chinese for Civil Rights (CCR), a community center providing services, advocacy, and grassroots organizing for the Chinese population, often supported local measures to address the concerns of the larger multiracial community, even when that support was occasionally in conflict with the immediate interests of the Chinese community as well as the broader Asian America community. Jonathan, CCR's director, recalled the organization's recent support for a new redistricting plan in San Francisco that would have allowed African Americans and Latinos to be elected in certain districts. A segment of the Chinese population strongly criticized CCR for not encouraging a plan that included stronger Chinese districts. The organization had a long history of making decisions that did not provide immediate material advantages for its core constituency but instead supported a broader multiracial movement for social change.[43] Jonathan described the resulting tensions:

> That's what is hard to explain to our constituency . . . that when you do coalition building, it has long-term benefits, because the average Chinese or Asian American immigrant says, "Why are we giving up this right now?" or, "Why aren't you being a stronger advocate for us?" or this or that. . . . But you know, our reply was that in the long run this was going to benefit us. If you draw an African American [community] out of it altogether, there will

be a long-term impact that will come back to haunt us, and it's very hard to explain that to your own community.

Although ethnic constituents may have disagreed with organizational leaders about their decisions to allocate support and resources to other racial groups, leaders found that following the principles of fairness, equality, and inclusion for all racial minority groups contributed to the larger goal of social justice and also helped them build strong organizational reputations, which benefited their ethnic communities in the long run.

Many leaders also mentioned that their organization was assessed by funders and other nonprofits based on what they had done in the community, who they had worked with, and the stances they had taken. Given that they were motivated to prioritize working outside of ethnic lines because of the broader benefits for the larger society and their own ethnic communities, some leaders negotiated the activation of panethnicity and managed the demands of their ethnic constituents by continuing to provide specialized programs and support policies that aided the Asian ethnic-specific and Asian American communities. Another strategy was to create another organization that would serve a diverse racial population. For most leaders, however, the demands of the constituency to maintain ethnic or panethnic practices won out because of institutional inertia; panracial ties were more difficult to sustain than panethnic ones unless leaders continued to nurture and maintain those ties.[44]

Leaders also dealt with tensions when attempting to expand boundaries to include other racial minorities by educating their own ethnic communities. Jonathan of CCR discussed the organization's responsibility to its members to help them adapt to living in American society: "One of our major roles here is to educate Chinese Americans and to make the community more progressive. It isn't just reaching out to African Americans, it's reaching back to Chinese immigrants, giving them education on civil rights issues and helping them to understand that they live in a multicultural society." Organizations like CCR contributed to a greater understanding between different groups, especially when partnerships were tied to long-term programs that brought different groups together in an interactive setting. In adopting panethnic practices, leaders of ethnic organizations could signal to constituents that ethnic boundaries were being maintained and ethnic legacies kept intact; by contrast, panracial work required that they overcome the durability of racial boundaries by educating ethnic group members and constituents about the shared fate of racial minority groups in the United States and the importance of organizing as a broad-based collective for social change.

THE PERMEABILITY AND STRENGTH OF ETHNIC BOUNDARIES

With the establishment and legitimacy of the panethnic organizational form, community-based ethnic organizations faced institutional pressures to adopt the panethnic model. Organizing as Asian Americans rendered Asian ethnic and immigrant communities more visible to elected officials, elites, funders, and mainstream institutions. Looking at the sample of ethnic organizations in the San Francisco–Oakland area and their engagement in panethnic practices, we can see how the panethnic model in the organizational field influenced ethnic organizations. Although we might expect that ethnic organizations in this region, with its deep history of Asian American activism and cooperation, would have easily conformed to a panethnic model, in fact panethnicity was not a natural outcome; as shown in this chapter and throughout this book, panethnicity had to be negotiated, constructed, and enacted by leaders and community members. Only half of the ethnic organizations in the sample had adopted panethnic practices, and they had mostly done so by supporting one another's campaigns, which was relatively low risk and did not involve extensive expenditures of resources. Other panethnic practices involved the inclusion of other Asian-origin groups in current programming and partnering across ethnic lines to develop campaigns or build new pan-Asian networks. For some organizations, these boundary-related organizational practices were transformative. Serving and advocating for other groups was not done to simply take advantage of funding opportunities; these ethnic organizations adopted inclusive mission statements, goals, programming, and staff, to signal a broader commitment to other Asian groups.

The widening of group boundaries to include others did not necessarily lead to the displacement of smaller group boundaries based on ethnicity or national origin. In fact, most ethnic organizations maintained their ethnic programs and worked to link expansive panethnic practices with ethnic interests and histories. Even when transformative ethnic organizations engaged in panethnic practices at multiple levels and were committed to the pan-Asian project, ethnic boundaries remained durable, if only symbolically, as nearly all were unwilling to change their organizational names to reflect the broader populations being served. This attests to the strength of ethnic boundaries. Remaining ethnic in name, organizations maintained their ethnic histories, roots, and culture in the face of assimilation, changing demographics, and institutional pressures to conform to a panethnic model. This is quite striking given that material boundaries expanded more easily, in the extension of services and programming, but symbolic boundaries remained strong. Thus, within the organizational field, ethnic group boundaries were both permeable and durable—social and symbolic distinctiveness between groups dissolved even as ethnicity was maintained.

Clearly, ethnic organizations can and do adopt panethnic practices, and according to their leaders, the demands associated with assimilation encourage the expansion of organizational boundaries. Given the changing needs of the first generation, the second generation, and the ethnic group as a whole, these organizations must shift their practices or risk losing their constituents. For the most part, leaders of East Asian organizations that provide services and advocacy for Chinese, Japanese, Korean, and Filipino populations adopt panethnic practices for two reasons: as a way to involve the younger generations who are interested in learning more about their panethnic identities, and as a response to successful ethnic group assimilation, which allows leaders to serve other populations within the pan-Asian community who have not yet experienced full assimilation and need advocacy. Linking the histories and experiences of East Asian groups with those of South Asians and Southeast Asians also helps to keep the ethnic legacies of communities alive. In contrast, leaders of ethnic organizations serving Laotian, Vietnamese, and other Southeast Asian groups work on expanding group boundaries in order to provide services for other newcomer groups because of the changing needs of the first generation. Issues related to assimilation, such as not yet having their own house in order, also keeps ethnic organizations from expanding their boundaries to include other Asian ethnic groups. At the same time, other factors—many of them related to an ethnic group's time in the United States—are contributing to organizational change, such as an organization's reputation, its access to funding, and its history.

This examination of the flexibility of group boundaries has also shown that it is difficult to expand organizational boundaries to include other racial groups. Nearly all ethnic organizations aspire to forging panethnic ties—or are at least open to it—but the same cannot be said for panracial work. Some leaders of Asian ethnic organizations do not acknowledge the experiences and histories shared with other racial minorities, and some assert clear distinctions. Leaders also claim that the second and later generations of their ethnic communities do not encourage or demand panracial programs or partnerships to fulfill their identity needs, as they do with respect to panethnic programs. Illustrating the durability of racial boundaries—and the differences between panethnicity and race—is the fact that leaders instead of members and constituents are the ones to spearhead organizational practices across racial lines.[45] The hallmark of panethnicity is the recognition of ethnic distinctions and the building of a broader shared identity.⁴⁶ Organizational leaders work to maintain ethnic distinctions when they engage in panethnic work, but they do not talk about working to maintain racial differences when engaging in panracial partnerships or alliances. The members of their organizations tend to view Asians, Latinos, and blacks as more "naturally" distinct from one another; if anything, leaders try to teach members about the commonalities and interests they share with other racial minorities and how to live within a multicultural society.

In short, the leaders of ethnic organizations play key roles in facilitating and maintaining expansive practices by prioritizing programs that incorporate multiple Asian-origin groups, developing ties between different ethnic communities, framing group members' interests, and reproducing the pan-Asian narrative. Most importantly, leaders help to construct community boundaries, develop inclusive programming, and work on behalf of expanded group affiliations, whether across ethnic or racial lines.

Chapter 6 | Panethnicity and Beyond

GIVEN THAT THE hallmark of panethnicity is its emphasis on solidarity through difference and that its success and longevity depend on the maintenance of ethnic identities, it is no wonder that the Asian American community and organizational leaders have spoken out against instances of racialization, such the 2012 Pew report.[1] Such media reports highlight the integration and assimilation of Asian Americans and thereby reinforce the model minority trope, erasing diversity within the category of Asian. It has been through concerted efforts and collective action based on a panethnic identity that Asian Americans have forged social change and begun to shift how policymakers, local officials, and the larger public understand the different needs and interests of the Asian American population.

By examining the conditions, processes, and mechanisms through which the category and identity of Asian American was used to organize different Asian-origin groups over the post-1968 era, this book has highlighted instances of collective organizing such as those surrounding the Pew report, but more importantly, it has revealed that group boundaries are not intractable or static—they are dynamic and can shift and change. I have asserted that broad social conditions such as federal policies related to immigration and civil rights and racial classification systems have been important for the expansion of boundaries. The liberalization of immigration laws brought increasing streams of immigrants from different parts of Asia into the United States, the extension of civil rights to racial minorities generated new political opportunities, and the racial categories created by the federal government were adopted by schools, in health care, and by other mainstream institutions. Yet these broader social changes did not naturally result in panethnicity.

Building on early theoretical work on panethnicity, which emphasized the importance of structural commonalities, I have also argued that a *structure* and a *narrative* must be in place to translate the broader forces of racialization, political opportunity, and demographic change into panethnicity.[2] Group interests and shared identities have to be constructed across ethnic, linguistic, and cultural lines before group identities and behaviors can align with racial categories. The *racialized boundary framework* that I have developed throughout the book focuses on how meso-level conditions shape group interaction and facilitate the formation of expansive group identities. It also contributes to a more complete understanding of panethnicity by highlighting the dynamic, layered nature of group boundaries, which is especially important when studying new immigrant groups within the United States that can organize along multiple dimensions of identity.

In short, this book has asserted that Asian American panethnicity during the post–civil rights era was a social accomplishment and negotiated process that occurred through: (1) racial segregation, a structural condition that reflected social difference and inequality in local labor markets, yet also created a context in which ethnic group members could interact, develop shared experiences and interests, and build solidarity across ethnic lines; (2) ethnic organizing, which provided an existing infrastructure that helped coordinate and build trust among different Asian-origin groups; and (3) the active role of community leaders and members in drawing on the structural conditions of labor market inequalities and building panethnic narratives about experiences of inequality and unfair treatment among Asian Americans that countered the model minority trope and stereotype. Figure 6.1 provides a visual representation of the argument: the development of network ties and trust, the construction of panethnic narratives and prioritization of inclusive programs, and an organizational infrastructure represent the mechanisms through which the proximate social conditions of racial segregation, active leaders, and ethnic organizing worked to produce panethnic outcomes.

THEORETICAL IMPLICATIONS

The evidence presented in this book has established that proximate conditions are indeed important in shaping when and where panethnicity emerges in both collective and organizational activity. The theoretical ideas about segregated conditions in labor markets giving rise to group solidarity within and among ethnic groups—because they foster common interests, networks, and identities—have been opposed here to competition models, which suggest that intergroup contact across racial lines generates competition and encourages racial groups to engage in collective action. Group solidarity and collective action emerge within a segregated context because not only do group members depend on the group itself—

Figure 6.1 The Mediating Conditions and Mechanisms That Encourage Panethnic Organizing

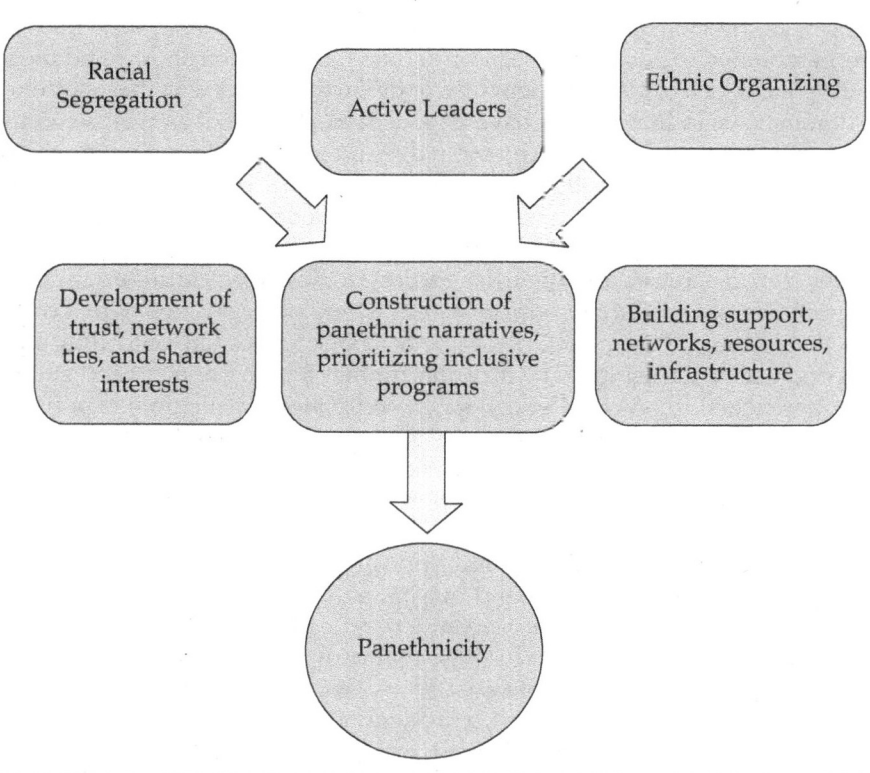

Source: Author's calculations.

they do not have access to the goods they demand except through the efforts of the collective—but such a context is conducive to the monitoring and sanctioning of group members if necessary.[3] Segregated conditions may also encourage dependence as ethnic or racial group members come to see that their life chances are shaped by their membership in the group.[4] Even though other factors, such as anti-Asian violence and racial profiling, may explain the urgency with which pan-Asian organizing is taking place, group solidarity facilitated by segregation is a necessary condition for the emergence of panethnic collective action.

Additionally, community leaders can draw upon the visible inequalities associated with a racially segregated occupational structure to create a panethnic narrative that they can use when articulating needs and developing campaigns. For instance, leaders cite the plight of low-wage workers who face unfair wages and poor working conditions and tie these contemporary experiences of labor discrimination to those of early Asian immigrants in the United States. They also deploy narratives about the underrepresentation of Asian Americans in certain parts of the economy and their subsequent lack of access to networks and power structures in these sectors. Although Asian immigrants have experienced residential as well as occupational segregation, it has been more difficult for activists and community leaders to construct panethnic narratives around the residential segregation of Asian Americans. Many Asians in the post-1968 era have been dispersed outside of ethnic enclaves. And those who reside in ethnic enclaves consider them desirable, since they have access in these social locations to community organizations, churches, restaurants, and other businesses that cater to their needs.[5] Ethnic enclaves are no longer associated with filth and second-class citizenship, but with opportunities for employment and ethnic entrepreneurship.[6] A racially segregated occupational structure—especially one with Asians concentrated near the bottom—is associated with clear economic inequalities upon which leaders can capitalize.

Though I did not find much support for the competition model, it has been used to explain conflict and collective action among dominant groups that are attempting to maintain their power and authority over resources, such as neighborhoods, jobs, and marital partners. When newcomers enter into once-segregated spaces, conflict and collective action on the part of dominant groups increase.[7] Given that competition has typically been understood as occurring "from above," its processes and dynamics do not easily apply to Asian Americans, a racial minority in the United States that is attempting to establish, not defend, group boundaries.[8]

Although segregation does explain the panethnic outcomes studied in this book, it may be more apt for understanding group solidarity—"the conscious identification by persons in an ethnic population as members of an ethnic group"—than conflict or exclusion movements.[9] Understanding the importance of segregation in producing conditions of dependence and control, and ultimately group solidarity, we can speculate that, when competition is introduced in such a context, collective action will occur. Following this logic, the segregation model may be more relevant to emergent group boundaries because it is able to explain how and why group boundaries form; the competition model, on the other hand, takes group boundaries as given and emphasizes the conditions that solidify preexisting boundaries.[10]

The segregation model derives from theoretical work on internal colonialism, which has been used to explain the rise of ethnic nationalism.[11] Cultural divisions of labor represent systems of stratification in which cultural or ethnic differences are aligned with class differences. Ethnic identity on the periphery becomes increasingly salient when the group is bounded within certain occupational niches and when life chances are increasingly determined by ethnic group membership.[12] New research from political science builds on and has in many ways revived these ideas, focusing on the "horizontal inequalities" between ethnic groups and states that can promote ethnic conflict.[13] These emerging studies examining political, economic, and social horizontal inequalities generally find that disadvantaged and advanced groups are more likely to be involved in conflict and collective action than groups that are closer to the national average. The social psychological process posited to be at work is one based on grievances, which emerge when group identities become salient and social comparisons result in antagonistic intergroup relations, sometimes triggering conflict.[14] Future research should expand on the idea of a cultural division of labor and look beyond labor markets to understand boundary dynamics within and outside of the U.S. context.

Furthermore, these theoretical ideas about the role of segregation in producing shared identities are consistent with current research on the contact hypothesis. Studies overwhelmingly demonstrate that intergroup contact between equal-status groups can increase empathy with the out-group, enhance positive emotions about the out-group, and reduce interactional anxiety.[15] All of these effects are necessary for building a shared collective identity among ethnic groups that did not originally see themselves as having much in common. Greater trust and a more differentiated view of the out-group also often emerge after contact between individuals of equal status. Within the context of segregation—that is, where racial groups are spatially organized in such a way that the ethnic groups sharing a racial category are likely to have more contact with one another than with other racial groups—contact across ethnic lines, among Chinese, Japanese, Koreans, Vietnamese, Indians, and other Asian ethnic groups, can lead to positive outcomes that should generalize to the groups involved as well as to new contact situations.[16]

In addition to segregation, ethnic organizations play a key role in panethnic organizing because of the support, resources, and networks they bring to the table, enabling group action across ethnic lines. Ethnic organizations and events also foster solidarity among ethnic communities that can later be translated into panethnic activity. These organizations based on collective identities not only provide a structural context for the development of a common culture and identity but also serve as "mobilizing structures."[17] By strengthening ethnic groups through advocacy and social service efforts, ethnic organizations increase community access to information, knowledge, and resources and provide social locations where mobilization can be generated. These organizations also facilitate solidarity by constructing inclusive ideologies and effective programming, and the communication networks they develop within ethnic communities cultivate fertile ground for collective action. Additionally, ethnic organizations organize material resources that make their social change and social service efforts more successful.

For some social movement scholars, it may not be surprising that past organizing efforts, which involve the mobilization of the resources required for successful collective action, have been important in the emergence of panethnicity.[18] They would expect past panethnic efforts to help generate current and future efforts. But what was unexpected is the fact that *ethnic* organizing, in the form of past events and the density of organizations, has encouraged panethnicity. This finding is consistent with the idea of group boundaries as layered: the assertion of one group boundary (say, one based on ethnicity) does not preclude the emergence of another (one based on a broader panethnic grouping). Understanding this relationship is key because it provides insights into the ways in which group boundaries are flexible and permeable rather than durable and static. Past research has emphasized the idea that group boundaries can shift and change.[19] Little empirical evidence has been found, however, for how layered identities operate in relation to one another and whether the relationship between ethnic and panethnic organizing is competitive or mutualistic.

Finally, the ideas presented here about how leaders generate and reinforce pan-Asian narratives, guide group interests, set priorities related to panethnic work, and ultimately work to organize different Asian-origin groups under a common framework also build on studies in social movements and interracial political coalitions. Past research has shown that leaders play a crucial role in the success of multiracial alliances because they generate shared interests and identities, forge ties between organizations and groups, and build trust.[20] Much of this research takes group boundaries as given and does not recognize that multiple, layered identities can be drawn upon when defining a community to achieve organizational goals. Ethnic and panethnic boundaries can be seen as mutually exclusive, but leaders work hard to ensure that members, constituents, policymakers, and the larger public understand that both boundaries and identities are important. Leaders are important in the panethnic collective action process because they construct and deploy a pan-Asian narrative about the shared needs and interests of Asian Americans as a social and political community while still recognizing and valuing ethnic differences to help generate pan-Asian protest and civic action. Where the panethnic model has become dominant as an organizational form that is recognizable to elites and policymakers, leaders are especially key when ethnic organizations shift their boundaries to include other Asian ethnic groups as members, constituents, and communities. They provide narratives about the expansion of group boundaries as a response to the needs of ethnic communities and work to link the past histories and experiences of one ethnic group to those of other ethnic groups in order to maintain an ethnic legacy. New research should focus on how leaders interpret and negotiate other forms of distinction or difference, such as legal and immigrant status, and how these forms affect panethnic group formations. The assumption is that these differences exist and challenge panethnicity, but we need more research to understand how particular boundaries are maintained or transversed and which actors are involved. As researchers, we cannot simply assume that ethnic, cultural, religious, linguistic, or citizenship differences keep groups from cooperating; we need to understand how and why group boundaries continue to be seen as durable and the conditions that encourage their maintenance.[21]

Taken together, community and organizational leaders continually participate in the construction of an Asian American community through the retelling and adoption of pan-Asian narratives, which bring diverse national-origin groups together, and through the partnerships, programming, and funding opportunities pursued between Asian ethnic groups. It may not be surprising that the narratives of leaders help to generate panethnic activity in light of "frame alignment processes," as social movement scholars call them, that channel grievances toward movement action.[22] Again, however, what is surprising is the fact that *ethnic* organizations and their leaders play a role in this process, given the assumptions about the durability of ethnic boundaries. We would readily expect leaders of panethnic organizations to create panethnic narratives and develop inclusive programming, but not necessarily leaders of ethnic organizations. Even if groups are structured in a way that encourages the development of trust and solidarity, that structure may not necessarily translate into cooperative efforts or a successful, enduring coalition unless leaders help to shape group members' interests and engage group members in mobilization efforts. Leaders of panethnic organizations are the most likely candidates to help with this framing and organizing work, but ethnic group boundaries are flexible enough that leaders of ethnic organizations play a key role in this process as well. Further work is needed to understand different frame alignment processes and how leaders use various strategies to diffuse conflicts.[23] Also, just as social movement scholars account for the mechanisms that mediate relationships among structural contexts and collective action outcomes, more case study research needs to be undertaken to gain further insights into the role of place and additional mechanisms and processes in shaping panethnic organizing.[24]

THE CONSEQUENCES OF PANETHNIC ORGANIZING FOR IDENTITY

This book has unearthed and confirmed key conditions and mechanisms that encourage panethnicity, but a question remains: what are the consequences of panethnic organizing for identity? It has been important to document the patterns of panethnic organizational emergence and collective action events because both have helped to secure resources and bring visibility to the Asian American community and its needs, but it is not clear whether and how such activities affect individuals' identities and behaviors. Past research has confirmed that a small minority of Asian Americans participate in protests and community civic action, and that panethnic organizations and events do not necessarily represent the entire Asian American community.[25] Nevertheless, individuals may still be influenced by how others organize and present the needs of the Asian American community in the public arena.

To adopt or choose an ethnic identity is to claim membership in a group or category, which often carries affective meaning.[26] Scholars have noted that panethnic identification has increased over the past few decades.[27] A nationally representative survey of over 5,000 Asian American adults in 2008 revealed that while a majority (67 percent) identified with ethnic-specific labels such as Chinese, Japanese, Korean, and Vietnamese, more than one in four respondents (27 percent) thought of themselves in panethnic terms, as Asian American.[28] When probed further, nearly half of all respondents indicated acceptance of this panethnic term as part of their identification.[29]

Does panethnic organizing shape the notion of a broader collective identity among individuals? Merging my data on organizations and events with 2008 National Asian American Survey (NAAS) data, I estimated logistic regression models to answer this question, and the results indicated that the density of panethnic organizations (but not events) in metropolitan areas in 2000 was indeed associated with a higher probability of panethnic identity in 2008 (see table A.7). In other words, individuals living in areas with more panethnic organizing in 2000 were more likely to identify as Asian American than with a national-origin group (such as Filipino or Filipino American) in 2008. While the effect of panethnic organizations was robust and the models controlled for a host of individual- and metropolitan-area-level variables, we must be careful when interpreting these results because there could be an issue with endogeneity: people who have stronger panethnic identities may choose to live in places where there are more panethnic organizations, such that the context of panethnic organizing may be reinforcing panethnic identities but not necessarily changing them. That said, it is likely that both processes are at work here—some individuals choose to live in places like San Francisco and Los Angeles because of the panethnic infrastructure of organizations and may even participate in panethnic organizing, and other individuals may be influenced by their surroundings and come to see themselves as having a panethnic identity.

I also analyzed NAAS data to understand whether panethnic organizing in local areas influenced formal political participation among Asian Americans. The civic and political participation of immigrant and ethnic groups is important precisely because of its broader implications for building social capital within local communities and ensuring civil rights and a participatory democracy.[30] The results show that the density of panethnic *organizations* was associated with a higher likelihood of working for or contributing to a political candidate, political party, or some other political campaign, and the number of panethnic *events* appeared to increase the likelihood of voting in 2004 (see table A.8). These results support past research, which also suggests organizations are key in mobilizing ethnic and racial communities to participate in formal politics, especially among those populations where voter turnout is lower than would be expected given their socioeconomic status and educational profile.[31] It is interesting to note that panethnic events (but not organizations) were associated with a higher likelihood of voting in the 2004 election, which suggests that publicly visible events that emphasize the shared experiences and histories of Asian Americans as a group can encourage participation in formal politics. When group members perceive that their votes will count because they are part of a larger (panethnic) voting bloc, it makes sense that they would be more likely to vote.

Panethnic organizations and events are important because they can provide a sense of empowerment and bring visibility to the needs and interests of Asian American communities, but as shown here, they also are significant because they influence how people think about themselves and how they behave, all of which ultimately helps to redefine racial categories and upend inequality.

BEYOND THE ASIAN AMERICAN CASE

It can be argued that the relationships elaborated by the racialized boundary framework may not necessarily apply to other groups. However, given that other groups in the United States and elsewhere have been racialized and have experienced segregation in the labor market and other institutional arenas, such conditions should heighten panethnic boundaries and collective action. Additionally, the flexibility of ethnic group boundaries and the mutual relationship between ethnic and panethnic organizing should hold when applied to other immigrant groups that experience racial and ethnic identities as salient. Thus, the racialized boundary approach could be productively applied in a comparative framework to understand the emergence of panethnicity.

Latinos are a potentially interesting case for comparison to Asians in the United States, considering that Latinos as a group are also racialized in American society.[32] The larger society does not differentiate between different national-origin populations from Latin America and sometimes conflates all Latinos with foreign-born Mexican Americans.[33] One main difference between the experience and outcome of panethnicity for Latinos compared to Asians is the broader phenotypical continuum that makes the process of racialization less uniform for Latinos. As we have seen, the identity of Asian American becomes significant because of ethnic groups' shared experiences of racial labeling and classification. That said, if we take into account the variation in skin color and tone among East and Southeast Asians as well as those from South or West Asia, the differences in the racialization process for Asians and Latinos may not be as stark.

In contrast to Asians in the United States, who speak over forty languages, Latinos share the common languages of English and Spanish, and which is likely to facilitate the formation of a panethnic group. Past relations between Latin American countries also do not seem to have been as problematic as relations between Japan and other Asian nations, which have complicated panethnic efforts. Another striking difference is that Latinos as a group have low average levels of educational and occupational attainment relative to Asian Americans. This difference has largely to do with the selectivity of the process through which many Asians arrived in the United States (see chapter 2) compared to the process of migration for Mexicans (the largest Hispanic/Latino national-origin group), which has been fueled by the demand for Mexican labor since the early 1900s.[34] Related to this migration history is that Latino populations currently face a hostile climate characterized by anti-immigrant sentiment, which could galvanize the Latino community and encourage organizing across ethnic lines.[35]

It is an empirical question, then, whether the same conditions that generate panethnicity among Asian Americans also provide analytical leverage in understanding how and when panethnic collective action emerges for Latinos. Nevertheless, I would argue that structural conditions such as racial segregation and ethnic organizing need to be in place so that the different Latino national-origin communities can build trust and solidarity, and that leaders are as necessary among Latino groups as they are among

Asian groups to guide group interests toward interethnic cooperation. I also suspect that ethnic organizing would enhance panethnic efforts among Latinos, since the ethnic efforts of the Mexican, Cuban, and Puerto Rican communities have a history of being transformed into broader panethnic efforts.

Could this approach be applied to groups that have not experienced panethnicity in the contemporary U.S. context? Thus far, African and Caribbean immigrants and U.S.-born blacks have not forged a common panethnic identity, even though, like Asians and Latinos, they have been racialized by the larger society such that distinctions between native-born and immigrant blacks are not often made by nonblacks.[36] A racialized boundary approach would be useful for understanding collective action among black immigrants because ethnic and racial boundaries are likely to be salient and should shape the ways in which they associate and affiliate with others. The layering of these group boundaries will undoubtedly come into play as new immigrants from different parts of Africa and the Caribbean continue to integrate into American society. Interestingly, new research suggests that for Nigerians in the United States and the United Kingdom, "African" is emerging as a panethnic identity associated with high educational attainment and strong religious values that the second generation has adopted to distinguish themselves from African Americans and Caribbean immigrants, yet national-origin identities also remain important when navigating institutions and everyday life.[37]

In regard to whites, even though many different European ethnic groups are included in the racial category of white, it is questionable whether these contemporary groups are panethnic because they do not necessarily share a sense of peoplehood or feel like they are part of a larger collective that has been created to fend off discrimination and disadvantage.[38] A white racial identity in the United States is typically associated with privilege and power, and ethnicity is called upon only when convenient, usually during holidays or rites of passage but not in daily life.[39] That said, with recent and projected demographic shifts resulting in larger numbers of majority-minority cities and states because of continuing immigration from Asia and Latin America, we may see new, defensive forms of white racial identity emerge.[40] Additionally, new waves of immigrants from Europe may result in the creation of a panethnic identity that is distinct from a white racial identity. Thus, it may make sense to examine intragroup dynamics, which can provide further understanding of the layering of identities—whether class- or ethnicity-based—for dominant groups, such as whites, and for groups that have been construed as monolithic, such as U.S. blacks.

The racialized boundary approach rests on the assumptions that race and ethnicity are both salient boundaries for group members and that the groups under study have not experienced full integration into the larger society because they remain occupationally segregated and, above all else, distinctive groups. Given these assumptions, such an approach may be useful to understanding panethnic organizing among groups such as Middle Eastern and Arab Americans, who are considered white by the U.S. Census but readily identify along ethnic or national-origin boundaries.[41] It may also be useful for examining the dynamics among groups that are just starting to form collective identities across national-origin and cultural groups, including a pan-Muslim identity in the United States and Europe among Arabs, Africans, and South Asians, a panethnic Roma identity in Spain and other parts of Europe, and a panethnic black movement in parts of Latin America.[42]

There is still much we do not know about changing boundaries and the formation of panethnic groups. Comparative case studies would take us far in getting at the precise mechanisms that underlie panethnic boundary formation. Comparisons are key here: Do the same mechanisms work for groups with different status positions? Why might some factors or processes be more important in one case and not another? The continued use of mixed-methods work to document and understand broader trends while honing in on the detailed everyday practices and perceptions related to panethnicity will produce theoretical and empirical advances.

BOUNDARY SHIFTING AND CHANGE

In the pre-1968 period, Asian immigrants responded to racialization by claiming to be white; they did not challenge the category of Asian itself, but attempted to engage in boundary crossing—the classic version of individual-level assimilation. Asians sought to be categorized as white and argued that they were white by virtue of their personal characteristics, such as high levels of education and moral character.[43] These attempts at boundary crossing were struck down by the U.S. Supreme Court as well as other local court systems. Asians also responded to racialization by claiming not to be a disparaged ethnic group—such as when Chinese and Korean Americans publicly claimed that they were not Japanese during World War II.[44] But in the post-1968 period, Asian Americans responded to racialization by challenging the category of Asian, redefining its meaning, and creating a new panethnic identity. Ethnic groups responded by expanding or widening their boundaries to include one another as part of a collective grouping as Asian Americans.[45] Ethnic group boundaries became permeable, but not necessarily less distinct.

Assimilation theorists interpret the development of panethnicity as part of the assimilation process, but I argue that the issue is more complicated because distinctions between ethnic groups are not necessarily fading away. The evidence presented in this book shows that when boundaries expand—such as with the shift from ethnicity to panethnicity—other group boundaries do not necessarily become displaced or attenuated. Instead, group boundaries can have a layered quality: some may be more salient than others under certain conditions. In fact, ethnicity and panethnicity are mutualistic: one does not diminish the other, and indeed they can even enhance each other (chapter 3). Additionally, the fact that leaders and organizations actively work to maintain ethnic differences when organizing on an ethnic as well as a panethnic basis highlights the flexible and durable nature of group boundaries.

So what does this all mean for Asian Americans in U.S. society? Some argue that Asians as a group are assimilating because of their high achievement rates and earnings, which are similar to those of whites, and because over the generations Asian Americans have become less distinct from whites on a number of key socioeconomic dimensions.[46] But others claim that Asian Americans are not moving toward assimilation, as they are still subject to racial profiling, hate crimes, and other forms of racial discrimination that deny them social citizenship and acceptance as Americans.[47] Both trends characterize the Asian American experience. I would argue that Asians are becoming central to—rather than on the margins of—the mainstream, especially within traditional immigrant destinations such as New York, Los Angeles, Chicago, and San Francisco, but that they must still deal with setbacks such as racial discrimination and misinformation as they move toward achieving a status as authentic Americans. Just as the assertion of panethnic boundaries does not erase ethnic boundaries and can even enhance them, the shift from ethnic to panethnic boundaries does not necessarily lead to assimilation. Panethnicity may be one step in the assimilation process, but it does not guarantee that Asian Americans will achieve full incorporation. As long as Asian Americans continue to be racialized as a model minority and as foreigners and boundaries between Asians and whites continue to be widely recognized, they will not achieve equal status in American society. Any decline in labor market segregation would suggest that Asian Americans are assimilating and that there is no need to continue to form new organizations to address experiences of social inequality and difference. However, other dimensions of inequality and difference not captured by labor market segregation might remain, motivating the formation of new organizations and the maintenance of panethnic identities.[48]

Nevertheless, what is clear is that in the twenty-first century race continues to matter in shaping how Asian Americans organize as a group and form individual and collective identities. This book has documented the ways in which Asian Americans have constructed a panethnic identity and organized accordingly to challenge inequalities. But some argue that using a racial category imposed by others as the basis for organizing efforts is problematic because doing so means that ethnic and immigrant groups are simply playing by the rules set by others. I argue that the struggle against the invidious distinctions created by race can take place using current racial categories. Panethnicity involves and recognizes the active role ethnic group members play in redefining the meaning of a racial label and taking part in constructing a broad-based collective identity.[49] A panethnic community also pays attention to the diverse needs and interests of its members and emphasizes that working together across ethnic lines is more powerful than going it alone. Moreover, the development of an Asian American identity can destabilize the model minority stereotype assigned to Asian Americans and disrupt the racialization of other groups, since racial groups are constructed relative to one another. An Asian American identity also offers a way to problematize the dominant construction of race in American society, and thereby redefines rather than reifies race. Altering widely agreed upon understandings of social categories can shape social interaction, create new forms of community and identity, and provide possibilities for change.[50] Through redefinition, ethnic group members are taking part in creating their own collective histories, cultures, and identities, which helps to make inequalities visible, calls for shifts in the distribution of resources, breaks down racial stereotypes, and ultimately contributes to a broader restructuring of the current racial hierarchy.

Appendix A | Variable Construction and Tables

NEARLY ALL OF the variables used in the regression analyses are measured at the metropolitan-area level and were constructed from U.S. census bound volumes and summary tape files, public use microdata samples (PUMS), state and metropolitan-area data books, the *Yearbook of Immigration Statistics* of the Immigration and Naturalization Service (INS), and the INS annual report. Table A.1 briefly describes the independent variables.

DETAILED DESCRIPTIONS OF SELECTED VARIABLES

I constructed a number of independent variables measuring economic competition, labor market segregation, threats against Asian Americans, financial and human capital, and political opportunities and resources in the local environment. The *unemployment ratios* comparing Asians to whites and nonwhites, as well as specific Asian ethnic groups to all other Asians, measure relative resources between the groups of interest. When the value of the ratio increases, the relative resources of the two groups (measured as the percentage unemployed) are becoming more equal and intergroup competition is predicted to erupt. For example, an increase in value of the Asian-nonwhite unemployment ratio indicates that either the nonwhite percentage unemployed is decreasing or the Asian percentage unemployed is increasing. In this situation, Asians are likely to feel threatened by the gains made by Latinos and blacks, and the result will be competition and collective action based on pan-national boundaries. Likewise, when relative gains are made by all other Asian groups, specific Asian groups should compete for resources, diminishing the ability of these groups to come together and engage in panethnic collective action.

Table A.1 The Independent Variables Used in the Regression Analyses

Independent Variable	Description
Immigration rate	Total number of new immigrants/total population
In-migration rate	Total number of non-Asian in-migrants/total population
Percentage unemployed	Percentage of civilian labor force unemployed, age sixteen to sixty-four
Poverty rate	Percentage in poverty
Unemployment ratio	Percentage unemployed Asian/percentage unemployed by racial or ethnic group
Labor market segregation	The degree to which Asians as a group and Asian ethnic groups are occupationally specialized
Labor market hierarchy	The degree to which Asians as a group and Asian ethnic groups are concentrated in low-status occupations
Change in labor market segregation	Change in the degree to which Asians as a group and Asian ethnic groups are occupationally specialized between t and $t-5$
Change in labor market hierarchy	Change in the degree to which Asians as a group and Asian ethnic groups are concentrated in low-status occupations between t and $t-5$
Population size (ln)	Natural log of total MSA population
Percentage Asian	Total number of Asians/total population
Heterogeneity index	Degree of diversity of Asian ethnic groups in area
Number of prior pan-Asian events	Number of prior pan-Asian collective action events
Number of pan-Asian organizations	Number of pan-Asian organizations present
Anti-Asian attacks	Number of prior attacks on Asians
Number of prior ethnic events	Number of prior events involving Asian ethnic group
Number of ethnic organizations	Number of Asian ethnic organizations present

Source: Author's compilation.
Note: All variables are measured at the metropolitan statistical area (MSA) level.

The non-Asian in-migration rate was calculated from the 5 percent PUMS regarding respondents' prior residence. If a respondent resided outside of the United States or in a different state or metropolitan area five years earlier, I coded the in-migrant variable as 1. I then calculated the number of non-Asian in-migrants and divided by the total metropolitan-area population. I also calculated the in-migration rate measuring the level of in-migration of *ethnically distinct* others within the Asian category as a percentage of the total metropolitan area.

The labor market/occupational segregation index measures the degree to which an ethnic group experiences occupational specialization in the following form,

$$(1/I) \times \Sigma_i | \ln(A_i / N_i) - [1/I \times \Sigma \ln(A_i / N_i)] |,$$

where A_i equals the number of workers from a specific Asian ethnic group in occupation i, N_i is the number of workers from all other Asian subgroups in occupation i, and I is the number of occupational categories.[1] When the value of the index increases, ethnic groups are more occupationally specialized. To measure the degree to which Asians as a group are concentrated in certain occupations, A_i equals the number of Asian workers and N_i equals the number of non-Asian workers. When the index increases, Asians experience high levels of occupational segregation relative to other racial groups. The advantage of this occupational segregation index is that it is not influenced by the ethnic and racial composition of the labor force or the size of different occupational categories.

The labor market/occupational hierarchy index measures the degree to which an ethnic group is concentrated in low-paying occupations in the following form,

$$A_{ls} / W_{ls} - (1/I \times \Sigma_i A_i / W_i),$$

where A_{ls} equals the total number of low-skill workers from a specific Asian subgroup, W_{ls} is the total number of low-skill workers from all other Asian subgroups, I is the number of occupational categories, A_i is the total number of Asian subgroup members in occupation i, and W_i is the total number of workers from all other Asian subgroups in occupation i.[2] When the index increases, there is more hierarchical segregation among Asian ethnic groups. I also calculated a measure of the extent to which Asians as a group are concentrated in low-paying occupations relative to all other racial groups. I used thirteen broad occupational census categories in the calculation of all occupational segregation indices at the metropolitan-area level.

In models predicting the formation of organizations and the rate of collective action events, I included a measure of *anti-Asian attacks* to capture racialization and threat processes at a local level. This cumulative count variable represents the number of attacks against Asian Americans in the previous month in a metropolitan statistical area (MSA). I used newspaper data to collect these data on occurrences of anti-Asian attacks. The newspaper articles had to specify that the attack was racially motivated (that is, that racist remarks were made by the perpetrator) for it to be counted as part of this variable. The number of prior ethnic and panethnic events refers to the number of ethnic or panethnic collective action events that occurred in each MSA between January 1, 1970 (the starting date of the sample) and the date of the current pan-Asian event. These variables were also constructed from newspaper data (see appendix B for more details on data collection).

To measure the political environment and potential opportunities for the founding of Asian American organizations, I created a national-level variable coded as 1 if the presidential administration in the previous year was Democratic (Democratic administration) and a state-level variable coded as 1 if more Democrats than Republicans were elected to Congress in the previous year (Democratic advantage). A Democratic advantage at the federal and state levels should influence the extent to which the political environment is open to the needs and interests of minority groups.

For the models predicting the formation of organizations, I also included a set of variables capturing the availability of resources at the federal and local levels. The first variable measures the annual amount of *federal grants* to state and local governments for community and regional development. These funds are locally administered to benefit low-income and minority groups in the community and often support organizations that address affordable housing, new job creation, and the expansion of business opportunities in urban areas. These funding figures are taken from the *Budget of the U.S. Government: Historical Tables,* presented in billions and measured at the national level. I also constructed a measure for *philanthropic funding,* which includes annual donations from corporations, individuals, and foundations. This information is reported at the national level in *Giving USA: The Annual Report on Philanthropy,* a publication of the American Association of Fund Raising Council (AAFRC) Trust for Philanthropy. These measures did not vary across metropolitan area for a given year, but varied over time and control for the possibility that an increase (or decrease) in resources at the national level influences the formation of panethnic organizations at the metro level. I reestimated these models with per capita income at the metropolitan-area level for each year (an additional measure of economic health of local areas), and the results were similar. Additionally, I constructed a variable measuring the percentage of Asians, ages twenty-five to forty-four, who have completed some college or higher (highly educated Asian American constituency), which measures the resources that such a community can bring to organize the community.

Table A.2 Zero-Inflated Poisson (ZIP) Regression Models Estimating the Effects of Independent Variables on the Formation of Pan-Asian Organizations, 1970–1998

Independent Variable	Regression Coefficient	Standard Error
Competition		
In-migration rate	5.82*	(4.23)
Unemployment ratio	5.47	(9.24)
Poverty rate	−0.11	(0.09)
Unemployment rate	11.32	(10.70)
Labor market segregation		
Racial segregation	0.24*	(0.18)
Racial hierarchy	3.63***	(0.76)
Racialization		
Attacks against Asians	0.66**	(0.25)
Resources and political opportunity		
Federal funding	−0.35	(0.37)
Philanthropic funding	−6.29***	(2.03)
Highly educated Asians	3.61*	(1.96)
Democratic administration	0.77***	(0.22)
Democratic advantage	0.12	(0.35)
Panethnic organizational density	0.23***	(0.03)
Controls		
Ethnic heterogeneity	5.21*	(2.73)
Percentage Asian	−4.19	(6.45)
Total population	0.69*	(0.38)
Intercept	10.30	(9.25)
−2 log likelihood	223.37	
McFadden's R-squared	0.45	

Source: Asian American National Organizations data set (Okamoto 2006)
Note: N = 870. Robust standard errors are presented in parentheses. The Poisson part of the model is shown here and estimates the non-zero-state probability as a Poisson function.
*$p < .05$; **$p < .01$; ***$p < .001$ (one-tailed tests)

Table A.3 The Effects of Ethnic-Specific Variables on the Formation of Pan-Asian Organizations, 1970–1998

Independent Variable	Model 1: Chinese	Model 2: Filipino	Model 3: Japanese	Model 4: Korean
Ethnic competition				
In-migration rate[a]	1.60***	6.25	0.82***	0.68
	(0.49)	(5.86)	(0.37)	(0.54)
Unemployment ratio	0.05	−0.45	−0.05	0.08
	(0.46)	(0.34)	(0.20)	(0.04)
Ethnic segregation				
Occupational segregation	−0.59	−0.38	−0.20	−0.52
	(0.34)	(0.34)	(0.22)	(0.33)
Occupational hierarchy	−0.03***	−0.04**	−0.02**	−0.11
	(0.01)	(0.02)	(0.01)	(0.06)
Intercept	1.31*	1.56*	1.40*	2.78
	(0.82)	(0.82)	(0.82)	(5.98)
−2 log-likelihood	217.54	219.84	221.71	226.17
McFadden's R-squared	0.46	0.46	0.45	0.44

Source: Asian American National Organizations data set (Okamoto 2006).
Note: N = 870. Results are from a zero-inflated Poisson regression model. Robust standard errors are presented in parentheses. All variables are measured at the metropolitan-area level. These models also include percentage Asian, size of metropolitan area, ethnic diversity, prior organizational foundings, and a host of other control variables (for details, see Okamoto 2006).
[a]The in-migration rate measures the percentage of noncoethnic Asians who moved to metropolitan area within the last five years.
*$p < .05$; **$p < .01$; ***$p < .001$ (two-tailed tests)

Table A.4 The Effects of Interethnic Competition and Segregation on the Rate of Pan-Asian Collective Action Events, 1970–1998

Independent Variable	Model 1: Chinese	Model 2: Filipinos	Model 3: Japanese	Model 4: Koreans
Economic conditions				
Immigration rate[a]	0.08	–0.12	0.02	0.11
	(0.06)	(0.08)	(0.03)	(0.10)
Unemployment ratio[b]	0.86	1.07	–0.07	–5.14**
	(1.33)	(0.96)	(0.08)	(0.21)
Occupational segregation				
Ethnic hierarchy[c]	–4.08	–3.71*	–7.17**	–8.09
	(3.37)	(1.92)	(2.94)	(13.7)
Change in ethnic labor force hierarchy	–8.91**	–5.05	3.06	–2.57
	(3.90)	(4.35)	(2.46)	(1.79)
–2 log-likelihood	308.14	325.21	311.88	317.51

Source: Asian American event data set (Okamoto 2003).
Note: Results are generated from an event history model. Number of uncensored spells = 59. Numbers in parentheses are estimated standard errors. All variables are measured at the metropolitan-area level. The four models test the effects of unemployment ratios, immigration rate, and occupational segregation for each national-origin group on the rate of pan-Asian collective action. The models include group-specific variables for Chinese, Filipinos, Japanese, and Koreans, respectively.
[a]The immigration rate measures the percentage of Asian immigrants in local areas who are non-coethnics.
[b]The unemployment ratio measures the relative resources of a specific Asian ethnic subgroup (measured as percentage unemployed) compared with all other Asian ethnic subgroups combined.
[c]Ethnic labor force hierarchy measures the degree to which a specific Asian ethnic subgroup is concentrated in low-status occupations relative to all other Asian ethnic subgroups combined.
*$p < .05$; **$p < .01$ (one-tailed tests)

Table A.5 The Effects of Interracial Competition and Segregation on the Rate of Pan-Asian Collective Action Events, 1970–1998

Independent Variable	Regression Coefficients	Standard Errors
Economic and demographic conditions		
Poverty rate	−0.29	(0.78)
Unemployment rate	−0.91	(1.71)
Unemployment ratio	−2.22**	(0.95)
Immigration rate	2.04	(2.70)
Labor market segregation		
Racial segregation	−1.63	(1.01)
Change in racial segregation	2.27**	(0.99)
Racialization		
Anti-Asian attacks	0.18	(1.54)
Control variables		
Ethnic heterogeneity	4.74	(4.29)
Ethnic heterogeneity-squared	−3.90	(2.97)
Log of population	2.11	(1.58)
Number of prior pan-Asian events	0.27	(0.17)
Number of pan-Asian organizations	0.77	(0.51)
Percentage Asian	−2.62*	(1.59)
Degrees of freedom	14	
−2 log-likelihood	316.37	

Source: Asian American event data set (Okamoto 2003).
Note: Number of uncensored spells = 59. Results are generated from an event history model. Numbers in parentheses are estimated standard errors. Racial segregation refers to the degree to which Asians as a group are concentrated—low-status occupations. All variables are measured at the metropolitan-area level.
$*p < .05; **p < .01$ (one-tailed tests)

Table A.6 Characteristics of Asian Ethnic Organizations by Boundary-Related Activity

	Remaining Ethnic (N)	Practicing Panethnicity (N)
Organizational type		
Civil rights	21.4% (3)	30.7% (4)
Community development	50.0 (7)	46.1 (6)
Arts/historical/cultural	21.4 (3)	0.0 (0)
Youth	0.0 (0)	15.4 (2)
Health	7.1 (1)	7.7 (1)
Organizational approach		
Advocacy	14.3 (2)	15.4 (2)
Direct services (DS)	35.7 (5)	38.5 (5)
Community organizing (CO)	14.3 (2)	0.0 (0)
Advocacy + DS + CO	14.3 (2)	46.1 (6)
Education/arts	21.4 (3)	0.0 (0)
Founding date		
Before 1970	14.3 (2)	15.4 (2)
1970–1980	14.3 (2)	76.9 (10)
1981–1990	28.6 (4)	7.7 (1)
1991–2000	42.8 (6)	0.0 (0)
Ethnicity		
Chinese	14.3 (2)	23.1 (3)
Filipino	21.4 (3)	7.7 (1)
Japanese	14.3 (2)	30.7 (4)
Korean	21.4 (3)	7.7 (1)
South Asian	14.3 (2)	0.0 (0)
Vietnamese/Lao/Cambodian/ Southeast Asian	14.3 (2)	30.7 (4)
Budget		
Less than $25,000	28.6 (4)	7.7 (1)
$35,000–$300,000	50.0 (7)	0.0 (0)
$350,000–$750,000	21.4 (3)	46.1 (6)
More than $1 million	0.0 (0)	46.1 (6)
Location		
San Francisco	85.7 (12)	69.2 (9)
Oakland	14.3 (2)	30.7 (4)

Source: Asian American Community-Based Organizations Sample (Okamoto 2004).
Notes: N = 27. The budget categories listed here reflect the four general categories that emerged from the data.

Table A.7 The Effects of Panethnic Organizing on the Panethnic Identity

Independent Variable	Regression Coefficient	Standard Error
Individual level		
Gender	0.18*	(0.78)
Education	0.31	(0.03)
Nativity (=1 if native-born)	−0.36**	(0.14)
Ethnicity	0.01	(0.81)
Metropolitan area level		
Percentage Asian	−0.68*	(0.41)
Racial heterogeneity	0.56	(0.02)
Panethnic organizations	0.03*	(0.16)
Panethnic events	0.07	(0.15)
Intercept	−1.61*	(0.71)

Source: Ramakrishnan et al., 2008.
Note: N = 3,027.
*$p \le .05$; **$p \le .01$ (two-tailed tests)

Table A.8 The Effects of Panethnic Organizing on Political Participation

Independent Variable	Campaigning	Contributing	Voting
Individual level			
Gender	0.22	−0.28***	−0.23**
	(0.18)	(0.11)	(0.07)
Education	0.29***	0.40***	0.17***
	(0.91)	(0.52)	(0.03)
Nativity (=1 if native-born)	0.76***	0.45**	0.62***
	(0.23)	(0.15)	(0.13)
Ability to speak English	0.29*	0.29***	0.03
	(0.15)	(0.08)	(0.05)
Ethnicity	0.02	0.04	0.13***
	(0.06)	(0.03)	(0.02)
Metropolitan area level			
Percentage Asian	0.18	0.09	0.71*
	(0.75)	(0.45)	(0.38)
Racial heterogeneity	3.00*	−0.09	−1.92**
	(1.42)	(0.75)	(0.61)
Panethnic organizations	0.04*	0.02*	−0.01
	(0.02)	(0.01)	(0.01)
Panethnic events	−0.01	0.02	0.19*
	(0.20)	(0.12)	(0.08)
Intercept	−8.45***	−4.52***	0.86
	(1.39)	(0.73)	(0.55)

Source: Ramakrishnan et al., 2008.
Note: N = 3,027.
*$p \le .05$; **$p \le .01$; ***$p \le .001$ (two-tailed tests)

Appendix B | Data Collection

THIS APPENDIX PROVIDES details about how I collected the data and the decisions I made along the way to build the organizations and collective action data sets and to gather interview and documentary data on Asian American organizations in San Francisco and Oakland.

ORGANIZATIONAL EMERGENCE

When I began this research, there was no systematic data set readily available on Asian American organizations, which are key players in politics, service, and advocacy. To document the evolution of the pan-Asian organizational field, I used the *Encyclopedia of Associations* (*EA*), a comprehensive public directory of nonprofit organizations published by Gale Research Company, to locate organizations with national memberships. Because *EA* is cumulative, it allows for an analysis of organizational trends over time.[1] Coding each annual volume allowed me to gather information about when new organizations entered the field, how organizational characteristics changed over time, and when current organizations ceased to exist. I was also able to update information about each organization in regard to its objectives, membership, areas of activity, budget, publication, and affiliations. Not included in this sample were organizations that disbanded or were founded before the starting point of the study and organizations that for all or part of their duration were located in other countries.

Researchers have extensively used *EA* as a data source to analyze organizations and as a sampling frame to conduct surveys of individual organizations.[2] While *EA* captures large, established organizations operating at the national level, it is likely to miss smaller organizations as well as those that are short-lived.[3] Social movement researchers also note that *EA* is biased toward organizations that use conventional tactics such as service and advocacy.[4] Although nonprofit databases such as *EA* do not report on all existing organizations, they do provide information about activity among large, national organizations over time, and that information was useful for my purposes in documenting the pan-Asian organizational field.

I included organizations in the sample if their members were Asian American or if they served an Asian American population. Many had "Asian" as part of their organizational name, but a few did not, such as American Citizens for Justice. I coded organizations such as the Society for Asian Art as panethnic because even though their membership was not confined to Asian ethnic groups, such organizations facilitated the development or maintenance of a panethnic framework through the dissemination of Asian history and culture. In other words, these organizations provided an institutional linkage between the different Asian ethnic groups, despite their linguistic, religious, and cultural differences. In the case of the Society for Asian Art, sharing a geographical region was often associated with a shared culture. I coded organizations such as the Korean National Association and the Organization of Chinese Americans as ethnic because they served or advocated for an ethnic-specific Asian population. I initially gathered data on the founding and longevity of ethnic organizations to understand the broader context within which pan-Asian organizations were forming, but soon found that they were a key part of the panethnicity story.

COLLECTIVE ACTION EVENTS

To document collective action over time, I followed in the footsteps of social movement and collective action researchers who have used newspapers to gather data on protests, civic activity, state repression, strikes, and violence.[5] Newspaper data provide details about the patterns, claims, and purposes related to events across different geographic locations and time periods—details that ultimately demonstrate how and when groups enact social boundaries.[6] Additionally, these data demonstrate the collective capacity of a group and the extent to which groups participate in political and civic life in the United States.[7] We learn about the "hard news"—the facts related to who, what, when, where, and why—and about how groups organize themselves, advocate, and make claims.

I collected data on ethnic and panethnic collective action events involving Asian Americans from three major newspapers, the *Los Angeles Times*, the *New York Times*, and the *Chicago Tribune*, over nearly three decades, capturing activity across the United States. I used relevant keywords such as

"Asian," "Asian American," "Chinese," "Japanese," "Korean," "Vietnamese," "Indian," "Filipino," "South Asian," "Southeast Asian," "protest," "demonstration," "rally," "campaign," "festival," and "celebration" to construct a systematic, reliable sample. Two or more Asian-origin groups engaging in coordinated group action, such as a protest, campaign, or celebration, was a form of panethnicity. I consider the data set to be a conservative, lower-bound estimate of pan-Asian activity; major mainstream newspapers are unlikely to capture all events that actually occur, but do cover those that are publicly visible and potentially relevant for social and political change.[8]

Media scholars suggest that since we mainly observe the world through the media, protests and other events that go unreported are in many ways "nonexistent."[9] Some even argue that studies focusing on events as political inputs that can shape the opinions of both public officials and the public—event data collected from the mass media—result in a higher level of validity than would the whole range of actual events.[10] All of this is not to say that protest and civic activities do not function in other ways, such as when they build community, efficacy, and resources. But for my purposes, the events in the data set represent visible events that serve as a strong leading indicator of the level of Asian American panethnicity across the United States and can provide insights into pan-national boundary formation processes.

The thirty metropolitan areas used in the regression analyses in chapters 3 and 4 represent over 75 percent of the entire Asian population residing in the United States. I selected these areas first and then gathered data on collective action events from the three national newspapers to examine variation in event activity over time and geographic location. Collective action events occurred outside of the thirty metropolitan areas during the time period under study, but I did not analyze them in the models. However, I did gather additional data on ethnic and panethnic collective action events from ethnic newspapers and other online sources to gain further information about these events and the events in the data set were representative of the full range of events that were not covered by the three national newspapers.

ORGANIZATIONS IN SAN FRANCISCO

To gain a sense of how panethnicity played out in local contexts, I wanted to find out how Asian American community-based organizations (CBOs) negotiated panethnicity. I chose San Francisco and Oakland as a site because of the area's history of Asian American activism and its reputation as a progressive region where many different Asian-origin groups reside. If panethnicity would be happening anywhere, it would be here. With help from Melanie Jones Gast and Jesse Rude, I created a comprehensive database of relevant Asian American CBOs in San Francisco and Oakland using telephone and online public listings and then gathered a purposive sample of forty CBOs, which included ethnic organizations representing Japanese, Chinese, Filipino, Korean, Southeast Asian, and Asian Indian populations as well as pan-Asian organizations that served multiple Asian-origin groups in San Francisco and Oakland. I first approached leaders of well-established organizations in the Asian American community and then asked for information about newer, smaller CBOs. Securing interviews with organizational leaders was relatively easy, possibly because of my status as a young Asian American professor at a local university.

In total, I conducted in-depth, semistructured interviews with forty-four executive and program directors and presidents from the forty CBOs in 2003 and 2004. Each interview was audiotaped and transcribed for data analysis. I focused on leaders because they had oversight of the programming and decisions about their organizations, particularly in the realm of coalition building and partnerships. One-third of the leaders were first-generation, and two-thirds were of the 1.5 generation or later. As mentioned in the text, I have used pseudonyms in this book to protect the identities of the organizations and the organizational leaders. In addition to the interview data, I also gathered public documents on the organizations in the sample and in the broader San Francisco Bay Area as a point of triangulation.

All of the ethnic community-based organizations in the sample were founded with the goal of serving a specific ethnic population that was lacking in services, programs, and advocacy from mainstream organizations. These ethnic CBOs functioned in a variety of ways and offered a multitude of services and programs to improve the social, economic, and political status and well-being of ethnic group members.

My analytical strategy included the coding of organizational documents and interview transcripts on programs, practices, partnerships, philosophies, and goals. I sorted the data based on themes and continued to narrow thematic codes and summaries until I began to see an organizational typology and narrative that best captured the organizations in the sample. When I entered the field, I was interested in documenting the partnerships and alliances that organizations form—and I was able to do that—but what emerged from the data was the key role that leaders play in developing, prioritizing, and carrying out organizational practices and priorities and the different ways leaders work across and carefully negotiate ethnic boundaries.

PANETHNIC IDENTITY AND INTERMARRIAGE

To understand whether panethnic organizing had any effect on panethnic identity and intermarriage, I used the restricted-use version of the 2008 National Asian American Survey (NAAS), which is a nationally representative survey of over 5,000 Asian Americans and provides information on panethnic identity and the geographic area where respondents reside.[11] I merged the panethnic event and organization data with the NAAS data by metropolitan area and limited the analysis to those individuals who resided in one of the thirty metropolitan areas with the largest Asian American populations. Controlling for a host of individual- and metropolitan-area-level variables, I estimated logistic and multinomial regression models. I decided not to use PUMS census data for this analysis because even though they provide a larger sample, they do not provide any information on panethnic identity, broadly and meaningfully defined, as compared to the 2008 NAAS.

Notes

CHAPTER 1

1. Pew Research Center (2012).
2. For more on Asians as a model minority, see Chou and Feagin (2008), Hurh and Kim (1989), S. Lee (1994), Suzuki (1989), Wu (2013), and Zia (2000).
3. In April 2014, the Pew Research Center released an updated edition of the 2012 report on Asian Americans in which it provided data on fourteen smaller Asian-origin groups.
4. See Dirlik (1996), Kibria (1998), and Palumbo-Liu (1999).
5. Examples outside of the U.S. context include the Kikimuyu in Kenya, the Moro in the Philippines, the Igbo in Nigeria, and the Malay in Malaysia; these ethnic groups were formed from smaller distinct groups based on caste, region, ancestral place of origin, and religion, and today they share kin, interests, and histories across these lines (see Horowitz 1985; Nagata 1981; Young 1976).
6. Alba (1990), Conzen et al. (1992), Doane (1997), Jacobsen (1998), and Sarna (1978). For a compelling argument about how European immigrants at the turn of the century in the United States faced discrimination but, for the most part, held social and political rights commensurate with Northern and Western Europeans, see Fox and Guglielmo (2012) This argument disrupts the notion that group boundaries expanded over time to include Europeans, since they were essentially white on arrival.
7. Beltrán (2010), Dávila (2012), Itzigsohn (2009), Lao-Montes and Dávila (2001), Mora (2014), Oboler (1995), and Padilla (1985).
8. Espiritu (1992), Lien (2001), Lowe (1996), Vo (2004), and Zia (2000).
9. Lowe (1991, 1996).
10. Takaki (1989); see also Chang (1997). "The Rape of Nanking," referred to as "the forgotten holocaust," was one of the most egregious war crimes. Japanese troops took over Shanghai in 1937 and brutally massacred over 300,000 civilians. The death toll from the city of Nanking alone exceeded the number of casualties in some European countries for the entire war (Chang 1997, 5).

During the same period, there were forced recruitments of mostly Korean, Chinese, and Japanese women, but also Filipino, Thai, Vietnamese, and Malaysian women, into sexual slavery by the Japanese military (Kawashima 2012). More than 200,000 women served as "comfort women."
11. Espiritu (1992) and Lopez and Espiritu (1990).
12. See Alba and Nee (2003), Bean and Stevens (2003), Roth (2012), and Waters (1999).
13. Omi (2001) and Omi and Winant (1994).
14. Bonilla-Silva (1997), Omi and Winant (1994), Saperstein et al. (2013), and Winant (2000).
15. See Espiritu (1992), Liu et al. (2008), Maeda (2009), Palumbo-Liu (1999), Vo (2004), and Wei (1993).
16. See Min (2008).
17. Although Asian ethnic groups may be concentrated in certain jobs and occupations owing to historical exclusion or contemporary discrimination, ethnic preferences and networks also play an important role in where ethnic groups are located in the occupational structure and where they are underrepresented (Waters 1999).
18. Geertz (1963) and Isaacs (1975).
19. Barth (1969), Cornell and Hartmann (1998), and Okamura (1981).
20. Weber (1968), 389.
21. Alba (1990), Horowitz (1985), Schermerhorn (1978), and Shibutani and Kwan (1965).
22. Barth (1969), 15.
23. Alba (2005), Lamont and Molnar (2002), Waters (1999), Yancey et al. (1976), and Zolberg and Woon (1999).
24. Epstein (1992), Lamont (1999), and Lamont and Molnar (2002).
25. Sanders (2002), 347.
26. Okamoto and Mora (2014).
27. Espiritu (1992), Nagel (1995), and Padilla (1985).
28. Kim and Lee (2001), Lien (2001), and Okamoto (2003).
29. Kibria (2003), Louie (2012), Massey and Sanchez (2010), and Tuan (1998).
30. Flores-Gonzalez (1999), Hein (2006), Itzigsohn (2004), Kibria (2003), and Tuan (1998).
31. Portes and Rumbaut (2001); see also Massey and Sanchez (2010). Richard Alba and Victor Nee (2003) contend that mainstream American society is not limited to white, middle-class culture and ideals. Different aspects of ethnic cultures have been incorporated into the mainstream over time, they argue, and continue to be accepted. It may be true that some ethnic practices, cuisine, and culture are now understood as part of American culture, but nonwhites are still not viewed as "true" Americans (see Kibria 2003; Schildkraut 2009; Song 2003; Tuan 1998).

32. Imoagene (2013) and Landale and Oroposa (2002); see also Kasinitz (1992) and Waters (1999).
33. Alba and Nee (2003), Bean and Stevens (2003), Portes and Rumbaut (2001), and Portes and Zhou (1993).
34. Alba and Nee (2003); see also Jung (2009), Rosenfeld (2002), Telles and Ortiz (2008), and Waldinger and Feliciano (2004).
35. Portes and Rumbaut (2001) and Portes and Zhou (1993).
36. Waters (1999) and Zhou and Bankston (1998).
37. Appadurai (1996), Brass (1997), Horowitz (1985), Laitin (1986, 1998), Posner (2005), and Wimmer (2008). The state has also attempted to expand group boundaries in the name of nationalism, which draws boundaries on an even larger scale making everyone a potential in-group member. But as history has shown, these attempts have not always been successful. In the former Yugoslavia, economic development, worker self-management, and equal rights for all citizens were expected to erode the traditional bases for national differences (Sekulic et al. 1994). Instead, increased fragmentation of identities along national lines was buttressed by an economic crisis in the 1980s, growing economic gaps between the republics, and a weak central government. Despite its state-building efforts, a national identity did not emerge in Yugoslavia, and ethnic conflict and violence erupted.
38. For groups such as the Malay in Malaysia, a panethnic grouping and identity stemmed from colonialism: a new, wider group boundary was assigned by colonial authorities with no regard for the conflicts and differences among already established ethnic groups such the Celebes, Borneo, Java, and Achenese. Today Malay is an administrative category used by the state and a panethnic label asserted by group members (Nagata 1981). Colonial authorities assigned several different ethnic groups to the Malay category in the mid-1800s, but a pan-Malay ethnicity only emerged with the dramatic increase in Chinese immigration in the early 1900s. The Malay differentiated themselves from newcomers and reinforced their shared culture, which included an adherence to Islam and knowledge of the Malay language (see Nagata 1981; Young 1976).
39. Omi and Winant (1994). On antimiscegenation laws, see Pascoe (2009); on immigration laws, see Ngai (2004).
40. See Morning (2009) and Nobles (2000).
41. Omi and Winant (1998), Winant (2000), and see Morning (2011).
42. Kim (1999).
43. N. Kim (2007).
44. Bashi (1998), Bonilla-Silva (1997), and Omi and Winant (1994).
45. During the 1980s, Mexicans and Puerto Ricans founded the Spanish Coalition for Jobs. a grassroots panethnic organization in Chicago to bring claims against companies that were discriminating against Spanish-speaking work-

ers (Padilla 1985). Even though Puerto Ricans and Mexicans had very different immigration and adaptation histories in the United States, they were able to effectively organize along a broader group boundary when federal affirmative action policies encouraged such action. Native Americans organized across tribal lines during the same period in response to race-based governmental policies. During the 1960s and 1970s, federal funds for minority programs, affirmative action, and land claim awards increased. Even though the racial category of Native American was created by the state, tribal members adopted this identity to take advantage of government programs. By 1978 more than $650 million had been paid out by the U.S. government in the form of land claim awards to American Indians. Tribal members also adopted supratribal identities with pride as the Red Power Movement grew in visibility and significance (Cornell 1988; Nagel 1995). Indian protest actions—such as the nearly yearlong takeover of Alcatraz Island in San Francisco Bay, the occupation of the U.S. Bureau of Indian Affairs in Washington, D.C., and the shoot-out at Pine Ridge Reservation in South Dakota—captured the attention of the larger public and raised a new panethnic consciousness among Native Americans (see Brass 1970, 1974; Chai 2005; Chandra 2004; Posner 2005; and Wimmer 2008; and Young 1976 for non-U.S. examples.

46. Espiritu (1992).
47. See Zia (2000).
48. Cornell (1990), Cornell and Hartmann (1998), Espiritu (1992), Nagel (1995), and Omi and Winant (1994).
49. The explanation of racialization as a consolidating force that generates new group formations and identities is consistent with the analyses of past scholars who studied how European immigrants became ethnic. Historians Jonathan Sarna (1978) and Kathleen Conzen and her colleagues (1992) argued that ascription and adversity led to boundary shifts among European immigrants. U.S. social institutions, such as the government, education system, and media, imposed ethnic group labels on European immigrant groups. Nativist hostility and xenophobic movements were not directed at separate groups based on region or dialect, but at ethnic groups. Over time, Silesians, Goralis, and Kashubes became Polish, and Sicilians, Calabrians, and Neopolitans were transformed into Italians (Alba 1985; Conner 1990). Eventually, these groups viewed themselves as part of distinct ethnic communities, and they created neighborhoods, organizations, and institutions based in broader ethno-national groupings.
50. Another reason 1968 was an important year for Asian Americans was that the Immigration and Nationality Act of 1965, which struck down national-origin quotas, was implemented.
51. Andrews (2004), Freeman (1975), McAdam (1982), McAdam and Su (2002), McCammon et al. (2001), Ryan (2013), and Taylor (1989).

52. Brilliant (2010), E. Lee (2006), Ngai (2004), and Skrentny (2002).
53. Hing (1994) and D. Lee (2012).
54. T. Lee (2007, 2008).
55. Brubaker (2004); see also Jenkins (1994), Loveman (1997), and Wimmer (2008).
56. Brubaker (2004), 169.
57. However, one cannot deny the importance of culture for understanding ethnicity and ethnic boundaries. Barth (1994, 18) himself acknowledged the role of culture in boundary processes when he stated that "central and culturally valued institutions and activities in an ethnic group may be deeply involved in its boundary maintenance." In a similar vein, Stephen Cornell (1996, 278) has argued that patterns of ethnic persistence and change depend on shared interests, institutions, and *culture*. The language, beliefs, practices, and symbolic structures shared by group members are often more stable than their interests, which may shift along with the context or circumstances. Cornell argues that an ethnic identity based on elaborate, shared accounts of how the world works can organize group action and shape ethnic transformations.
58. Banton (1983), Blalock (1967), Bonacich (1972), Nagel (1995), and Olzak (1992).
59. Medrano (1994), Nielsen (1980), Olzak (1982, 1990, 1992), and Ragin (1979).
60. Hechter (1978, 1999); see also Cederman, Weidmann, and Gleditsch (2011), Gellner (2009), and Stewart (2008, 2010). An ethnic group may be concentrated in certain jobs and occupations owing to historical exclusion or contemporary discrimination. If immigrant groups have been historically excluded from certain trades or occupations, they do not have the social networks to help them gain entry into those sectors of the labor market. Contemporary discrimination operates in similar ways, keeping ethnic groups from gaining access to particular jobs, occupations, and industries (Pager, Western, and Bonikowski 2009). But ethnic preferences and networks also play an important role in where ethnic groups are located in the occupational structure and where they are underrepresented (Waters 1999). Some immigrants arrive in the United States with advanced credentials and some financial capital, but language often keeps them from working as professionals in the mainstream labor market. These immigrants may enter particular ethnic niches, such as restaurants, nail salons, or budget motels, because of closed opportunities in other sectors of the economy. Finally, immigration legislation and recruitment efforts by U.S. organizations also affect the concentration of ethnic groups in occupational positions. For example, Asians are overrepresented in professional occupations in the health, technology, and science sectors because of the priority placed by U.S. immigration policy on filling the shortage of skilled workers in computer and biotechnology companies as well as in universities.
61. Cornell and Hartmann (1998).
62. Min (2008).

63. See Chou and Feagin (2008) and Zia (2000).
64. South Asians—a term that generally refers to those who have immigrated from or link their ancestry to India, Pakistan, Nepal, Bhutan, Bangladesh, Sri Lanka, or Maldives—are viewed as phenotypically different from East Asian groups such as Chinese, Japanese, and Koreans. Given that skin color affects how people are labeled and how they identify themselves, these differences could make it more difficult to create a common identity across these diverse groups.
65. Barnes and Bennett (2002).
66. Hoeffel et al. (2012).
67. Espiritu and Ong (1994) and Chung (2007).
68. Jiménez (2008), Kasinitz et al. (2008), and Ochoa (2004).
69. Yen Le Espiritu (2004) argues that global structures of inequality are critical to our understanding of panethnicity and its uneven adoption by ethnic group members. Even though panethnic identities are made in the American context, U.S. engagement in foreign countries influences migration flows, indirectly affecting the process of group formation.
70. Hein (2006) and Hing (1994, 2000).
71. Espiritu (2004).
72. Hurh and Kim (1989), Sakamoto et al. (2009), and Xie and Goyette (2004).
73. Timothy Egan, "Little Asia on the Hill," *New York Times*, January 7, 2007; Espenshade and Radford (2009).
74. U.S. Census Bureau (2006).
75. Ngo and Lee (2007).
76. See Bobo and Tuan (2006), Forman and Lewis (2006), and Waters (1999); see also Ebert and Okamoto (2013) and Wong et al. (2011). Although survey data can tell us whether an individual participated in a protest or worked with others to solve a problem in the community, they are limited because they are often cross-sectional and do not provide details regarding where and when these activities took place, who was involved, and what issues were at stake. Additionally, by design, survey data capture the participation of a sample of individuals rather than the group-based forms of social action that are key for understanding group boundary formation and change.
77. McAdam et al. (1996), Okamoto and Ebert (2010), and Olzak (1992).
78. See Baumgartner (2005) and Minkoff (1995, 1999).
79. Other researchers who have used newspaper data to understand trends in events over time include: Gurr (2000), Koopmans et al. (2005), McAdam and Su (2002), Myers (1997, 2000), Olzak (1992), Rucht, Koopmans, and Neidhardt (1998), Sampson et al. (2005), Olzak and Shanahan (2003), Smith et al. (2001), Soule et al. (1999), Tarrow (1989), and Van Dyke, Soule, and Taylor (2004).
80. See Earl et al. (2004) and Ortiz et al. (2005).
81. On the *EA* data set, see Andrews and Edwards (2004) and Baumgartner

(2005); on the use of newspaper data, see Oliver and Myers (1999), Koopmans and Rucht (2002), and Rucht, Koopmans, and Neidhardt (1999).
82. These public documents served as an additional point of data triangulation to further understand and confirm patterns of panethnic practices and the content of organizational narratives.
83. For more on collective identity from a social movements perspective, see Laraña et al. (2009), Polletta and Jasper (2001), and Taylor (1989).

CHAPTER 2

1. Takaki (1989).
2. Bloemraad and Ueda (2005) and E. Lee (2006).
3. Ancheta (1998), Daniels (1988), Jacobsen (1998), Lopez (2006), and Ngai (2004). The Immigration and Nationality Act of 1952 (the McCarran-Walter Act) abolished all racial requirements for citizenship (see Hing 1994; Ichioka 1988).
4. Hing (1994), Jacobsen (1998), Lopez (2006), and Ngai (2004). The Asiatic Barred Zone included the Middle East and parts of China and Mongolia on the western border and Malaysia, Indonesia, and Singapore on the eastern border. The Chinese Exclusion Act of 1882 had also included a provision that barred Chinese immigrants from naturalization rights (Bloemraad and Ueda 2005).
5. Ngai (2004).
6. See C. Lee (2013). An earlier law, the National Origins Quota Act (NOQA) of 1921, had deemed that laborers from Asia could not enter the United States, but under the new legislation labor status did not matter. NOQA placed numerical limits on immigration and established a quota system based on national origins. Specifically, the act limited the number of immigrants allowed into the United States to 3 percent of their national-origin group residing in the United States in 1910. The groups that benefited from this new legislation were those from countries that had large numbers in the United States by 1910. The losers were groups that had smaller or no representation of their populations in the United States in the early twentieth century. The Johnson-Reed Act of 1924, which replaced NOQA when it expired, reduced each country's annual quota to 2 percent of its emigrants already in the United States in 1890, an earlier period when immigrant populations were more heavily Northern and Western European. Under this legislation, China, Japan, and Korea received no quotas, virtually ending immigration from these countries. By 1924, even U.S. citizens could not bring their Asian wives to the United States (see Hing 1994, 2012; C. Lee 2013).
7. For example, Japanese American farmers transferred their land to their U.S.-born children after the enactment of the 1913 Alien Land Law, which prohibited "aliens ineligible to citizenship" from owning property (Ichioka 1984).

8. Chun (1998).
9. Motomura (2006) and Takaki (1989, 1993).
10. Chan (1991b), Daniels (1988), and Kwong (2001).
11. Almaguer (1994), Higham (2002), and Jacobsen (1998). In his book on racial formation in California, Tomas Almaguer (1994) points out that the perception of Chinese immigrants was shaped by whites' attitudes toward slavery. The Chinese were viewed as unfree laborers who posed a threat to whites' free labor status.
12. Kwong (1987).
13. Almaguer (1994).
14. Zhang (1998).
15. Jacobsen (1998), Okihiro (1994), and Takaki (2000).
16. C. Lee (2013).
17. E. Lee (2006). Teachers, students, and merchants were exempt from this law, but they still faced a small quota.
18. Jacobson (1999).
19. C. Lee (2013) and Motomura (2006).
20. Daniels (1988), 116.
21. AFL (1908).
22. In 1893 the San Francisco Board of Education passed a resolution that ordered all persons of the Japanese race to attend a segregated school for the Chinese, but then overturned its own decision, declaring that the Japanese were not "Mongolian" (Daniels 1988). Under pressure from labor unionists, the issue was revisited in 1906, when the board decided to force Japanese and Korean students to attend the Chinese school. The story made national headlines because the Japanese government intervened on behalf of Japanese immigrants in the United States. President Theodore Roosevelt urged that the policy be rescinded for fear of offending Japan, a rising world power. The school board agreed in return for a promise by President Roosevelt to stem Japanese immigration, which led to the negotiation of the Gentlemen's Agreement with Japan in 1907 and 1908 (see also C. Lee 2013; Motomura 2006).
23. Ngai (2004).
24. Among the first Filipino immigrants to the United States in the early 1900s were elite students, or *pensionados*, who were sponsored by the U.S. government and educated in American universities. Part of a U.S. nation-building project, these immigrants returned to the Philippines to run the economic and political institutions in their homeland (see Cordova, Cordova, and Acena 1983; Espiritu 1995; Lasker 1931; Melendy 1977).
25. California Building Trades Council (1928).
26. Ngai (2004).
27. E. Lee (2008). The new law also limited Filipino immigration to an annual

quota of fifty persons. The minimum quota for all countries under the Immigration Act of 1924 was one hundred. Filipinos who entered Hawaii as plantation laborers were exempt from the quota but were prohibited from remigrating to the U.S. mainland. The 1934 Tydings-McDuffie Act was more extreme than past exclusion laws because it did not exempt family members and wives, which significantly constrained the ability of Filipino immigrants to start families.

28. Jung (2002).
29. Jung (2006) and Okihiro (1994).
30. Beechert (1985) and Chan (1991a).
31. Walter G. Smith, "Japanese Stinkers," *Pacific Commercial Advertiser*, January 20, 1906.
32. Moon-Kie Jung (2002, 2006) argues that Japanese and Filipinos in prewar Hawaii were viewed as separate races and faced different racisms—the Japanese were racialized as disloyal subjects, while Filipinos were seen as primitive and inferior. Thus, it is not surprising that Japanese and Filipinos in Hawaii organized along ethnic lines to address labor grievances.
33. Takaki (1989).
34. Beechert (1985).
35. Ichioka (1988).
36. Chen (2000) and Ichioka (1988).
37. Azuma (1994); see also Fearon and Laitin (1996) and Laitin (1998); on in-group policing, see Brubaker and Laitin (1998).
38. Ichioka (1988), 176.
39. Azuma (1998, 2000).
40. See Daniels (1988) and Ichioka (1988).
41. Azuma (1994).
42. Japanese immigrants entered agriculture because they were excluded from other trades, but also because community leaders believed that farming would give laborers an economic stake in the United States and provide a transition to permanent settlement (Ichioka 1988). They began as laborers in the fields and eventually became contract farmers and sharecroppers. Japanese immigrants were successful in generating new crops, and each year saw an increase in the total acreage they farmed (Daniels 1988; Ichioka 1988). The Alien Land Laws in California, first implemented in 1913, forbade the owning of property and the leasing of land for more than three years by "aliens ineligible to citizenship." Several states, including Texas, Oregon, and Washington, passed similar land laws.
43. *Nichibei Shimbun*, May 5, 1937.
44. Azuma (1998).
45. Kim (1999).
46. Hurh (1998). Korean animosity toward Japan long preceded the early 1900s:

a history of repeated invasions and royal assassinations dated back to the 1600s.
47. Korean immigrants first arrived in Hawaii as migrant workers in the early 1900s, but migration from Korea soon stopped when Japan took over Korea's trade and foreign affairs in 1905 and annexed Korea in 1910. Under The Japan-Korea Treaty of 1905 (also known as the Eulsa treaty), Korea became a protectorate of Japan, thereby entering into an unequal relationship with Japan. The legality of that treaty was questionable, and in 1965 Japan and South Korea declared it "null and void." In a joint statement in 2005, officials of South Korea and North Korea reiterated their stance that the Eulsa treaty was null and void because of coercion by the Japanese.
48. Kim (2011), Min (1992), and Takaki (1989, 279–80).
49. Takaki (1989), 282.
50. Chen (2000), 200.
51. Ngai (2004).
52. Chen (2000).
53. Azuma (1994).
54. Daniels (1988).
55. See Azuma (1994) and Takaki (1989).
56. Asian Americans' labor history included a few prominent panethnic incidents, but they did not lead to long-term, positive intergroup relations (see Jung 2006).
57. Despite the success of the Chinese Exclusion Act and the Gentlemen's Agreement in prohibiting new immigrants from China and Japan, many Asian laborers still remained in the United States.
58. Johnson (1996) and Nee (1973).
59. Cordova et al. (1983), Daniels (1988), and Takaki (1989). The first Chinatowns that arose in the 1880s were not like the immigrant enclaves of Italians or Poles. They did not represent a fleeting, transitory stage in immigrant assimilation but were urban slums where Chinese and other Asian immigrants were forced to live and work (Zhou 1992). These segregated areas were inhabited mainly by men, which also differentiated them from immigrant enclaves during the turn of the century (Kwong 1996).
60. On Asian immigrants as undesirable "others," see Kwong (1996). Although Asian ethnic groups tended to live in separate communities, occasionally those communities overlapped, for instance, Koreans lived in Chinatown, and Hindus resided in Japanese boardinghouses (see Leonard 1992).
61. Chen (2000).
62. Chan (1991a) and Kwong (1984).
63. On family and clan lines, see Kwong (1984). On huiguans, see Daniels (1990) and Lai (1987, 2004). For an extensive discussion of the huiguan system and

its development in the United States in Chinese American communities, see Lai (2004).
64. Lyman (1970.
65. Kitano and Daniels (1988).
66. Chan (1991a,1991b) and Lai (2004).
67. Lai (2004).
68. Chan (1991b).
69. Chen 2000.
70. Leonard (1992) and Melendy (1977).
71. Takaki (1989), 186.
72. Chan (1991a).
73. Ichioka (1977).
74. Fugita and O'Brien (1991), 55; Modell (1977).
75. Ichioka (1977).
76. Azuma (1994) and Daniels (1988).
77. Choy (1979).
78. Takaki (1989).
79. I. Kim (2007), R. Kim (2011), Lien (2001), and Takaki (1989).
80. Chan (1991a) and Melendy (1977).
81. Kim (1977) and Takaki (1994).
82. Chin and Kim (1999), 32.
83. Canlas (2002) and Melendy (1977).
84. On Manilatowns, see McWilliams (1942). On racial discrimination, see Melendy (1977).
85. Leonard (1992).
86. Ibid., 33.
87. Jensen (1988) and Takaki (1989).
88. Chan (1991a).
89. Juergensmeyer (1978, 1981).
90. Singh (2000).
91. Ichioka (1990), Kwong (1987), and Lien (2001).
92. According to leaders in Hawaii, evacuating one-third of Hawaii's population was simply not possible; without Japanese labor, the economy of the islands would have collapsed. On the West Coast, the Japanese were still viewed as economic threats to white farmers and laborers and were not necessary to keep the economy running. For more on the Japanese American experience in Hawaii, see Ogawa and Fox (1986).
93. Robinson and Robinson (2009).
94. Daniels (1993) and Irons (1993). The U.S. government's wartime policy toward Japanese Americans diverged sharply from its treatment of Japanese Americans in Hawaii and German and Italian Americans, which was based on individual selection and investigation (Ngai 2004, 175).

95. Ichioka (1989).
96. Takaki (1989).
97. Ibid.
98. Nee (1973) and Zhou (2010).
99. Lau (2007) and E. Lee (2008). Chinese immigrants could enter the United States, but the annual immigration quota for China was only 105.
100. Nevertheless, applicants encountered barriers to citizenship: they were required to present documentation of their legal entry into the United States and pass tests of their English competency and knowledge of American history and the Constitution (Hing 1994).
101. Takaki (1989), 368.
102. Skrentny (2002).
103. King (2000), E. Lee (2003), and Reimers (1985).
104. See Liu, Geron, and Lai (2008) and Maeda (2009).
105. Maeda (2009) and Wei (1993).
106. Maeda (2009).
107. Omatsu (1994) and Wei (1993).
108. Armstrong (2002), Bernstein (1997), Cohen (1985), and Melucci (1985, 1989).
109. See Carmichael and Hamilton (1967), Nagel (1996), and Rosales (2000).
110. Liu et al. (2008).
111. Maeda (2009), 68.
112. Umemoto (1989) and Wei (1993).
113. Blauner (1972) and Omatsu (1994). For more on the Asian American organizations and individuals involved in the TWLF and the development of different strands of the Asian American movement on the West and East Coasts, see Wei (1993).
114. Louie and Omatsu (2001), 281.
115. Maeda (2009) and Okihiro (1994). It is interesting to note that participation in a broader-based movement across racial lines led to the development of a group-specific identity and movement among Asian Americans; for more details, see Maeda (2009).
116. Geron (2003) and Liu et al. (2008).
117. Maeda (2009), 99 and Wei (1993).
118. Wei (1993) and Zia (2000).
119. Louie and Omatsu (2001), 118.
120. Liu et al. (2008), Maeda (2009), and Umemoto (1989).
121. Espiritu (1992) and Zia (2000).
122. Liu et al. (2008) and Wei (1993).
123. Louie and Omatsu (2001), 114.
124. Kawashima (2012).
125. Habal (2007).

Notes   187

126. Ho (2000) and Yip (2000).
127. Geron (2003).
128. Liu and Geron (2008).
129. Eventually responding to community pressure, the owners of the site of the old I-Hotel later sold it to the Chinatown Community Development Center, which completed the construction of a new building for low-income housing and a community center to commemorate the I-Hotel tenants in 2005.
130. Maeda (2009), 30.
131. Takaki (1989).
132. See Lien (2001), Okamoto (2003), and Vo (2004). This resonates with the work of Paul DiMaggio and Walter Powell (1983), who suggest that organizations tend to alter their practices and structures to mimic those in the organizational field in order to obtain institutional legitimacy.
133. Nakanishi and LaForteza (1984).
134. Espiritu (1992).
135. Jones-Correa (2007).
136. Fox and Guglielmo (2012).
137. Conley (1999) and Oliver and Shapiro (2006).
138. See Lee, Ramakrishnan, and Ramírez (2006), Telles and Ortiz (2008), and Tuan (1998).
139. The new immigration policy also implemented an annual cap of 170,000 immigrants from the Eastern Hemisphere and 120,000 from the Western Hemisphere.
140. S. Lee (1993).
141. Gibson and Jung (2002) and Junn (2007).
142. U.S. Office of Management and Budget (1977).
143. Nobles (2000).
144. Katzen (1997) and Prewitt (2005).
145. In 1990 respondents were also able to check the box "Other Asian or Pacific Islander"; if they did, they were instructed to write in one group, such as "Hmong, Fijian, Laotian, Tongan, Pakistani, Cambodian, and so on" (Bennett 2000). In 1990 and 2010, ethnic groupings such as Chinese, Japanese, Filipino, Korean, and Vietnamese appeared as boxes that respondents could check in response to questions about their race. The U.S. census acknowledges that the race categories used in the race question include both racial and national-origin groups (see USA Map Stats, "Race," available at: http://www.fedstats.gov/qf/meta/long_RHI425207.htm).
146. Omi and Winant (1994).
147. Shiao (1998, 2004).
148. Ong (2003), Rumbaut (2000), and Shiao (1998).
149. See Espiritu (1992).

150. Shiao (1998), 37.
151. See Espiritu (1992).
152. Jeung (2005), Espiritu and Ong (1994), Shiao (2004), and Wong (2006).
153. Espiritu (1992) also points out that funding agencies prefer to fund a multiethnic project or coalition rather than several ethnic-specific projects because such a strategy is more fiscally sound and avoids ethnic politics.

CHAPTER 3

1. Chan (1991a) and Jacobsen (1998).
2. Ngai (2004) and Takaki (1989).
3. Espiritu (1992) and Omi and Winant (1994).
4. Lien (2001), Martinez (2008), Okamoto (2003), and Wong (2006). For more on the Asian American movement, see Espiritu (1992), Liu et al. (2008), Maeda (2009), and Wei (1993). For more on the Latino and Chicano movements, see Oboler (1995), Padilla (1985), and Rosales (2000).
5. See McAdam et al. (1996) and Minkoff and McCarthy (2005).
6. McCarthy et al. (1996) and Clemens (1996); see also Clemens and Minkoff (2004).
7. See also Espiritu (1992), Liu et al. (2008), Omatsu (1994), and Wei (1993).
8. For *Encyclopedia of Associations*, see Gale Research Company (1965–2000). For more details about the data collection process, see appendix B. I thank Kim Ebert for the use of her data on Hispanic and black organizations, which were also gleaned from the *Encyclopedia of Associations*.
9. The count of panethnic organizations for the Asian, Latino/Hispanic, and black/African American populations deliberately excludes ethnic organizations that serve these populations. There were 168 ethnic organizations that served the Asian population, 34 serving specific Latino ethnic groups, and 14 national organizations dedicated to African national-origin or immigrant groups.
10. Some of the early organizations and those that were founded later under a panethnic banner had fewer than twenty members while others had tens of thousands of members, but most reported their membership in the hundreds.
11. Maeda (2009) and Wei (1993).
12. Lu (2009).
13. This example could be interpreted as Asian Americans being spurred to form an alternative group because they felt threatened by Latinos and frustrated that attention was centered primarily on Hispanics and Spanish-English bilingualism. Given the limited historical materials available to me, I interpret the formation of this organization as fulfilling a need for the Asian American community. The newly formed NAAPAE collaborated with and gained infor-

mation from NABE, and if Asian Americans viewed Latinos as a threat, such cooperation would have been unlikely.
14. Espiritu (1992) and Zia (2000).
15. See Geron et al. (2001) and Liu and Geron (2008).
16. Habal (2007).
17. Espiritu (1992) and Nobles (2000).
18. Grønbjerg and Smith (1999) and Marwell (2007).
19. Grønbjerg (2001), 292.
20. Ong (2003).
21. Because typically there is a lag time between an organization's founding and its appearance in the *Encyclopedia of Associations*, it is likely that the data undercount the number of pan-Asian organizations that were formed in the latter part of the 1990s.
22. Only a handful of national pan-Asian organizations have also been formed outside of the thirty major metropolitan areas. For example, some organizations affiliated with academic professions, such as the Asian American Psychological Association, are located at college campuses in locations like Ithaca, New York, and Bloomington, Indiana.
23. Espiritu (1992).
24. See Banton (1983), Nagel (1996), and Olzak (1992).
25. Okamoto (2003, 2006).
26. Hechter (1978, 1999); see also Cederman et al. (2011), Gellner (2009), and Stewart (2008).
27. Okamoto (2003, 2006). Even though the segregation and competition models suggest different causal mechanisms for understanding panethnicity, we can view these processes as interdependent: when a group dominates an occupational niche or is concentrated in certain parts of the labor market, other groups may challenge that monopoly, thereby leading to intergroup competition. At the same time, competition also shapes occupational segregation. As ethnic groups attempt to stake out secure positions of their own, they may engage in competitive tactics that involve ethnic clustering in the labor market to consolidate resources.
28. Okamoto and Mora (2014).
29. Once an ethnic group enters a particular niche and comes to dominate it, ethnic networks aid in securing jobs in the same industry for coethnics (see Sanders 2000; Waters 1999). The process becomes self-sustaining and reproduces ethnic clustering in the new economy (Waldinger 1994, 1996).
30. Kwong (1987), ch. 2.
31. Leonard (1992) and Takaki (1989).
32. Azuma (2000) and Jung (2006).
33. Daniels (1988) and Kwong (1987).

34. Abelmann and Lie (2009), Bonacich (1973), Joyce (2003), J. Lee (1999, 2002), Min (1996, 2008), and Stryker (1974).
35. Jimenez and Horowitz (2013) and Saito and Horton (1994).
36. Horton (1995), Saito (1998), and Saito and Horton (1994).
37. Gold (1994).
38. Min (2008).
39. Bonacich (1994), Bonacich and Appelbaum (2000), and Gold (1994).
40. Junn (2007) and C. Lee (2013).
41. Khandelwal (2002) and Min (2006).
42. See Kanjanapan (1995). This trend of admitting professional workers continued as policymakers signed a new immigration policy into law in 1990 that expanded employment-based preferences and allowed for temporary worker visas (H-1Bs). In 2005 Asian immigrants made up more than one-third of new immigrants awarded lawful permanent residence (LPR)—the next largest percentage was from Mexico (14 percent)—and they accounted for more than half (53 percent) of those who obtained LPR status on the basis of being a priority or skilled worker (Junn 2007). Thus, U.S. employers' continued demand for scientific and technical workers combined with changes in U.S. immigration law to bring a disproportionately large number of Asians into the country on the basis of employment preferences.
43. Tang (1996).
44. Haines (1983) and Rumbaut (2001).
45. Bach and Bach (1980), Espiritu (2004), Rumbaut (2000), and Rutledge (1992).
46. See Gold (1994).
47. On globalization, see Ong, Bonacich, and Cheng (1994) and Wilson (1986). On Asian American occupations, see Xie and Goyette (2004).
48. In 2010 Asian Americans were about 4.7 percent of the labor force (Allard 2011).
49. Researchers have recently tried to compile comprehensive lists of organizations that serve immigrant and ethnic populations in metropolitan areas (see Cordero-Guzmán 2005; Okamoto et al. 2011). These data are useful because they provide a mix of local, national, and community organizations but are limited to only a few metropolitan areas and are cross-sectional, capturing a snapshot in time.
50. See Olzak (1992).
51. These variables measure the level of governmental and philanthropic resources available to ethnic and racial minorities, the extent to which the political environment is open to the needs and interests of minority groups at federal and local levels, the density of current pan-Asian organizations that may help foster new organizations with the potential to grow, the total population of the metropolitan area, the percentage Asian, and the ethnic diversity

within the Asian population. For additional details regarding variable construction, see Okamoto (2006).
52. Occupational *hierarchies* tend to persist, not necessarily because of group adherence to ethnic networks and culture, but because groups at the upper levels of the hierarchy often profit from the labor of those beneath them (Hechter 2000). In my analyses, I include measures of occupational *specialization* and occupational *hierarchy*, but with the current data I am unable to determine whether it is group adherence to culture at work, or group relegation to certain occupational positions. Given past work on ethnic networks and occupational mobility (see Waldinger 1994; Waters 1999), it is likely that both processes are at work; the fact remains, however, that Asians are still disadvantaged by being located at the bottom of the occupational structure.
53. See Hurh and Kim (1989), Pew Research Center (2012), and Zhou (2004).
54. S. Lee (1998), Reeves and Bennett (2004), and Xie and Goyette (2004).
55. See Hein (2006), Min (2006), Ong, Bonacich, and Cheng (1994), Rumbaut (2000), and Xie and Goyette (2004).
56. See Olzak (1992), Olzak and Shanahan (1996), and Soule (1992).
57. Hannan and Freeman (1989) and Minkoff (1995).
58. Espiritu (1992).
59. While not the focus of the analysis, it should also be noted that political opportunities at the federal level and an educated Asian population in metropolitan areas have shaped the formation of pan-Asian organizations as well. Interestingly, higher levels of philanthropic funding hindered the formation of panethnic organizations. Given that Asian American nonprofit organizations receive a small percentage of funds from private foundations and donors (Kimura 1990; Shiao 1998), it is likely that philanthropic funds are directed toward other groups that are able to frame their needs and interests as more compelling. If so, this would dampen Asians' ability to garner financial support to start organizations. In regard to the educated Asian population, metropolitan areas with higher proportions of Asian Americans with a college degree are associated with higher levels of pan-Asian organizational formation, which supports a resource mobilization framework (Edwards and McCarthy 2004; McCarthy and Zald 1977).
60. Beck and Tolnay (1995), Bergesen and Herman (1998), McVeigh (1999), Olzak (1989, 1990, 1992), Olzak and Shanahan (1996), Olzak, Shanahan, and McEneaney (1996), Soule (1992), and Soule and Van Dyke (1999).
61. Olzak (1992) and Olzak, Shanahan, and West (1994).
62. See Almaguer (1994) and Bonilla-Silva (1999).
63. Kim and Lee (2001) and Okamoto and Gast (2013); see also chapter 5. There is another reason why the competition model may not be supported: it takes salient ethnic identities for granted. In other words, increasing intergroup

contact and declining economic opportunities in *any* context may not result in collective action (Belanger and Pinard 1991). Given the right conditions (that is, when ethnic and racial identities have been made salient), competition mechanisms may be useful.

64. Alba et al. (1999) and Kim and White (2010).
65. Fong (1994), Horton (1995), and Zhou (2009).
66. Li (2009) and Zhou, Tseng, and Kim (2008).
67. See Espiritu (1992) and Shiao (1998).
68. Chung (2007) and Omatsu (1994). Legal advocacy organizations also targeted industries and occupational sectors where Asians were overrepresented, such as the low-wage service (such as nail salons, garment factories, restaurants, and hotels) and transportation (taxi drivers, bus drivers, airport screeners) industries, and experienced wage theft, discrimination, and unsafe working conditions.
69. Chun (2011).
70. Delloro et al. (2010) and Wong (2000).
71. Delloro et al. (2010).
72. Ibid., 9.
73. Pew Research Center (2012).
74. Asian American and Pacific Islanders in Philanthropy (AAPIP), "Who We Are—Why AAPIP?," available at: http://aapip.org/who-we-are/why-aapip (accessed February 8, 2013).
75. Min and Kim (1999), Sun and Starosta (2006), Takei and Sakamoto (2008), and Woo (2000).
76. Hirschman and Wong (1984) and Kim and Sakamoto (2010); see also Zeng and Xie (2004).

CHAPTER 4

1. Aguirre and Lio (2008), Espiritu (1992), Liu et al. (2008), Okamoto (2003), and Vo (2004).
2. Das Gupta (2006), Liu and Geron (2008), Min (2008), Park (2001), Shah (2012), and Zia (2000).
3. Lien (2001) and Liu et al. (2008).
4. Benford (1992), McAdam and Snow (1997), Olzak (1992, 2004), and Okamoto (2003).
5. Ebert and Okamoto (2013), L. Kurashige (2002), Sampson et al. (2005), and Shutika (2008).
6. Morris and Staggenborg (2004); see also Goldstone (2001) and Robnett (1997).
7. Of course, some events reported by the national press occurred outside of the thirty metropolitan areas. In fact, visible panethnic events took place in loca-

tions such as Arlington, Virginia, and Syracuse, New York, during the post-1968 era. See appendix A for details on the construction of the data set.
8. See Koopmans and Rucht (2002), Oliver and Myers (1999), and Rucht et al. (1999).
9. Jenkins, Jacobs, and Agnone (2003); see also McAdam (1982) and Morris (2000).
10. Deirdre Carmody, "Thousands in Chinatown March in Police Protest: Report to City Hall," *New York Times,* May 20, 1975.
11. Leslie Maitland, "2,500 Chinese Protest Alleged Policy Beating Hero," *New York Times,* May 12, 1975.
12. Liu and Geron (2008) and Zia (2000).
13. Habal (2007) and Kurashige (2010).
14. Laguerre (2000) and Liu and Geron (2008).
15. Liu et al. (2008).
16. Suga (2004).
17. Omatsu (1994); see also Brilliant (2010).
18. Espiritu (1992).
19. Ibid.; Zia (2000).
20. See S. Kurashige (2002) and Zia (2000).
21. Los Angeles and New York had the highest number of collective action events involving Asian Americans and captured the majority of the panethnic events in the sample.
22. Aguirre and Lio (2008), Lien (2001), Yoshikawa (1994), and Zia (2000).
23. Most of the pan-Asian events were relatively large in size, with the majority falling within the range of 100 to 5,000 participants. Given that larger events are more likely to be covered in newspapers, this may be why many of the events involved multiple ethnic groups.
24. Espiritu (1992), Kurashige (2000), Omatsu (1994), Vo (2004), and Zia (2000). According to FBI statistics, the incidence of reported hate crimes committed against Asians steadily increased throughout the 1990s across the country, from 217 in 1992 to 437 in 1997, with three racially motivated murders in 1999: Joseph Ileto, a Filipino American in California; Naoki Kamijima, a Japanese American in Illinois; and Won-Joon Yoon, a Korean graduate student in Indiana (NAPALC 1998; Perry 2002).
25. K. Connie Kang, "Asian American Groups Organize to Fight Measure," *Los Angeles Times,* October 9, 1994; Kim and Lee (2001).
26. Okamoto (2003).
27. The proportion of ethnic protest and civic collective action events differed from the proportion of events organized along panethnic lines: over half (54 percent) of the events with an ethnic claim or purpose were commemorations, festivals, or celebrations, and a bit less than half (46 percent) of the ethnic events were protests, demonstrations, or marches. The sequencing of

protest and civic events also differed: panethnic protest events seemed to be a precursor to panethnic civic events, but ethnic civic events were more prevalent and preceded protest events in the 1970s and 1980s, and then throughout the 1990s; both types of collective action seemed to occur together.

28. See Ebert and Okamoto (2013), L. Kurashige (2002), King-O'Riain (2006), and Sampson et al. (2005).
29. David Haldane, "Event Promotes Asian Unity Celebration: People from Various Cultures Gather at Mile Square Park for the Two-Day Festival, the First of Its Kind in Orange County," *Los Angeles Times*, August 9, 1992.
30. Martin A. David, "Dancewatching: Asian Festival: A Collaboration," *Los Angeles Times*, May 27, 1984.
31. Continuing rollbacks in civil rights at the federal level may not have been the only reason for the decrease in panethnic collective action, which could also have been related to the rise of nonprofit organizations that served Asian Americans by addressing policymakers through advocacy and lobbying rather than grassroots organizing.
32. See Hayashi (2010) and Irons (1993).
33. Hosokawa (1982).
34. Liu et al. (2008).
35. Shortly after the commission released its report in 1983, the Japanese American community filed a $25 billion class-action lawsuit against the U.S. government, seeking reparations for 120,000 Japanese Americans who were interned during World War II. Reparation payments were to compensate for the loss of freedom, property, livelihood, and dignity. The lawsuit ultimately failed, but it paved the way for the 1988 Civil Liberties Act.
36. The legislation represented a formal apology for the forced relocation of 120,000 Japanese Americans and designated that payments of $20,000 would be made to each of the 60,000 surviving Japanese Americans who had been interned. A year after it was signed into law, the Japanese American community organized rallies and demonstrations because reparation payments had not yet been released and former internees who were eligible to receive payments were dying at a rate of more than 200 a month; see Jonathan Gaw, "Reparations Delay Hit in Little Tokyo Rally," *Los Angeles Times*, August 6, 1989). The Japanese American community continues to keep alive the collective memory of the internment because it is a key element of Japanese American identity. Other forms of collective organizing, such as pilgrimages to internment camp sites and commemoration ceremonies, help Japanese Americans remember their past so as to ensure that internment never happens again.
37. Espiritu (2004) and Ong (2003).
38. Gonzalves (1995) and Vergara (1997).
39. Yang (2001).

40. Paul Feldman, "L.A. Sikhs Stage March, Liken Raid on Shrine to 'Attack on Vatican': SIKHS: Protest March." *Los Angeles Times*, June 18, 1984; K. Connie Kang, "Human Rights Groups Protest Alleged Abuses in South Korea," *Los Angeles Times*, October 3, 1992, 3; John H. Lee, "Koreans End Sympathy Hunger Strike," *Los Angeles Times*, August 3, 1989; and Zhao (1998).
41. Mark Gladstone, "Chinese Protest in Little Tokyo Against Japanese Textbooks," *Los Angeles Times*, September 19, 1982.
42. K. Connie Kang, "Protesters Decry Japan's New History Textbooks," *Los Angeles Times*, April 18, 2001; and "Apology Sought for Japanese Atrocities," *Los Angeles Times*, August 18, 2001.
43. See Liu and Geron (2008).
44. Takaki (1989).
45. Liu et al. (2008), 134.
46. Quon (2001), 216.
47. See Okamoto (2010).
48. Vivian S. Toy, "Councilwoman Apologizes for Comments about Asians," *New York Times*, May 3, 1996.
49. Cualoping (2011).
50. See Olzak et al. (1996) and Spilerman (1971).
51. See Sonenshein (1989, 2001) and Morris and Staggenborg (2004).
52. See de la Garza (1992) and Itzigsohn and Dore-Cabral (2000).
53. Espiritu (1992) and Zia (2000).
54. See M. Kim (2007).
55. K. Connie Kang, "Asian Americans Rally for Unity," *Los Angeles Times*, September 11, 1996.
56. Ibid.
57. Irene Chang, "Asians Protest Census Follow-up Procedures," *Los Angeles Times*, July 3, 1990.
58. Ibid.
59. The fight for ethnic enumeration continues today: activists, academics, and researchers are working to support state mandates to collect data disaggregated by ethnic group. California AB 1088, which was signed into law by Governor Jerry Brown in California in October 2011, requires that any state agency, board, or commission that collects demographic data must collect data by Asian American and Native Hawaiian/Pacific Islander subgroup. Additionally, the state's Department of Industrial Relations and Department of Fair Employment and Housing must also collect data by these subgroups.
60. Chang, "Asians Protest Census Follow-up Procedures."
61. Espenshade and Chung (2005) and Takagi (1992).
62. Danico and Ng (2004) and Takeda (2001).
63. Ryan Kim, "Asian Americans Rally, Protest at UC Davis: Students Ask for More Services and Protection," *SF Gate*, February 18, 2001, available at: http://

www.sfgate.com/education/article/Asian-Americans-Rally-Protest-at-UC-Davis-2950689.php (accessed March 4, 2013).
64. Kristina Lindgren, "UC Irvine Asian-American Studies Demanded," *Los Angeles Times*, April 23, 1993; De Tran and Matt Laitt, "UC Irvine Protest Ends in Accord on Asian Studies Program," *Los Angeles Times*, June 11, 1993.
65. Omatsu (1994); Pam Prasarttongosoth, "Northwestern U Hunger Strike Over: Still No Asian American Studies Program," *The Thistle* 9(6), 1995), available at: http://www.mit.edu/activities/thistle/v9/9.06/2northwestern.html (accessed November 3, 2012).
66. Tuan (1998). For example, in 1994 Asian Americans in New York protested a CBS news report about the extensive Chinese spy network in the United States and demanded a public apology. The report exaggerated the issue and suggested that there was a significant number of spies among recent Chinese immigrants. After months of protest, CBS made a public apology to the Asian American community during primetime broadcasting, which, at the time, was unprecedented.
67. Turnbull (2003).
68. Julie D. Soo, "National Day of Protest for Wen Ho Lee: Cities to Join Forces on Behalf of Incarcerated Scientist," *AsianWeek*, June 8, 2000, available at: http://www.asianweek.com/2000/06/08/national-day-of-protest-for-wen-ho-lee-2/ (accessed July 10, 2012).
69. Naomi Nakamura, "Free Wen Ho Lee," *Fight Back News*, July 1, 2000, available at: http://www2.ljworld.com/news/2002/sep/13/wen_ho_lee/ (accessed August 5, 2010).
70. Tuan (1998) and Zia (2000).

CHAPTER 5

1. See Espiritu (1992) and Shiao (1998).
2. See appendix A for details on the organizational sample and data collection. I recognize that South Asians represent a panethnic group comprising different ethnic groups. The leaders representing this population identified their organizations as South Asian, but the membership was predominantly Indian.
3. Kaufman (2003), Okamoto and Gast (2013), Regalado (1995), and Sonenshein (2001).
4. Okamoto and Gast (2013).
5. See Breton (1964), Cordero-Guzmán (2005), Portes, Escobar, and Arana (2008), and Zhou (2000, 2009).
6. Sanders (2000) and Zhou (2000).
7. On the Bay Area interethnic and interracial coalitions to combat racial inequality, see Liu et al. (2008), Maeda (2009), Omatsu (1994), Louie and Omatsu (2001), and Wei (1993). On the campus movement of the 1960s, see Liu et al.

(2008). Anti-imperialist resistance movements in Asia, Africa, and Latin America provided a backdrop to radical politics in the United States, and the black power movement popularized the concept of "internal colonialism," which explicitly linked the oppression of Third World peoples abroad with those in the United States (Blauner 1972; Omatsu 1994).
8. Geron (2003) and Liu et al. (2008).
9. Rumbaut (2000)
10. U.S. Census Bureau (2010).
11. Iceland et al. (2002).
12. De Graauw (2008, 2012), de Graauw et al. (2013), Silverman et al. (2009), and Okamoto, Gast, and Feldman (2012). In 2006, it has been estimated, there were about 7,000 registered nonprofits in San Francisco; of these, more than 40 percent had $25,000 or more in annual revenues (see Silverman et al. 2009).
13. In fiscal year 2011–2012, the San Francisco Department of Children, Family, and Youth allocated almost $69 million in strategic funding to other city departments and to about 200 community-based organizations that provided social and support services.
14. DiMaggio and Powell (1983).
15. See Galaskiewicz and Bielefeld (1998).
16. See Espiritu (1992), Espiritu and Ong (1994), and Shiao (1998).
17. Espiritu and Ong (1994). In fact, Espiritu (1992) discovered that funding administrators preferred pan-Asian collaborations over ethnic projects: it was more cost-effective to fund one panethnic project than several ethnic-specific ones.
18. DiMaggio and Powell (1983).
19. Ibid.; Meyer and Rowan (1977).
20. Chan (1991a) and Daniels (1988).
21. Gee (1999).
22. Hosokawa (1982).
23. Grønjberg (1986).
24. Espiritu (1992).
25. See Chung (2005), Louie (2004), and Waters (1999).
26. Massey (1985).
27. Fong (1994) and Li (2009).
28. See Chambré and Fatt (2002) and Singh, Tucker, and House (1986).
29. Espiritu (1992) and Espiritu and Ong (1994); see also Ong (2003), Otis (2001), Shankar and Srikanth (1998), and Taing (2005).
30. See Chang (1997) and Zia (2000).
31. These organizations are still serving their primary ethnic group—the newcomers make up only about one-quarter of their clients—and that may be why they did not encounter controversy when they expanded their services.
32. See Okamoto and Gast (2013).
33. See Jones-Correa (2001).

34. Organizational leaders did not talk about religion as a divide among Asian ethnic groups. If anything, sharing a progressive ideology, an understanding of histories, or status as a low-income immigrant or refugee group was more important than sharing religious beliefs or traditions.
35. Alba and Nee (2003), Lee and Fernandez (1998), Okamoto (2007), and Kim and Sakamoto (2010).
36. In fact, many Japanese American organizations serve the local community by providing youth programs, legal aid, artist networks, and community centers. There are also a number of organizations primarily focused on preserving the cultural history and heritage of Japantown even though the Japanese American population is associated with relatively high levels of social and economic assimilation.
37. See Okamoto and Gast (2013).
38. The fact that few ethnic organizations change their name to reflect their panethnic practices further confirms the idea that panethnicity should not be measured and understood in only one way (for example, as pan-Asian organizations or events), because there are clear limits to doing so. Other forms and expressions of panethnicity are important to examine, as I do here, precisely because panethnicity is manifested in ways that we might not expect at the outset.
39. *AsianWeek*, May 2, 2001.
40. The possibility of unique names being beneficial for organizations serving Cambodians and Vietnamese may also be related to refugee status. Additionally, as noted here, many leaders believed that having a unique name would help garner funding, although this belief might seem to be in conflict with earlier claims that having a pan-Asian orientation helped secure foundation grants. My data indicate that it was mostly Southeast Asian organizations that emphasized unique names to help garner attention from funders, so this could have been an issue regarding their place in the ethnic-racial hierarchy. It is also likely that this pattern of branding reflects the funding audience. Public and private foundations recognize the panethnic label, while local public funding agencies are likely to have a better sense of the differences within the local Asian American community. So organizations may tend to focus on branding and unique names when they are competing for local funds or attention.
41. Only one organization in the larger sample successfully changed its name, and my interviewees from this organization claimed that it occurred without controversy. The main reason for the change was to increase outreach to other populations in need, such as Southeast Asians and Pacific Islanders, and to effectively serve a broader Asian American population. Given that part of the original name had been in Japanese, some staff found that they continually had to explain their target population to funders. The organization did not

have a membership base, but it had been in existence for over twenty-five years.
42. A Chinese American civil rights organization, the Chinese American Coalition (CAC), expanded its boundaries to include other groups in its programming and mission. The organization decided not to change its name, but shifted its mission to advance the *social, political*, and *economic well-being* of Asian Pacific Americans.
43. CCR supported the decision of the San Francisco Unified School District (SFUSD) to adopt a race-based admissions policy to address racial segregation in educational institutions, including a predominantly Chinese magnet school that was considered one of the best high schools in the nation. CCR supported SFUSD's decision because race-based policies would ensure that other racial groups such as African Americans and Latinos would have an equal opportunity to attend the high school. It was a controversial position, but CCR's director felt that it would serve the Chinese community in the long run.
44. For ethnic organizations engaged in panracial work, deciding whether to make a broader name change to include other racial groups has not been controversial because most of these organizations rarely attempt such a change, perhaps owing in part to the fact that they maintain a clear ethnic agenda in regard to programming and services.
45. Okamoto and Gast (2013).
46. Okamoto and Mora (2014).

CHAPTER 6

1. Pew Research Center (2012).
2. For the earlier work, see Cornell (1990) and Lopez and Espiritu (1990).
3. Hechter (1986) and Fearon and Laitin (1996).
4. Hechter (1978, 1986). Even if dependence on the group is high, solidarity can be achieved only when the group has control capacity, the ability to monitor and sanction group members in order to dissuade free-riding and encourage compliance. A group is less likely to achieve its collective goals if group members free-ride. Segregated spatial locations such as labor markets are conducive to monitoring and sanctioning because interaction is dense among group members who are often phenotypically distinct from the majority group (and therefore visible). Thus, reputation and gossip are effective in ensuring that group members will remain obligated to the group.
5. See Fong (1994), Horton (1995), and Zhou (2009).
6. Li (2009) and Zhou, Tseng, and Kim (2008).
7. See Olzak (1992), Olzak et al. (1994), and Soule (1992).
8. See also Bobo and Hutchings (1996).

9. Olzak (1992), 6.
10. Hechter and Okamoto (2001) and Okamoto (2003). Even though the segregation and competition models suggest different causal mechanisms for understanding panethnicity, we can view these processes not only as interdependent but as part of the same historical process (see Okamoto 2003).
11. Hechter (1999, 2000).
12. Hechter and Levy (1994), 185–86.
13. Cederman et al. (2011) and Stewart (2008).
14. Cederman et al. (2011), Gurr (2000), and Horowitz (1985); see also Tajfel and Turner (1979).
15. Hewstone (1996), Pettigrew and Tropp (2012), and Tropp and Pettigrew (2005).
16. See Pettigrew and Tropp (2006, 2012). On the other hand, intergroup contact can also be negative. While negative contact may have occurred between Asians and other racial groups may have occurred, I found no evidence that it led to panethnic group formation.
17. McCarthy (1996); see also Andrews (2002), Clemens and Minkoff (2004), and McCammon et al. (2001).
18. Edwards and McCarthy (2004), McCarthy and Zald (1977), and Olzak (1992).
19. Barth (1969), Cornell and Hartmann (2006), Lamont and Molnar (2002), and Okamura (1981).
20. See Browning et al. (1984), Meier and Stewart (1991), Roth (2003), Sonenshein (1989, 1993), Diaz-Veizades and Chang (1996), and Regalado (1995).
21. See Brubaker (2004).
22. Benford and Snow (2000) and Snow et al. (1986).
23. Mora (2014) and Okamoto and Mora (2014).
24. See Andrews (2004), Cunningham (2012), McCammon (2012), and Meyer (2004).
25. On the participation of Asian Americans in protests and collective action events, see Wong et al. (2011). On the representativeness of the Asian Americans involved in these actions, see Espiritu (1992) and Espiritu and Ong (1994); see also chapter 5. California's Proposition 187, a statewide ballot initiative proposing to prohibit undocumented immigrants from access to public services such as health care and education, provides a useful example. Asian American organizers on both sides of the debate generated support, but the organizations and groups opposed to the proposition were more visible through their volunteer and protest efforts in the public arena. More than sixty Asian ethnic organizations formed a coalition to fight against the proposition and deployed panethnic and panracial narratives at protest events. When it came time to vote, 57 percent of Asian American voters supported the ballot initiative to prohibit undocumented immigrants' access to public services compared to 64 percent of whites, 56 percent of African Americans, and 31 percent of Latinos (Martin 1995). This fact suggests that panethnic efforts in the public sphere did not necessarily represent the majority of Asian

Americans, which highlights the complicated nature of panethnicity as a political force and the diversity within the panethnic community (see T. Lee 2007).
26. Cornell and Hartmann (2006) and Song (2003)
27. Fraga et al. (2012).
28. Wong et al. (2011).
29. See also Lien et al. (2003).
30. Skocpol and Fiorina (1999).
31. Bloemraad (2006), Ramakrishnan and Bloemraad (2008), Wong (2006), and Wong et al. (2011).
32. Telles and Ortiz (2008).
33. See Jiménez (2008) and Ochoa (2004).
34. Massey, Durand, and Malone (2002), Ngai (2004), and Telles and Ortiz (2008).
35. Massey and Sanchez (2010), Perea (1997), and Santa Ana (2002).
36. Waters (1999); see also Foerster (2004). There does not seem to be a dominant narrative that either West Indian and African immigrant leaders or African American leaders are developing to bolster a panethnic identity and grouping among this diverse population, perhaps because the category of "black" is taken for granted.
37. Imoagene (2013).
38. Doane (1997) and Omi and Winant (1994); see also McDermott (2006).
39. Gans (1979) and Waters (1990). However, the experience of working-class whites suggests that this privilege is not enjoyed by all whites in all contexts (McDermott 2006; McDermott and Samson 2015).
40. Berbrier (1998) and Omi (2001).
41. Ajrouch and Jamal (2007) and Kulczycki and Lobo (2002).
42. On the panethnic movement among Muslims, see Jamal (2008), Bakalian and Bozorgmehr (2009), Leonard (2005), Leweling (2005), Love (2009), and Meer (2012). On the panethnic Roma movement, see Ladányi and Szelényi (2006) and Prieto-Flores and Sordé-Martí (2011). On the panethnic black movement, see Htun (2004) and Telles (2014).
43. Lopez (1996) and Ngai (2004).
44. R. Kim (2011) and Takaki (1989).
45. Boundary blurring (when the social profile of a boundary becomes less distinct) and boundary shifting (when a boundary is relocated so that former outsiders become insiders) did not occur in the traditional sense of the boundary between racial minority or immigrant group and the dominant group becoming less distinct or shifting so that minority groups are included in the mainstream (Zolberg and Woon 1999).
46. Alba and Nee (2003).
47. Chou and Feagin (2010), N. Kim (2007), and Zhou (2004).
48. If Asian Americans do achieve equal status on a number of different dimen-

sions, a panethnic identity could remain, especially if the United States moves toward a culturally pluralist society where ethnic, religious, and cultural differences are equally valued.

49. One task of panethnicity is redefining racial categories; Chinese and Vietnamese, for instance, may continue to feel some distinctions from one another, despite the fact that the larger society categorizes them as Asian. But identifying with a panethnic identity that has been created to challenge racial stereotypes and unfair treatment is different from simply identifying as Asian. One way to understand this distinction is through an examination of organizing: when community leaders and members use the label and category of Asian, inequalities are clearly being challenged.

50. Panethnic efforts alone will not eradicate racial inequality, but they are one way to challenge how race is understood, enacted, and used in everyday life. Broader structural changes are necessary to further break down racial ideologies and inequalities, but panethnic collective and organizational activities represent one step in the process.

APPENDIX A

1. On the labor market/occupational segregation index, see Charles (1992) and Charles and Grusky (1995).
2. On the labor market/occupational hierarchy index, see Diez Medrano (1994).

APPENDIX B

1. See Baumgartner (2005) and Minkoff (1999, 2002).
2. Baumgartner and Jones (2003), Knoke (1990), Minkoff (1995, 1997), Smith (1992), and Sutton et al. (1994).
3. Andrews and Edwards (2004) and Baumgartner (2005).
4. Brulle et al. (2007) and Minkoff (2002).
5. Gurr (2000), Koopmans et al. (2005), McAdam and Su (2002), Myers (1997, 2000), Olzak (1992), Rucht, Koopmans, and Neidhardt (1999), Sampson et al. (2005), Shanahan et al. (2008), Smith et al. (2001), Soule et al. (1999), Tarrow (1989), and Van Dyke, Soule, and Taylor (2004).
6. See Earl et al. (2004), Koopmans (1999), Olzak (1989), Rucht et al. (1999), and Rucht and Ohlemacher (1992).
7. See Ramakrishnan and Bloemraad (2008) and Okamoto and Ebert (2010).
8. See Koopmans and Rucht (2002), Oliver and Myers (1999), and Rucht et al. (1999).
9. Koopmans and Rucht (2002), 252.
10. Rucht et al. (1999).
11. Ramakrishnan et al. (2008) and Wong et al. (2011).

References

Abelmann, Nancy, and John Lie. 2009. *Blue Dreams: Korean Americans and the Los Angeles Riots*. Cambridge, Mass.: Harvard University Press.

Aguirre, Adalberto, and Shoon Lio. 2008. "Spaces of Mobilization: The Asian American/Pacific Islander Struggle for Social Justice." *Social Justice* 112: 1–17.

Ajrouch, Kristine J., and Amaney Jamal. 2007. "Assimilating to a White Identity: The Case of Arab Americans." *International Migration Review* 41: 860–79.

Alba, Richard D. 1985."The Twilight of Ethnicity among Americans of European Ancestry: The Case of Italians." *Ethnic and Racial Studies* 8(1): 134–58.

———. 1990. *Ethnic Identity: The Transformation of White America*. New Haven, Conn.: Yale University Press.

———. 2005. "Bright vs. Blurred Boundaries: Second-Generation Assimilation and Exclusion in France, Germany, and the United States." *Ethnic and Racial Studies* 28: 20–49.

Alba, Richard D., and Victor Nee. 2003. *Remaking the American Mainstream: Assimilation and Contemporary Immigration*. Cambridge, Mass.: Harvard University Press.

Alba, Richard D., John R. Logan, Brian J. Stults, Gilbert Marzan, and Wenquan Zhang. 1999. "Immigrant Groups in the Suburbs: A Reexamination of Suburbanization and Spatial Assimilation." *American Sociological Review* 64(3): 446–60.

Allard, Mary Dorina. 2011. "Asians in the U.S. Labor Force: Profile of a Diverse Population." Washington: U.S. Department of Labor, Bureau of Labor Statistics, Division of Labor Force Statistics.

Almaguer, Tomas. 1994. *Racial Fault Lines: The Historical Origins of White Supremacy in California*. Berkeley: University of California Press.

American Federation of Labor Building and Construction Trades Department. 1908. *Report of Proceedings of the Annual Convention, Volume I*. Dayton, Ohio: Lander and Elwell.

Ancheta, Angelo N. 1998. *Race, Rights, and the Asian American Experience*. New Brunswick, N.J.: Rutgers University Press.

Andrews, Kenneth T. 2002. "Movement-Countermovement Dynamics and the Emergence of New Institutions: The Case of 'White Flight' Schools in Mississippi." *Social Forces* 80(3): 911–36.

———. 2004. *Freedom Is a Constant Struggle: The Mississippi Civil Rights Movement and Its Legacy.* Chicago: University of Chicago Press.

Andrews, Kenneth T., and Bob Edwards. 2004. "Advocacy Organizations in the U.S. Political Process." *Annual Review of Sociology* 30: 479–506.

Appadurai, Arjun. 1996. *Modernity at Large: Cultural Dimensions of Globalization.* Vol. 1. Minneapolis: University of Minnesota Press.

Armstrong, Elizabeth A. 2002. *Forging Gay Identities: Organizing Sexuality in San Francisco, 1950–1994.* Chicago: University of Chicago Press.

Azuma, Eiichiro. 1994. "Interethnic Conflict Under Racial Subordination: Japanese Immigrants and Their Asian Neighbors in Walnut-Grove, California, 1908–1941." *Amerasia Journal* 20: 27–56.

———. 1998. "Racial Struggle, Immigrant Nationalism, and Ethnic Identity: Japanese and Filipinos in the California Delta." *Pacific Historical Review* 67: 163–99.

———. 2000. "Interstitial Lives: Race, Community, and History among Japanese Immigrants Caught Between Japan and the United States, 1885–1941." Ph.D. diss., University of California, Los Angeles.

Bach, Robert L., and Jennifer B. Bach. 1980. "Employment Patterns of Southeast Asian Refugees." *Monthly Labor Review* 103(10): 31–38.

Bakalian, Anny, and Medhi Bozorgmehr. 2009. *Backlash 9/11: Middle Eastern and Muslim Americans Respond.* Berkeley: University of California Press.

Banton, Michael P. 1983. *Racial and Ethnic Competition.* Cambridge: Cambridge University Press.

Barnes, Jessica S., and Claudette E. Bennett. 2002. "The Asian Population." Washington: U.S. Census Bureau.

Barth, Fredrik. 1969. "Introduction." In *Ethnic Groups and Boundaries,* ed. Fredrik Barth. Boston: Little, Brown and Co.

———. 1994. "Enduring and Emerging Issues in the Analysis of Ethnicity." In *The Anthropology of Ethnicity: Beyond "Ethnic Groups and Boundaries,"* ed. Hans Vermeulen and Cara Govers. Amsterdam: Het Spinhuis.

Bashi, Vilna. 1998. "Racial Categories Matter Because Racial Hierarchies Matter: A Commentary." *Ethnic and Racial Studies* 21(5): 959–68.

Baumgartner, Frank R. 2005. "The Growth and Diversity of U.S. Associations, 1956–2004: Analyzing Trends Using the Encyclopedia of Associations." Working paper. Chapel Hill: University of North Carolina.

Bean, Frank D., and Gillian Stevens. 2003. *America's Newcomers and the Dynamics of Diversity.* New York: Russell Sage Foundation.

Beck, E. M., and Stewart E. Tolnay. 1995. *A Festival of Violence: An Analysis of Southern Lynchings, 1882–1930.* Urbana: University of Illinois Press.

Beechert, Edward D. 1985. *Working in Hawaii: A Labor History*. Honolulu: University of Hawaii Press.

Belanger, Sarah, and Maurice Pinard. 1991. "Ethnic Movements and the Competition Model: Some Missing Links." *American Sociological Review* 56: 446–57.

Beltrán, Cristina. 2010. *The Trouble with Unity: Latino Politics and the Creation of Identity*. New York: Oxford University Press.

Benford, Robert D. 1992. "Social Movements." In *Encyclopedia of Sociology*, ed. Edgar Borgatta and Maria Borgatta. New York: MacMillan.

Benford, Robert D., and David A. Snow. 2000. "Framing Processes and Social Movements: An Overview and Assessment." *Annual Review of Sociology* 26: 611–39.

Bennett, Claudette. 2000. "Racial Categories Used in the Decennial Censuses, 1790 to Present." *Government Information Quarterly* 17(2): 161–80.

Berbrier, Mitch. 1998. "White Supremacists and the (Pan-)Ethnic Imperative: On 'European-Americans' and 'White Student Unions.'" *Sociological Inquiry* 68(4): 498–516.

Bergesen, Albert, and Max Herman. 1998. "Immigration, Race, and Riot: The 1992 Los Angeles Uprising." *American Sociological Review* 63(1): 39–54.

Bernstein, Mary. 1997. "Celebration and Suppression: The Strategic Uses of Identity by the Lesbian and Gay Movement." *American Journal of Sociology* 103: 531–65.

Blalock, Hubert M. 1967. *Toward a Theory of Minority Group Relations*. New York: Wiley.

Blauner, Bob. 1972. *Racial Oppression in America*. New York: Harper & Row.

Bloemraad, Irene. 2006. *Becoming a Citizen: Incorporating Immigrants and Refugees in the United States and Canada*. Berkeley: University of California Press.

Bloemraad, Irene, and Reed Ueda. 2005. "Naturalization and Nationality." In *A Companion to American Immigration*, ed. Reed Ueda. Malden, Mass.: Blackwell.

Bobo, Lawrence D., and Vincent L. Hutchings. 1996. "Perceptions of Racial Group Competition: Extending Blumer's Theory of Group Position to a Multiracial Context." *American Sociological Review* 61(6): 951–72.

Bobo, Lawrence D., and Mia Tuan. 2006. *Prejudice in Politics: Group Position, Public Opinion, and the Wisconsin Treaty Rights Dispute*. Cambridge, Mass.: Harvard University Press.

Bonacich, Edna. 1972. "A Theory of Ethnic Antagonism: The Split Labor Market." *American Sociological Review* 37: 547–59.

———. 1973. "A Theory of Middleman Minorities." *American Sociological Review* 37: 583–94.

———. 1994. "Asians in the Los Angeles Garment Industry." In *The New Asian Im-*

migration in Los Angeles and Global Restructuring, ed. Paul Ong, Edna Bonacich, and Lucie Cheng. Philadelphia: Temple University Press.

Bonacich, Edna, and Richard P. Appelbaum. 2000. *Behind the Label: Inequality in the Los Angeles Apparel Industry*. Berkeley: University of California Press.

Bonilla-Silva, Eduardo. 1997. "Rethinking Racism: Toward a Structural Interpretation." *American Sociological Review* 62: 465–80.

———. 1999. "The Essential Social Fact of Race." *American Sociological Review* 64(6): 899–906.

Brass, Paul R. 1970. "Muslim Separatism in the United Provinces: Social Context and Political Strategy Before Partition." *Economic and Political Weekly*, 5(3–5): 167–86.

———. 1974. *Language and Politics in North India*. London: Cambridge University Press.

———. 1997. *Theft of an Idol: Text and Context in the Representation of Collective Violence*. Princeton, N.J.: Princeton University Press.

Breton, Raymond. 1964. "Institutional Completeness of Ethnic Communities and the Personal Relations of Immigrants." *American Journal of Sociology* 70: 193–205.

Brilliant, Mark. 2010. *The Color of America Has Changed: How Racial Diversity Shaped Civil Rights Reform in California, 1941–1978*. Oxford: Oxford University Press.

Browning, Rufus P., Dale Rogers Marshall, and David H. Tabb. 1984. *Protest Is Not Enough: The Struggle of Blacks and Hispanics for Equality in Urban Politics*. Berkeley: University of California Press.

Brubaker, Rogers. 2004. *Ethnicity Without Groups*. Cambridge, Mass.: Harvard University Press.

Brubaker, Rogers, and David Laitin. 1998. "Ethnic and Nationalist Violence." *Annual Review of Sociology* 24: 423–52.

Brulle, Robert, Liesel Hall Turner, Jason Carmichael, and J. Craig Jenkins. 2007. "Measuring Social Movement Organization Populations: A Comprehensive Census of U.S. Environmental Movement Organizations." *Mobilization* 12: 255–70.

California Building Trades Council. 1928. *Organized Labor: Official Publication of the Building and Construction Trades Council of San Francisco*. Sacramento, Calif.: California Building Trades Council (May 12).

Canlas, M. C. 2002. "Tabi Po, Respect for Those Who Came Before: Filipinos in South of Market, San Francisco." *Race, Poverty, and the Environment* 9(1): 44–46.

Carmichael, Stokely, and Charles V. Hamilton. 1967. *Black Power: The Politics of Liberation in America*. New York: Random House.

Cederman, Lars-Erik, Nils B. Weidmann, and Kristian Skrede Gleditsch. 2011. "Horizontal Inequalities and Ethnonationalist Civil War: A Global Comparison." *American Political Science Review* 105: 478–95.

Chai, Sun-Ki. 2005. "Predicting Ethnic Boundaries." *European Sociological Review* 21: 375–91.
Chambré, Susan M., and Naomi Fatt. 2002. "Beyond the Liability of Newness: Nonprofit Organizations in an Emerging Policy Domain." *Nonprofit and Voluntary Sector Quarterly* 31(4): 502–24.
Chan, Sucheng. 1991a. *Asian Americans: An Interpretive History.* New York: Twayne Publishers.
———. 1991b. *Entry Denied: Exclusion and the Chinese Community in America, 1882–1943.* Philadelphia: Temple University Press.
Chandra, Kanchan. 2004. *Why Ethnic Parties Succeed.* New York: Cambridge University Press.
Chang, Iris. 1997. *The Rape of Nanking.* New York: Basic Books.
Charles, Maria. 1992. "Cross-National Variation in Occupational Sex Segregation." *American Sociological Review* 57(4): 483–503.
Charles, Maria, and David Grusky. 1995. "Models for Describing the Underlying Structure of Sex Segregation." *American Journal of Sociology* 100(4): 931–71.
Chen, Yong. 2000. *Chinese San Francisco, 1850–1943: A Trans-Pacific Community.* Stanford, Calif.: Stanford University Press.
Chin, Soo-Young, and Dora Yum Kim. 1999. *Doing What Had to Be Done: The Life Narrative of Dora Yum Kim.* Philadelphia: Temple University Press.
Chou, Rosalind S., and Joe R. Feagin. 2008. *The Myth of the Model Minority: Asian Americans Facing Racism.* Boulder, Colo.: Paradigm.
Choy, Bong-Yuon. 1979. *Koreans in America.* Chicago: Nelson-Hall.
Chun, Gloria H. 1998. "'Go West . . . to China': Chinese American Identity in the 1930s." In *Claiming America: Constructing Chinese American Identities During the Exclusion Era,* ed. K. Scott Wong and Sucheng Chan. Philadelphia: Temple University Press.
Chun, Jennifer Jihye. 2011. "Living Outside the Cup: Asian Immigrant Women Workers Fighting for Change." Oakland, Calif.: Asian Immigrant Women Advocates.
Chung, Angie Y. 2005. "'Politics Without the Politics': The Evolving Political Cultures of Ethnic Nonprofits in Koreatown, Los Angeles." *Journal of Ethnic and Migration Studies* 31(5): 911–29.
———. 2007. *Legacies of Struggle: Conflict and Cooperation in Korean American Politics.* Stanford, Calif.: Stanford University Press.
Clemens, Elisabeth S. 1996. "Organizational Form as Frame: Collective Identity and Political Strategy in the American Labor Movement, 1880–1920." In *Comparative Perspectives on Social Movements: Political Opportunities, Mobilizing Structures, and Cultural Framings,* ed. Doug McAdam, John D. McCarthy, and Mayer N. Zald. New York: Cambridge University Press.
Clemens, Elisabeth S., and Debra C. Minkoff. 2004. "Beyond the Iron Law: Rethinking the Place of Organizations in Social Movement Research." In *The*

Blackwell Companion to Social Movements, ed. David Snow, Sarah Soule, and Hanspeter Kriesi. Malden, Mass.: Blackwell.
Cohen, Jean L. 1985. "Strategy or Identity: New Theoretical Paradigms and Contemporary Social Movements." *Social Research* 52(4): 663–716.
Conley, Dalton. 1999. *Being Black, Living in the Red: Race, Wealth, and Social Policy in America.* Berkeley: University of California Press.
Connor, Walker. 1990. "When Is a Nation?" *Ethnic and Racial Studies* 13(1): 92–103.
Conzen, Kathleen Neils, David A. Gerber, Ewa Morawska, George E. Pozzetta, and Rudolph J. Vecoli. 1992. "The Invention of Ethnicity: A Perspective from the U.S.A." *Journal of American Ethnic History* 12: 3–41.
Cordero-Guzmán, Héctor R. 2005. "Community-Based Organisations and Migration in New York City." *Journal of Ethnic and Migration Studies* 31: 889–909.
Cordova, Fred, Dorothy Laigo Cordova, and Albert A. Acena. 1983. *Filipinos, Forgotten Asian Americans: A Pictorial Essay, 1763–Circa 1963.* Dubuque, Iowa: Kendall Hunt Publishing.
Cornell, Stephen. 1988. *The Return of the Native: American Indian Political Resurgence.* New York: Oxford University Press.
———. 1990. "Land, Labor, and Group Formation: Blacks and Indians in the United States." *Ethnic and Racial Studies* 13: 368–88.
———. 1996. "The Variable Ties That Bind: Content and Circumstance in Ethnic Processes." *Ethnic and Racial Studies* 19: 265–89.
Cornell, Stephen, and Douglas Hartmann. 1998. *Ethnicity and Race: Making Identities in a Changing World.* Thousand Oaks, Calif.: Pine Forge Press.
———. 2006. *Ethnicity and Race: Making Identities in a Changing World.* 2nd ed. Thousand Oaks, Calif.: Pine Forge Press.
Cualoping, Irene. 2011. "Asian American Coalition of Chicago Announces Celebrity Presenters, Keynote Speaker, and Awardees for 28th Annual Lunar New Year Celebration" (press release). Chicago: Asian American Coalition of Chicago.
Cunningham, David. 2012. *Klansville, USA: The Rise and Fall of the Civil Rights-era Ku Klux Klan.* New York: Oxford University Press.
Danico, Mary Yu, and Franklin Ng. 2004. *Asian American Issues.* Westport, Conn.: Greenwood.
Daniels, Roger. 1988. *Asian America: Chinese and Japanese in the United States Since 1850.* Seattle: University of Washington Press.
———. 1990. *Coming to America: A History of Immigration and Ethnicity in American Life.* New York: HarperCollins.
———. 1993. *Prisoners Without a Trial: Japanese Americans in World War II.* New York: Hill and Wang.
Das Gupta, Monisha. 2006. *Unruly Immigrants: Rights, Activism, and Transnational South Asian Politics in the United States.* Durham, N.C.: Duke University Press.

Dávila, Arlene. 2012. *Latinos, Inc.: The Marketing and Making of a People*. Berkeley: University of California Press.

De Graauw, Els. 2008. "Nonprofit Organizations: Agents of Immigrant Political Incorporation in Urban America." In *Civic Hopes and Political Realities: Immigrants, Community Organizations, and Political Engagement*, ed. S. Karthick Ramakrishnan and Irene Bloemraad. New York: Russell Sage Foundation.

———. 2012. "The Inclusive City: Public-Private Partnerships and Immigrant Rights in San Francisco." In *Remaking Urban Citizenship: Organizations, Institutions, and the Right to the City*, ed. Michael Peter Smith and Michael McQuarrie. New Brunswick, N.J.: Transaction Publishers.

De Graauw, Els, Shannon Gleeson, and Irene Bloemraad. 2013. "Funding Immigrant Organizations: Suburban Free Riding and Local Civic Presence." *American Journal of Sociology*, 119(1), 75–130.

de la Garza, R. O. 1992. "From Rhetoric to Reality: Latinos and the 1988 Election in Review." In *From Rhetoric to Reality: Latino Politics in the 1988 Elections*, ed. R. de La Garza, L. DeSipio, pp. 171–81. Boulder, Colo.: Westview Press.

Delloro, John, Caroline Fan, Lucia Lin, Malcolm Amado Uno, and Kent Wong. 2010. *Breaking Ground, Breaking Silence: Report from the First National Asian Pacific American Workers' Rights Hearing*. Washington, D.C., and Los Angeles: UCLA Labor Center and Asian Pacific American Labor Alliance.

Diaz-Veizades, Jeannette, and Edward T. Chang 1996. "Building Cross-Cultural Coalitions: A Case-Study of the Black-Korean Alliance and the Latino-Black Roundtable." *Ethnic and Racial Studies* 19: 680–700.

Diez Medrano, Juan. 1994. "The Effects of Ethnic Segregation and Ethnic Competition on Political Mobilization in the Basque Country, 1988." *American Sociological Review* 59(6): 873–89.

DiMaggio, Paul J., and Walter W. Powell. 1983. "The Iron Cage Revisited: Institutional Isomorphism and Collective Rationality in Organizational Fields." *American Sociological Review* 48: 147–60.

Dirlik, Arif. 1996. "Asian on the Rim: Transnational Capital and Local Community in the Making of Contemporary Asian America." *Amerasia Journal* 22(3): 1–24.

Doane, Ashley W., Jr. 1997. "Dominant Group Ethnic Identity in the United States: The Role of 'Hidden' Ethnicity in Intergroup Relations." *Sociological Quarterly* 38: 375–97.

Earl, Jennifer, Andrew Martin, John D. McCarthy, and Sarah A. Soule. 2004. "The Use of Newspaper Data in the Study of Collective Action." *Annual Review of Sociology* 30: 65–80.

Ebert, Kim, and Dina G. Okamoto. 2013. "Social Citizenship, Integration, and Collective Action: Immigrant Civic Engagement in the United States." *Social Forces* 91(4): 1267–92.

Edwards, Bob, and John D. McCarthy. 2004. "Resources and Social Movement Mobilization." In *The Blackwell Companion to Social Movements*, ed. David Snow, Sarah Soule, and Hanspeter Kriesi. Malden, Mass.: Blackwell.

Epstein, Cynthia Fuchs. 1992. "Tinkerbells and Pin-ups: The Construction and Reconstruction of Gender Boundaries at Work." In *Cultivating Differences: Symbolic Boundaries and the Making of Inequality*, ed. Michèle Lamont and Marcel Fournier. Chicago: University of Chicago Press.

Espenshade, Thomas J., and C. Y. Chung. 2005. "The Opportunity Cost of Admission Preferences at Elite Universities." *Social Science Quarterly*, 86(2), 293–305.

Espenshade, Thomas J., and Alexandria Walton Radford. 2009. *No Longer Separate, Not Yet Equal: Race and Class in Elite College Admission and Campus Life*. Princeton, N.J.: Princeton University Press.

Espiritu, Yen Le. 1992. *Asian American Panethnicity: Bridging Institutions and Identities*. Philadelphia: Temple University Press.

———. 1995. *Filipino American Lives*. Philadelphia: Temple University Press.

———. 2004. "Asian American Panethnicity: Contemporary National and Transnational Possibilities." In *Not Just Black and White: Historical and Contemporary Perspectives on Immigration, Race, and Ethnicity in the United States*, ed. N. Foner and G. M. Fredrickson. New York: Russell Sage Foundation.

Espiritu, Yen Le, and Paul Ong. 1994. "Class Constraints on Racial Solidarity Among Asian Americans." In *The New Asian Immigration in Los Angeles and Global Restructuring*, ed. P. M. Ong, E. Bonacich, and L. Cheng. Philadelphia: Temple University Press.

Fearon, James D., and David Laitin. 1996. "Explaining Interethnic Cooperation." *American Political Science Review* 4: 715–35.

Flores-Gonzalez, Nilda. 1999. "The Racialization of Latinos: The Meaning of Latino Identity for the Second Generation." *Latino Studies Journal* 10: 3–31.

Foerster, Amy. 2004. "Race, Identity, and Belonging: 'Blackness' and the Struggle for Solidarity in a Multiethnic Labor Union." *Social Problems* 51: 386–409.

Fong, Timothy. 1994. *The First Suburban Chinatown: The Remaking of Monterey Park*. Philadelphia: Temple University Press.

Forman, Tyrone A., and Amanda E. Lewis. 2006. "Racial Apathy and Hurricane Katrina: The Social Anatomy of Prejudice in the Post–Civil Rights Era." *Du Bois Review* 3(1): 175–202.

Fox, Cybelle, and Thomas A. Guglielmo. 2012. "Defining America's Racial Boundaries: Blacks, Mexicans, and European Immigrants, 1890–1945." *American Journal of Sociology* 118: 327–79.

Fraga, Luis R., John A. Garcia, Rodney E. Hero, Michael Jones-Correa, Valerie Martinez-Ebbers, and Gary M. Segura. 2012. *Latinos in the New Millenium: An Almanac of Opinion, Behavior, and Policy Preferences*. New York: Cambridge University Press.

Freeman, Jo. 1975. *The Politics of Women's Liberation: A Case Study of an Emerging Social Movement and Its Relation to the Policy Process*. New York: Longman.

Fugita, Stephen S., and David J. O'Brien. 1991. *Japanese American Ethnicity: The Persistence of Community*. Seattle: University of Washington Press.

Galaskiewicz, Joseph, and Wolfgang Bielefeld. 1998. *Nonprofit Organizations in an Age of Uncertainty: A Study of Organizational Change*. New Brunswick, N.J.: Transaction Publishers.

Gale Research Company. 1965–2010. *Encyclopedia of Associations: National Organizations of the U.S.* Detroit, Mich.: Gale Group.

Gans, Herbert J. 1979. "Symbolic Ethnicity: The Future of Ethnic Groups and Cultures in America." *Ethnic and Racial Studies* 2: 1–20.

Gee, Nancy Ann. 1999. "A Brief History of the Chinese American Citizens Alliance." San Francisco: Chinese American Citizens Alliance–Portland Lodge.

Geertz, Clifford. 1963. *Peddlers and Princes: Social Change and Economic Modernization in Two Indonesian Towns*. Chicago: University of Chicago Press.

Gellner, E. 2009. *Nations and Nationalism*. Ithaca, N.Y.: Cornell University Press.

Geron, Kim. 2003. "Serve the People: An Exploration of the Asian American Movement." In *Asian American Politics: Law, Participation, and Policy*, ed. Don T. Nakanishi and James S. Lai. Lanham, Md.: Rowman & Littlefield.

Geron, Kim, Enrique de la Cruz, Leland T. Saito, and Jaideep Singh. 2001. "Asian Pacific Americans' Social Movements and Interest Groups." *Political Science and Politics* 34(3): 619–24.

Gibson, Campbell, and Kay Jung. 2002. "Appendix C. Asian and Pacific Islander by Category. Historical Census Statistics on Population Totals by Race, 1790 to 1990, and by Hispanic Origin, 1970 to 1990, for the United States, Regions, Divisions, and States." Washington: U.S. Census Bureau, Population Division.

Gold, Steve. 1994. "Chinese-Vietnamese Entrepreneurs in California." In *New Asian Immigration in Los Angeles and Global Restructuring*, ed. Paul M. Ong, Edna Bonacich, and Lucie Cheng. Philadelphia: Temple University Press.

Goldstone, Jack A. 2001. "Toward a Fourth Generation of Revolutionary Theory." *Annual Review of Political Science* 4: 139–87.

Gonzalves, Theo. 1995. "'We Hold a Neatly Folded Hope': Filipino Veterans of World War II on Citizenship and Political Obligation." *Amerasia Journal* 21(3): 155–74.

Grønbjerg, Kirsten A. 1986. *Responding to Community Needs: The Missions and Programs of Chicago Nonprofit Organizations*. Washington, D.C.: Urban Institute.

———. 2001. "The U.S. Nonprofit Human Service Sector: A Creeping Revolution." *Nonprofit and Voluntary Sector Quarterly* 30: 276.

Grønbjerg, Kirsten A., and Steven Rathgeb Smith. 1999. "Nonprofit Organizations and Public Policies in the Delivery of Human Services." In *Philanthropy and the Nonprofit Sector in a Changing America*, ed. Charles T. Clotfelter and Thomas Ehrlich. Bloomington: Indiana University Press.

Gurr, Ted. 2000. *People Versus States: Minorities at Risk in the New Century*. Washington, D.C.: Endowment of the United States Institute of Peace.

Habal, Estella. 2007. *San Francisco's International Hotel: Mobilizing the Filipino American Community in the Anti-Eviction Movement*. Philadelphia: Temple University Press.

Hannan, Michael T., and John Freeman. 1989. *Organizational Ecology*. Cambridge, Mass.: Harvard University Press.

Hayashi, Brian Masaru. 2010. *Democratizing the Enemy: The Japanese American Internment*. Princeton, N.J.: Princeton University Press.

Hechter, Michael. 1978. "Group Formation and Cultural Division of Labor." *American Journal of Sociology* 84: 293–318.

———. 1986. *The Principles of Group Solidarity*. Berkeley: University of California Press.

———. 1999. *Internal Colonialism: The Celtic Fringe in British National Development, 1536–1966*. New Brunswick, N.J.: Transaction Publishers.

———. 2000. *Containing Nationalism*. Oxford: Oxford University Press.

Hechter, Michael, and M. Levy. 1994. "Ethno-regional movements in the West." In *Nationalism*, eds. J. Hutchinson and A. D. Smith. New York: Oxford University Press.

Hechter, Michael, and Dina Okamoto. 2001. "Political Consequences of Minority Group Formation." *Annual Review of Political Science* 4: 189–215.

Hein, Jeremy. 2006. *Ethnic Origins: The Adaptation of Cambodian and Hmong Refugees in Four American Cities*. New York: Russell Sage Foundation.

Hewstone, M. 1996. "Contact and Categorization: Social Psychological Interventions to Change Intergroup Relations." In *Stereotypes and Stereotyping*, eds. C. Neil Macrae, Charles Stangor, and Miles Hewstone. New York: Guilford Press.

Higham, John. 2002. *Strangers in the Land: Patterns of American Nativism, 1860–1925*. New Brunswick, N.J.: Rutgers University Press.

Hing, Bill Ong. 1994. *Making and Remaking Asian America Through Immigration Policy, 1850–1990*. Stanford, Calif.: Stanford University Press.

———. 2000. *To Be an American: Cultural Pluralism and the Rhetoric of Assimilation*. New York: New York University Press.

———. 2012. *Defining America: Through Immigration Policy*. Philadelphia: Temple University Press.

Hirschman, Charles, and Morrison G. Wong. 1984. "Socioeconomic Gains of Asian Americans, Blacks, and Hispanics: 1960–1976." *American Journal of Sociology* 90(3): 584–607.

Ho, Fred. 2000. "Fists for Revolution: The Revolutionary History of I Wor Kuen, League of Revolutionary Struggle." In *Legacy to Liberation: Politics and Culture of Revolutionary Asian Pacific America*, ed. F. Ho, C. Antonio, D. Fujino, and S. Yip. San Francisco and Edinburgh, Scotland: Big Red Media and AK Press.

Hoeffel, Elizabeth M., Sonya Rastogi, Myoung Ouk Kim, and Hasan Shahid. 2012. "The Asian Population: 2010." Washington: U.S. Census Bureau.

Horowitz, Donald. 1985. *Ethnic Groups in Conflict.* Berkeley: University of California Press.

Horton, John. 1995. *The Politics of Diversity: Immigration, Resistance, and Change in Monterey Park, California.* Philadelphia: Temple University Press.

Hosokawa, Bill. 1982. *JACL: In Quest of Justice.* New York: William Morrow and Co.

Htun, Mala. 2004. "From Racial Democracy to Affirmative Action: Changing State Policy on Race in Brazil." *Latin American Research Review* 39: 60–89.

Hurh, Won M. 1998. *The Korean Americans.* Westport, Conn.: Greenwood.

Hurh, Won Moo, and K. Chung Kim. 1989. "The Success Image of Asian Americans: Its Validity, and Its Practical and Theoretical Implications." *Ethnic and Racial Studies* 12: 512–38.

Iceland, John, Daniel H. Weinberg, and Erika Steinmetz. 2002. *U.S. Census Bureau, Series CENSR-3, Racial and Ethnic Residential Segregation in the United States: 1980–2000.* Washington: U.S. Government Printing Office

Ichioka, Yuji. 1977. "Japanese Associations and the Japanese Government: A Special Relationship, 1909–1926." *Pacific Historical Review* 46: 409–37.

———. 1984. "Japanese Immigrant Response to the 1920 California Alien Land Law." *Agricultural History* 58(2): 157–78.

———. 1988. *The Issei: The World of the First Generation Japanese Immigrants, 1885–1924.* New York: Free Press.

———. 1989. *Views from Within: The Japanese American Evacuation and Resettlement Study.* Los Angeles: UCLA Asian American Studies Center.

———. 1990. "Japanese Immigrant Nationalism: The Issei and the Sino-Japanese War, 1937–1941." *California History* 69(3): 260–75.

Imoagene, Onoso. 2013. "In Search of Green Pastures: Second-Generation Adults of Nigerian Descent in the U.S. and U.K." Unpublished book manuscript. Philadelphia: University of Pennsylvania.

Irons, Peter. 1993. *Justice at War: The Story of the Japanese American Internment Cases.* New York: Oxford University Press.

Isaacs, Harold Robert. 1975. *Idols of the Tribe: Group Identity and Political Change.* New York: Harper & Row.

Itzigsohn, José. 2004. "The Formation of Latino and Latina Panethnic Identities." In *Not Just Black and White: Historical and Contemporary Perspectives on Immigration, Race, and Ethnicity in the United States,* ed. Nancy Foner and George M. Fredrickson. New York: Russell Sage Foundation.

———. 2009. *Encountering American Faultlines: Race, Class, and the Dominican Experience in Providence.* New York: Russell Sage Foundation.

Itzigsohn, José, and Carlos Dore-Cabral. 2000. "Competing Identities? Race, Ethnicity and Panethnicity among Dominicans in the United States." *Sociological Forum* 15: 225–46.

Jacobsen, Matthew Frye. 1998. *Whiteness of a Different Color: European Immigrants and the Alchemy of Race.* Cambridge, Mass.: Harvard University Press.

Jamal, Amaney. 2008. "Civil Liberties and the Otherization of Arab and Muslim Americans." In *Race and Arab Americans Before and After 9/11: From Invisible Citizens to Visible Subjects,* ed. Jamal Amaney and Nadine Naber. Syracuse, N.Y.: Syracuse University Press.

Jenkins, J. Craig, David Jacobs, and Jon Agnone. 2003. "Political Opportunities and African-American Protest, 1948–1997." *American Journal of Sociology* 109: 277–303.

Jenkins, Richard. 1994. "Rethinking Ethnicity: Identity, Categorization, and Power." *Ethnic and Racial Studies* 17: 197–223.

Jensen, Joan M. 1988. *Passage from India: Asian Indian Immigrants in North America.* New Haven, Conn.: Yale University Press.

Jeung, Russell. 2005. *Faithful Generations: Race and New Asian American Churches.* New Brunswick, N.J.: Rutgers University Press.

Jiménez, Tomás R. 2008. "Mexican Immigrant Replenishment and the Continuing Significance of Ethnicity and Race." *American Journal of Sociology* 113(6): 1527–67.

Jimenez, Tomas R., and Adam L. Horowitz. 2013. "When White Is Just Alright: How Immigrants Redefine Achievement and Reconfigure the Ethnoracial Hierarchy." *American Sociological Review* 78(5): 849–71.

Johnson, Kevin R. 1996. "'Aliens' and the U.S. Immigration Laws: The Social and Legal Construction of Nonpersons." *University of Miami Inter-American Law Review* 28(2): 263–92.

Jones-Correa, Michael. 2001. *Governing American Cities: Interethnic Coalitions, Competition, and Conflict.* New York: Russell Sage Foundation.

———. 2007. "Fuzzy Distinctions and Blurred Boundaries: Transnational, Ethnic, and Immigrant Politics." In *Latino Politics: Identity, Mobilization, and Representation,* ed. Rodolfo Espino, David L. Leal, and Kenneth J. Meier. Charlottesville, Va., University of Virginia Press.

Joyce, Patrick D. 2003. *No Fire Next Time: Black-Korean Conflicts and the Future of America's Cities.* Ithaca, N.Y.: Cornell University Press.

Juergensmeyer, Mark. 1978. "The Ghadar Syndrome: Nationalism in an Immigrant Community." *Center for South and Southeast Asian Studies Review* 1: 9–13.

———. 1981. "The Ghadar Syndrome: Ethnic Anger and Nationalist Pride." *Population Review* 25: 48–58.

Jung, Moon-Kie. 2002. "Different Racisms and the Differences They Make: Race and 'Asian Workers' of Prewar Hawai'i." *Critical Sociology* 28(1–2): 77–100.

———. 2006. *Reworking Race: The Making of Hawaii's Interracial Labor Movement.* New York: Columbia University Press.

———. 2009. "The Racial Unconscious of Assimilation Theory." *Du Bois Review* 6(2): 375–95.

Junn, Jane. 2007. "From Coolie to Model Minority: U.S. Immigration Policy and the Construction of Racial Identity." *DuBois Review* 4: 355–73.

Kanjanapan, Wilawan. 1995. "The Immigration of Asian Professionals to the United States: 1988–1990." *International Migration Review* 29(1): 7–32.

Kasinitz, Philip. 1992. *Caribbean New York: Black Immigrants and the Politics of Race*. Ithaca, N.Y.: Cornell University Press.

Kasinitz, Philip, John H. Mollenkopf, Mary C. Waters, and Jennifer Holdway. 2008. *Inheriting the City: The Children of Immigrants Come of Age*. New York: Russell Sage Foundation.

Katzen, Sally. 1997. Prepared statement of Sally Katzen, Administrator, Office of Information and Regulatory Affairs, Office of Management and Budget, before the House Committee on Government Reform and Oversight, Subcommittee on Government Management, Information, and Technology, April 23, 1997.

Kaufmann, Karen M. 2003. "Cracks in the Rainbow: Group Commonality as a Basis for Latino and African-American Political Coalitions." *Political Research Quarterly* 56(2): 199–210.

Kawashima, Yoshimi. 2012. "Gidra: The Voice of the Asian American Movement." *Discovernikkei*. Available at: http://www.discovernikkei.org/en/journal/2012/1/12/gidra/ (accessed January 12, 2012).

Khandelwal, Madhulika S. 2002. *Becoming American, Being Indian: An Immigrant Community in New York City*. Ithaca, N.Y.: Cornell University Press.

Kíbría, Nazli. 1998. "The Contested Meanings of 'Asian American': Racial Dilemmas in the Contemporary U.S." *Ethnic and Racial Studies* 21: 939–58.

——. 2003. *Becoming Asian American: Second-Generation Chinese and Korean American Identities*. Baltimore: Johns Hopkins University Press.

Kim, Ann H., and Michael J. White. 2010. "Panethnicity, Ethnic Diversity, and Residential Segregation." *American Journal of Sociology* 115: 1558–96.

Kim, ChangHwan, and Arthur Sakamoto. 2010. "Have Asian American Men Achieved Labor Market Parity with White Men?" *American Sociological Review* 75(6): 934–57.

Kim, Claire Jean. 1999. "The Racial Triangulation of Asian Americans." *Politics & Society* 27(1): 105–38.

Kim, Claire Jean, and Taeku Lee. 2001. "Interracial Politics: Asian Americans and Other Communities of Color." *PS: Political Science and Politics* 34: 631–37.

Kim, Hyung-chan. 1977. "The History and Role of the Church in the Korean American Community." In *The Korean Diaspora: Historical and Sociological Studies of Korean Immigration and Assimilation in North America*, ed. Hyung-chan Kim. Santa Barbara, Calif.: ABC-Clio.

Kim, Ilpyong J. 2007. *Korean-Americans: Past, Present, and Future*. Elizabeth, N.J.: Hollym International.

Kim, Marlene. 2007. "The Economic Status of Asian Americans." In *Race and Economic Opportunity in the 21st Century*, ed. Marlene Kim. London: Routledge.

Kim, Nadia. 2007. "Critical Thoughts on Asian American Assimilation in the Whitening Literature." *Social Forces* 86(2): 561–74.

Kim, Richard S. 2011. *The Quest for Statehood: Korean Immigrant Nationalism and US Sovereignty, 1905–1945*. New York: Oxford University Press.

Kimura, Naomi. 1990. "A Study of Charitable Giving and Financial Support to Asian Pacific Human Service Organizations in Los Angeles." Los Angeles: Special Services for Groups.

King, Desmond. 2000. *Making Americans: Immigration, Race, and the Origins of the Diverse Democracy*. Cambridge, Mass.: Harvard University Press.

King-O'Riain, Rebecca Chiyoko. 2006. *Pure Beauty: Judging Race in Japanese American Beauty Pageants*. Minneapolis: University of Minnesota Press.

Kitano, Harry H. L., and Roger Daniels. 1988. *Asian Americans: Emerging Minorities*. Englewood Cliffs, N.J.: Prentice-Hall.

Knoke, David. 1990. *Organizing for Collective Action: The Political Economies of Associations*. New York: Aldine de Gruyter.

Koopmans, Ruud. 1999. "The Use of Protest Events Data in Cross-National Research: Comparability, Sampling Methods, and Robustness." In *Acts of Dissent: New Developments in the Study of Protest*, ed. Dieter Rucht, Ruud Koopmans, and Friedhelm Neidhardt. Lanham, Md.: Rowman and Littlefield.

Koopmans, Ruud, and Dieter Rucht. 2002. "Protest Event Analysis." In *Methods of Social Movement Research*, ed. Bert Klandermans and Suzanne Staggenborg. Minneapolis: University of Minnesota Press.

Koopmans, Ruud, Paul Statham, Marco Giugni, and Florence Passy. 2005. *Contested Citizenship: Immigration and Cultural Diversity in Europe*. Minneapolis: University of Minnesota Press.

Kulczycki, Andrzej, and Arun Peter Lobo. 2002. "Patterns, Determinants, and Implications of Intermarriage Among Arab Americans." *Journal of Marriage and the Family* 64: 202–10.

Kurashige, Lon. 2002. *Japanese American Celebration and Conflict: A History of Ethnic Identity and Festival, 1934–1990*. Berkeley: University of California Press.

Kurashige, Scott. 2000. "Pan-ethnicity and Community Organizing: Asian Americans United's Campaign Against Anti-Asian Violence." *Journal of Asian American Studies* 3: 163–90.

———. 2002. "Detroit and the Legacy of Vincent Chin." *Amerasia Journal* 28(3): 51–55.

———. 2010. *The Shifting Grounds of Race: Black and Japanese Americans in the Making of Multiethnic Los Angeles*. Princeton, N.J.: Princeton University Press.

Kwong, Julia. 1984. "Ethnic Organizations and Community Transformation: The Chinese in Winnipeg." *Ethnic and Racial Studies* 7(3): 374–86.

Kwong, Peter. 1987. *The New Chinatown*. New York: Hill and Wang.

———. 1996. *The New Chinatown*. New York: Hill and Wang.
———. 2001. *Chinatown, New York: Labor and Politics, 1930–1950*. New York: New Press.
Ladányi J., and Szelényi, I. 2006. *Patterns of Exclusion: Constructing Gypsy Ethnicity and the Making of an Underclass in Transitional Societies of Europe*. New York: Columbia University Press.
Laguerre, Michel S. 2000. *The Global Ethnopolis: Chinatown, Japantown, and Manilatown in American Society*. New York: St. Martin's Press.
Lai, Mark Him. 1987. "Historical Development of the Chinese Consolidated Benevolent Association/*Huiguan* System." In *Chinese American: History and Perspectives, 1987*. San Francisco: Chinese Historical Society of America.
———. 2004. *Becoming Chinese American: A History of Communities and Institutions*. Walnut Creek, Calif.: Altamira Press.
Laitin, David D. 1986. *Hegemony and Culture: Politics and Change Among the Yoruba*. Chicago: University of Chicago Press.
———. 1998. *Identity in Formation: The Russian-Speaking Populations in the Near Abroad*. Vol. 22. Ithaca, N.Y.: Cornell University Press.
Lamont, Michele. 1999. *The Cultural Territories of Race: Black and White Boundaries*. New York: Russell Sage Foundation.
Lamont, Michèle, and Virag Molnar. 2002. "The Study of Boundaries in the Social Sciences." *Annual Review of Sociology* 28: 167–95.
Landale, Nancy S., and Ralph Salvatore Oropesa. 2002. "White, Black, or Puerto Rican? Racial Self-Identification among Mainland and Island Puerto Ricans." *Social Forces* 81(1): 231–54.
Laó-Montes, Agustín, and Arlene M. Dávila, eds. 2001. *Mambo Montage: The Latinization of New York*. New York: Columbia University Press.
Laraña, Enrique, Hank Johnston, and Joseph R. Gusfield, eds. 2009. *New Social Movements: From Ideology to Identity*. Philadelphia, Pa.: Temple University Press.
Lasker, Bruno. 1931. *Filipino Immigration*. New York: Arno Press.
Lau, Estelle T. 2007. *Paper Families: Identity, Immigration Administration, and Chinese Exclusion*. Durham, N.C.: Duke University Press
Lee, Catherine. 2013. *Fictive Kinship: Family Reunification and the Meaning of Race and Nation in American Immigration*. New York: Russell Sage Foundation.
Lee, Dawn Tu. 2012. "The Continuing Salience of Panethnicity: Neo-Asian Americanness, Higher Education, Multiculturalism, and Youth Performances of Asian American Identity." Ph.D. diss., University of California–Davis, Cultural Studies Program.
Lee, Erika. 2003. *At America's Gates: Chinese Immigration During the Exclusion Era, 1882–1943*. Chapel Hill: University of North Carolina Press.
———. 2006. "A Nation of Immigrants and a Gatekeeping Nation: American Immigration Law and Policy." In *A Companion to American Immigration*, ed. Reed Ueda. Malden, Mass.: Blackwell.

Lee, Jennifer. 1999. Retail Niche Domination among African American, Jewish, and Korean Entrepreneurs: Competition, Coethnic Advantage and Disadvantage. *American Behavioral Scientist* 42(9): 1398–1416.

———. 2002. "From Civil Relations to Racial Conflict: Merchant-Customer Interactions in Urban America." *American Sociological Review* 67(1): 77–98.

Lee, Sharon M. 1993. "Racial Classifications in the U.S. Census: 1890–1990." *Ethnic and Racial Studies* 16(1): 75–94.

———. 1998. "Asian Americans: Diverse and Growing." *Population Bulletin* 53(2): 1–40.

Lee, Sharon M., and Marilyn Fernandez. 1998. "Trends in Asian American Racial/Ethnic Intermarriage: A Comparison of 1980 and 1990 Census Data." *Sociological Perspectives* 41: 323–42.

Lee, Stacey J. 1994. "Behind the Model-Minority Stereotype: Voices of High- and Low-Achieving Asian American Students." *Anthropology and Education Quarterly* 25(4): 413–29.

Lee, Taeku. 2007. "From Shared Demographic Categories to Common Political Destinies." *Du Bois Review: Social Science and Research on Race* 4(2): 433–56.

———. 2008. "Race, Immigration, and the Identity-to-Politics Link." *Annual Review of Political Science* 11: 457–78.

Lee, Taeku, S. Karthick Ramakrishnan, and Ricardo Ramirez. 2006. "Introduction." In *Transforming Politics, Transforming America: The Political and Civic Incorporation of Immigrants in the United States*, ed. Taeku Lee, S. Karthick Ramakrishnan, and Ricardo Ramírez. Charlottesville: University of Virginia Press.

Leonard, Karen. 1992. *Making Ethnic Choices: California's Punjabi Mexican Americans*. Philadelphia: Temple University Press.

———. 2005. "Introduction: Young American Muslim Identities." *The Muslim World* 95: 473–77.

Leweling, Tara. 2005. *Exploring Muslim Diaspora Communities in Europe through a Social Movement Lens: Some Initial Thoughts*. Monterey, Calif: Naval Postgraduate School Center for Contemporary Conflict.

Li, Wei. 2009. *Ethnoburb: The New Ethnic Community in Urban America*. Honolulu: University of Hawaii Press.

Lien, Pei-te. 2001. *The Making of Asian America Through Political Participation*. Philadelphia: Temple University Press.

Lien, Pei-te, M. Margaret Conway, and Janelle Wong. 2003. "The Contours and Sources of Ethnic Identity Choices Among Asian Americans." *Social Science Quarterly* 84: 461–81.

Liu, Michael, and Kim Geron. 2008. "Changing Neighborhood: Ethnic Enclaves and the Struggle for Social Justice." *Social Justice* 35: 18–35.

Liu, Michael, Kim Geron, and Tracy Lai. 2008. *The Snake Dance of Asian American Activism: Community, Vision, and Power in the Struggle for Social Justice, 1945–2000*. Lanham, Md.: Lexington Books.

Lopez, David, and Yen Le Espiritu. 1990. "Panethnicity in the United States: A Theoretical Framework." *Ethnic and Racial Studies* 13: 198–224.

Lopez, Ian F. Haney. 1996. *White by Law: The Legal Construction of Race.* New York: New York University Press.

———. 2006. *White by Law: The Legal Construction of Race.* New York: New York University Press.

Louie, Steven G., and Glenn K. Omatsu. 2001. *Asian Americans: The Movement and the Moment.* Los Angeles: UCLA Asian American Studies.

Louie, Vivian S. 2004. *Compelled to Excel: Immigration, Education, and Opportunity Among Chinese Americans.* Stanford, Calif.: Stanford University Press.

———. 2012. *Keeping the Immigrant Bargain: The Costs and Rewards of Success in America.* New York: Russell Sage Foundation.

Love, Evan. 2009. "Confronting Islamophobia in the United States: Framing Civil Rights Activism among Middle Eastern Americans." *Patterns of Prejudice* 43(3–4): 401–25.

Loveman, Mara. 1997. "Is 'Race' Essential?" *American Sociological Review* 64: 891–98.

Lowe, Lisa. 1991. "Heterogeneity, Hybridity, Multiplicity: Marking Asian American Differences." *Diaspora: A Journal of Transnational Studies* 1(1): 24–44.

———. 1996. *On Asian American Cultural Politics.* Durham, N.C.: Duke University Press.

Lu, Janet. 2009. "A History of the National Association for Asian and Pacific American Education: Serving Asian and Pacific Islander Communities in the United States and Canada Since 1977." Available at: http://www.naapae.net/ (accessed February 17, 2012).

Lyman, Stanford M. 1970. *The Asian in the West.* Reno: University of Nevada, Western Studies Center, Desert Research Institute.

Maeda, Daryl. 2009. *Chains of Babylon: The Rise of Asian America.* Minneapolis: University of Minnesota Press.

Martin, Philip. 1995. "Proposition 187 in California." *International Migration Review* 29(1): 258–59.

Martinez, Lisa M. 2008. "The Individual and Contextual Determinants of Protest Among Latinos." *Mobilization* 13: 189–204.

Marwell, Niccle. 2007. *Bargaining for Brooklyn: Community Organizations in the Entrepreneurial City.* Chicago: University of Chicago Press.

Massey, Douglas S. 1985. "Ethnic Residential Segregation: A Theoretical Synthesis and Empirical Review." *Sociology and Social Research* 69(3): 315–50.

Massey, Douglas S., Jorge Durand, and Nolan J. Malone. 2002. *Beyond Smoke and Mirrors: Mexican Immigration in an Era of Economic Integration.* New York: Russell Sage Foundation.

Massey Douglas S., and Magaly Sanchez. 2010. *Brokered Boundaries: Creating Immigrant Identity in Anti-Immigrant Times.* New York: Russell Sage Foundation.

McAdam, Doug. 1982. *Political Process and the Development of Black Insurgency, 1930–1970*. Chicago: University of Chicago Press.

McAdam, Doug, John D. McCarthy, and Mayer N. Zald, eds. 1996. *Comparative Perspectives on Social Movements: Political Opportunities, Mobilizing Structures, and Cultural Framings*. Cambridge: Cambridge University Press.

McAdam, Doug, and David A. Snow eds. 1997. "Introduction—Social Movements: Conceptual and Theoretical Issues." *Social Movements: Readings on their Emergence, Mobilization, and Dynamics*. Los Angeles: Roxbury.

McAdam, Doug, and Yang Su. 2002. "The War at Home: Antiwar Protests and Congressional Voting, 1965 to 1973." *American Sociological Review* 67(5): 696–721.

McCammon, Holly J. 2012. *The US Women's Jury Movements and Strategic Adaptation: A More Just Verdict*. Cambridge University Press.

McCammon, Holly J., Karen E. Campbell, Ellen M. Granberg, and Christine Mowery. 2001. "How Movements Win: Gendered Opportunity Structures and US Women's Suffrage Movements, 1866 to 1919." *American Sociological Review* 66(1): 49–70.

McCarthy, John D. 1996. "Constraints and Opportunities in Adopting, Adapting, and Inventing." In *Comparative Perspectives on Social Movements: Political Opportunities, Mobilizing Structures, and Cultural Framings*, eds. Doug McAdam, John D. McCarthy, and Mayer N. Zald. Cambridge, England: Cambridge University Press.

McCarthy, John D., Clark McPhail, and Jackie Smith. 1996. "Images of Protest: Dimensions of Selection Bias in Media Coverage of Washington Demonstrations, 1982 and 1991." *American Sociological Review* 61: 478–99.

McCarthy, John D., and Mayer N. Zald. 1977. "Resource Mobilization and Social Movements: A Partial Theory." *American Journal of Sociology* 82(6): 1212–41.

McDermott, Monica. 2006. *Working-Class White: The Making and Unmaking of Race Relations*. Berkeley: University of California Press.

McDermott, Monica, and Frank L. Samson. 2005. "White Racial and Ethnic Identity in the United States." *Annual Review of Sociology* 31: 245–61.

McVeigh, Rory. 1999. "Structural Incentives for Conservative Mobilization: Power Devaluation and the Rise of the Ku Klux Klan, 1915–1925." *Social Forces* 77(4): 1461–96.

McWilliams, Carey. 1942. *Brothers Under the Skin*. Boston: Little, Brown.

Medrano, Juan Diaz. 1994. "The Effects of Ethnic Segregation and Ethnic Competition on Political Mobilization in the Basque Country, 1988." *American Sociological Review* 59: 873–89.

Meer, Nasar. 2012. "Misrecognising Muslim Consciousness in Europe." *Ethnicities* 12(2): 178–96.

Meier, Kenneth J., and Joseph Stewart Jr. 1991. "Cooperation and Conflict in Multiracial School Districts." *Journal of Politics* 53: 1123–33.

Melendy, H. Brett. 1977. *Asians in America: Filipinos, Koreans, and East Indians*. Boston: Twayne Publishers.

Melucci, Alberto. 1985. "The Symbolic Challenge of Contemporary Movements." *Social Research* 52: 789–816.

———. 1989. *Nomads of the Present: Social Movements and Individual Needs in Contemporary Society*. Philadelphia: Temple University Press.

Meyer, David S. 2004. "Protest and Political Opportunities." *Annual Review of Sociology* 30: 125–45.

Meyer, John W., and Brian Rowan. 1977. "Institutionalized Organizations: Formal Structure as Myth and Ceremony." *American Journal of Sociology* 83(2): 340–63.

Min, Pyong Gap. 1992. "The Structure and Social Functions of Korean Immigrant Churches in the United States." *International Migration Review* 26(4): 1370–94.

———. 1996. *Caught in the Middle: Korean Merchants in America's Multiethnic Cities*. Berkeley: University of California Press.

———, ed. 2006. *Asian Americans: Contemporary Trends and Issues*. Thousand Oaks, Calif.: Sage Publications.

———. 2008. *Ethnic Solidarity for Economic Survival: Korean Greengrocers in New York City*. New York: Russell Sage Foundation.

Min, Pyong Gap, and Rose Kim, eds. 1999. *Struggle for Ethnic Identity: Narratives by Asian American Professionals*. Walnut Creek, Calif.: Rowman Altamira.

Minkoff, Debra. 1995. *Organizing for Equality: The Evolution of Women's and Racial-Ethnic Organizations in America, 1955–1985*. New Brunswick, N.J.: Rutgers University Press.

———. 1997. "The Sequencing of Social Movements." *American Sociological Review* 62: 779–99.

———. 1999. "Bending with the Wind: Strategic Change and Adaptation by Women's and Racial Minority Organizations 1." *American Journal of Sociology* 104(6): 1666–1703.

———. 2002. "The Emergence of Hybrid Organizational Forms: Combining Identity-Based Service Provision and Political Action." *Nonprofit and Voluntary Sector Quarterly* 31(3): 377–401.

Minkoff, Debra C., and John D. McCarthy. 2005. "Reinvigorating the Study of Organizational Processes in Social Movements." *Mobilization: An International Quarterly* 10(2): 289–308.

Modell, John. 1977. *The Economics and Politics of Racial Accommodation: The Japanese of Los Angeles, 1900–1942*. Champaign: University of Illinois Press.

Mora, G. Cristina. 2014. *Making Hispanics: How Activists, Bureaucrats, and Media Constructed a New American*. Chicago: University of Chicago Press.

Morning, Ann. 2009. "Toward a Sociology of Racial Conceptualization for the 21st Century." *Social Forces* 87(3): 1167–92.

———. 2011. *The Nature of Race: How Scientists Think and Teach about Human Difference*. Berkeley: University of California Press.

Morris, Aldon D., and Suzanne Staggenborg. 2004. "Leadership in Social Movements." In *The Blackwell Companion to Social Movements*, ed. David A. Snow, Sarah A. Soule, and Hanspeter Kriesi. Malden, Mass.: Blackwell.

Morris, Irwin L. 2000. "African American Voting on Proposition 187: Rethinking the Prevalence of Interminority Conflict." *Political Research Quarterly* 53: 77–98.

Motomura, Hiroshi. 2006. *Americans in Waiting: The Lost Story of Immigration and Citizenship in the United States*. New York: Oxford University Press.

Myers, Daniel. 1997. "Racial Rioting in the 1960s: An Event History Analysis of Local Conditions." *American Sociological Review* 62: 94–112.

———. 2000. "The Diffusion of Collective Violence: Infectiousness, Susceptibility, and Mass Media Networks." *American Journal of Sociology* 106(1): 173–208.

Nagata, Judith. 1981. "In Defense of Ethnic Boundaries: The Changing Myths and Charters of Malay Identity." In *Ethnic Change*, ed. Charles F. Keyes. Seattle: University of Washington Press.

Nagel, Joane. 1995. "American Indian Ethnic Renewal: Politics and the Resurgence of Identity." *American Sociological Review* 60: 947–65.

———. 1996. *American Indian Ethnic Renewal: Red Power and the Resurgence of Identity and Culture*. New York: Oxford University Press.

Nakanishi, Don T., and Bernie C. LaForteza. 1984. *The National Asian American Roster, 1984*. Los Angeles: UCLA Asian American Studies Center.

National Asian Pacific American Legal Consortium (NAPALC). 1998. "Audit of Violence Against Asian Pacific Americans: 1998 Annual Report." Washington, D.C.: NAPALC.

Nee, Victor. 1973. *Longtime Californ': A Documentary Study of an American Chinatown*. Stanford, Calif.: Stanford University Press.

Ngai, Mae M. 2004. *Impossible Subjects: Illegal Aliens and the Making of Modern America*. Princeton, N.J.: Princeton University Press.

Ngo, Bic, and Stacey J. Lee. 2007. "Complicating the Image of Model Minority Success: A Review of Southeast Asian American Education." *Review of Educational Research* 77(4): 415–53.

Nielsen, François. 1980. "Flemish Movement in Belgium After World War II: A Dynamic Analysis." *American Sociological Review* 45: 76–94.

Nobles, Melissa. 2000. *Shades of Citizenship: Race and the Census in Modern Politics*. Stanford, Calif.: Stanford University Press.

Oboler, Suzanne. 1995. *Ethnic Labels, Latino Lives: Identity and the Politics of (Re)Presentation in the United States*. Minneapolis: University of Minnesota Press.

Ochoa, Gilda. 2004. *Becoming Neighbors in a Mexican American Community: Power, Conflict, and Solidarity*. Austin: University of Texas Press.

Ogawa, Dennis M., and Evarts C. Fox Jr. 1986. "Japanese American Internment and Relocation: The Hawaii Experience." In *Japanese Americans: From Relocation to Redress*, ed. Roger Daniels, Sandra C. Taylor, and Harry H. L. Kitano. Salt Lake City: University of Utah Press.

Okamoto, Dina G. 2003. "Toward a Theory of Panethnicity: Explaining Asian American Collective Action." *American Sociological Review* 68(6): 811–42.

———. 2004. "Asian American Community-Based Organizations." Unpublished data.

———. 2006. "Institutional Panethnicity: Boundary Formation in Asian American Organizing." *Social Forces* 85: 1–25.

———. 2007. "Marrying Out: A Boundary Approach to Understanding the Marital Integration of Asian Americans." *Social Science Research* 36: 1391–1414.

———. 2010. "Organizing across Ethnic Boundaries in the Post-Civil Rights Era: Asian American Panethnic Coalitions." In *Strategic Alliances: Coalition Building and Social Movements*, eds. Nella Van Dyke and Holly McCammon. Minneapolis: Minnesota University Press, Social Movements Series.

Okamoto, Dina G., and Kim Ebert. 2010. "Beyond the Ballot: Immigrant Collective Action in Gateways and New Destinations in the United States." *Social Problems* 57: 529–58.

Okamoto, Dina G., Kim Ebert, and Carla Violet. 2011. "¿El Campeón de Los Hispanos? Comparing the Coverage of Latino/a Collective Action in Spanish- and English-Language Newspapers." *Latino Studies: Special Issue on Latinos and the Media* 9: 219–41.

Okamoto, Dina, and Melanie Jones Gast. 2013. "Racial Inclusion or Accommodation?" *Du Bois Review* 10(1): 131–53.

Okamoto, Dina G., Melanie Jones Gast, and Valerie Feldman. 2012. "Managing Diversity in Youth-Serving Organizations." Paper presented at the Annual Meeting of the American Sociological Association, Denver, Colo.

Okamoto, Dina, and G. Cristina Mora. 2014. "Panetnicity." *Annual Review of Sociology* 10: 1–21.

Okamura, Jonathan Y. 1981. "Situational Ethnicity." *Ethnic and Racial Studies* 4(4): 452–65.

Okihiro, Gary. 1994. *Margins and Mainstreams: Asians in American History and Culture*. Seattle: University of Washington Press.

Oliver, Melvin L., and Thomas M. Shapiro. 2006. *Black Wealth, White Wealth: A New Perspective on Racial Inequality*. New York: Taylor & Francis.

Oliver, Pamela E., and Daniel J. Myers. 1999. "How Events Enter the Public Sphere: Conflict, Location, and Sponsorship in Local Newspaper Coverage of Public Events." *American Journal of Sociology* 105(1): 38–87.

Olzak, Susan. 1982. "Ethnic Mobilization in Quebec." *Ethnic and Racial Studies* 5: 253–75.

———. 1989. "Analysis of Events in the Study of Collective Action." *Annual Review of Sociology* 15: 119–41.

———. 1990. "The Political Context of Competition: Lynching and Urban Racial Violence, 1882–1914." *Social Forces* 69(2): 395–421.

———. 1992. *The Dynamics of Ethnic Competition and Conflict*. Palo Alto, Calif.: Stanford University Press.

———. 2004. "Ethnic and Nationalist Movements." In *The Blackwell Companion to Social Movements*, ed. David Snow, Sarah Soule, and Hanspeter Kriesi. Malden, Mass.: Blackwell.

Olzak, Susan, and Suzanne Shanahan. 1996. "Deprivation and Race Riots: An Extension of Spilerman's Analysis." *Social Forces* 74: 931–61.

Olzak, Susan, Suzanne Shanahan, and Elizabeth H. McEneaney. 1996. "Poverty, Segregation, and Race Riots: 1960 to 1993." *American Sociological Review* 61(4): 590–613.

Olzak, Susan, Suzanne Shanahan, and Elizabeth West. 1994. "School-Desegregation, Interracial Exposure, and Antibusing Activity in Contemporary Urban America." *American Journal of Sociology* 100(1): 196–241.

Omatsu, Glenn. 1994. "The 'Four Prisons' and the Movements of Liberation." In *The State of Asian America: Activism and Resistance in the 1990s*, ed. Karin Aguilar-San Juan. Boston: South End Press.

Omi, Michael A. 2001. "The Changing Meaning of Race." *America Becoming: Racial Trends and Their Consequences* 1: 243–63.

Omi, Michael, and Howard Winant. 1994. *Racial Formation in the United States: From the 1960s to the 1990s*. New York: Routledge.

Ong, Aihwa. 2003. *Buddha Is Hiding: Refugees, Citizenship, the New America*. Berkeley: University of California Press.

Ong, Paul M., Edna Bonacich, and Lucie Cheng. 1994. *The New Asian Immigration in Los Angeles and Global Restructuring*. Philadelphia: Temple University Press.

Ortiz, David G., David J. Myers, Eugene N. Walls, and Maria-Elena D. Diaz. 2005. "Where Do We Stand With Newspaper Data?" *Mobilization* 10: 397–419.

Otis, Eileen. 2001. "The Reach and Limits of Asian Panethnic Identity: The Dynamics of Gender, Race, and Class in a Community-Based Organization." *Qualitative Sociology* 24: 349–79.

Padilla, Felix M. 1985. *Latino Ethnic Consciousness: The Case of Mexican Americans and Puerto Ricans in Chicago*. Notre Dame, Ind.: University of Notre Dame Press.

Palumbo-Liu, David. 1999. *Asian/American: Historical Crossings of a Racial Frontier*. Stanford, Calif.: Stanford University Press.

Park, Edward J. W. 2001. "Community Divided: Korean American Politics in Post–Civil Unrest Los Angeles." In *Asian and Latino Immigrants in a Restructuring Economy*, ed. Marta Lopez-Garza and David R. Diaz. Stanford, Calif.: Stanford University Press.

Pascoe, Peggy. 2009. *What Comes Naturally: Miscegenation Law and the Making of Race in America*. Oxford: Oxford University Press.

Perea, Juan F., ed. 1997. *Immigrants Out! The New Nativism and the Anti-Immigrant Impulse in the United States*. New York: New York University Press.

Perry, Barbara. 2002. "Defending the Color Line: Racially and Ethnically Motivated Hate Crime." *American Behavioral Scientist* 46: 72–92.

Pettigrew, Thomas F., and Linda R. Tropp. 2006. "A Meta-Analytic Test of Intergroup Contact Theory." *Journal of Personality and Social Psychology* 90(5): 751–83.

———. 2012. *When Groups Meet: The Dynamics of Intergroup Contact*. New York: Psychology Press.

Pew Research Center. 2012. "The Rise of Asian Americans." Washington, D.C.: Pew Research Social and Demographic Trends (June 19). Available at: http://www.pewsocialtrends.org/2012/06/19/the-rise-of-asian-americans/ (accessed March 14, 2012).

Polletta, Francesca, and James Jasper. 2001. "Collective Identity in Social Movements." *Annual Review of Sociology* 27: 283–305.

Portes, Alejandro, Cristina Escobar, and Renelinda Arana. 2008. "Bridging the Gap: Transnational and Ethnic Organizations in the Political Incorporation of Immigrants in the United States." *Ethnic and Racial Studies* 31(6): 1056–90.

Portes, Alejandro, and Rubén G. Rumbaut. 2001. *Legacies: The Story of the Immigrant Second Generation*. Berkeley: University of California Press.

Portes, Alejandro, and Min Zhou. 1993. "The New Second Generation: Segmented Assimilation and Its Variants." *Annals of the American Academy of Political and Social Science* 530: 74–96.

Posner, Daniel. 2005. *Institutions and Ethnic Politics in Africa*. New York: Cambridge University Press.

Prewitt, Kenneth. 2005. "Racial Classification in America: Where Do We Go From Here?" *Daedalus* 134(1): 5–17.

Prieto-Flores, Oscar, and Teresa Sordé-Martí. 2011. "The Institutionalization of Panethnicity from the Grassroots Standpoint in a European Context: The Case of Gitanos and Roma Immigrants in Barcelona." *Ethnicities* 11: 202–17.

Quon, Merilynne Hamano. 2001. "Individually We Contributed, Together We Made a Difference." In *Asian Americans: The Movement and the Moment*, ed. Steve Louie and Glenn Omatsu. Los Angeles: UCLA Asian American Studies Center Press.

Ragin, Charles. 1979. "Ethnic Political Mobilization: The Welsh Case." *American Sociological Review* 44: 619–35.

Ramakrishnan, S. Karthick, and Irene Bloemraad, eds. 2008. *Civic Hopes and Political Realities: Community Organizations and Political Engagement among Immigrants in the U.S. and Abroad*. New York: Russell Sage Foundation.

Ramakrishnan, Karthick, Jane Junn, Taeku Lee, and Janelle Wong. 2008. National Asian American Survey [Computer file]. ICPSR31481-v2. Ann Arbor, Mich.: Inter-University Consortium for Political and Social Research [distributor], 2012-07-19. doi:10.3886/ICPSR31481.v2.

Reeves, Terrance J., and Claudette E. Bennett. 2004. "We the People: Asians in the United States. Census 2000 Special Reports. Washington U.S. Census Bureau.

Regalado, James A. 1995. "Creating Multicultural Harmony? A Critical Perspective on Coalition-Building Efforts in Los Angeles." In *Multiethnic Coalition Building in Los Angeles*, ed. Eui-Young Yu and Edward T. Chang. Los Angeles: California State University, Institute for Asian American and Pacific American Studies.

Reimers, David M. 1985. *Still the Golden Door: The Third World Comes to America*. New York: Columbia University Press.

Robinson, Greg. 2009. *By Order of the President: FDR and the Internment of Japanese Americans*. Boston, Mass.: Harvard University Press.

Robnett, Belinda. 1997. *How Long? How Long? African-American Women in the Struggle for Civil Rights*. New York: Oxford University Press.

Rosales, Francisco Arturo, ed. 2000. *Testimonio: A Documentary History of the Mexican American Struggle for Civil Rights*. Houston: Arte Publico Press.

Rosenfeld, Michael J. 2002. "Measures of Assimilation in the Marriage Market: Mexican Americans 1970–1990." *Journal of Marriage and Family* 64(1): 152–62.

Roth, Silke. 2003. *Building Movement Bridges: The Coalition of Labor Union Women*. Westport, Conn.: Praeger.

Roth, Wendy. 2012. *Race Migrations: Latinos and the Cultural Transformation of Race*. Stanford, Calif.: Stanford University Press.

Rucht, Dieter, Ruud Koopmans, and Friedhelm Neidhardt. 1999. *Acts of Dissent: New Developments in the Study of Protest*. New York: Rowman & Littlefield.

Rucht, Dieter, and Thomas Ohlemacher. 1992. "Protest Event Data: Collection, Uses, and Perspectives." In *Studying Collective Action*, ed. Ron Eyerman and Mario Diani. Beverly Hills, Calif.: Sage Publications.

Rumbaut, Rubén. 2000. "Immigration Research in the United States: Social Origins and Future Orientations." In *Immigration Research for a New Century: Multidisciplinary Perspectives*, ed. Nancy Foner, Rubén G. Rumbaut, and Steven J. Gold. New York: Russell Sage Foundation.

Rutledge, Paul. 1992. *The Vietnamese Experience in America*. Bloomington: Indiana University Press.

Ryan, Barbara. 2013. *Feminism and the Women's Movement: Dynamics of Change in Social Movement Ideology and Activism*. New York: Routledge.

Saito, Leland T. 1998. *Race and Politics: Asian Americans, Latinos, and Whites in a Los Angeles Suburb*. Champaign: University of Illinois Press.

Saito, Leland T., and John Horton. 1994. "The New Chinese Immigration and the Rise of Asian American Politics in Monterey Park, California." In *The New Asian Immigration in Los Angeles and Global Restructuring*, ed. Paul M. Ong, Edna Bonacich, and Lucie Cheng. Philadelphia: Temple University Press.

Sakamoto, Arthur, Kimberly A. Goyette, and ChangHwan Kim. 2009. "Socioeconomic Attainments of Asian Americans." *Annual Review of Sociology* 35: 255–76.

Sampson, Robert J., Doug McAdam, Heather MacIndoe, and Simon Weffer. 2005. "Civil Society Reconsidered: The Durable Nature and Community Structure of Collective Civic Action." *American Journal of Sociology* 111: 673–714.

Sanders, Jimy M. 2000. "Ethnic Boundaries and Identity in Plural Societies." *Annual Review of Sociology* 28: 327–57.
Santa Ana, Otto. 2002. *Brown Tide Rising: Metaphors of Latinos in Contemporary American Public Discourse*. Austin, Tex.: University of Texas Press.
Saperstein, Aliya, Andrew M. Penner, and Ryan Light. 2013. "Racial Formation in Perspective: Connecting Individuals, Institutions, and Power Relations." *Annual Review of Sociology* 39: 359–78.
Sarna, Jonathan D. 1978. "From Immigrants to Ethnics: Toward a New Theory of Ethnicization." *Ethnicity* 5: 370–78.
Schermerhorn, Richard A. 1978. *Comparative Ethnic Relations: A Framework for Theory and Research*. Chicago: University of Chicago Press.
Shah, Bindi. 2012. *Laotian Daughters: Working Toward Community, Belonging, and Environmental Justice*. Philadelphia: Temple University Press.
Shankar, Lavina Dhingra, and Rajini Srikanth. 1998. *A Part, Yet Apart: South Asians in Asian America*. Philadelphia: Temple University Press.
Shiao, Jiannbin Lee. 1998. "The Nature of the Nonprofit Sector: Professionalism Versus Identity Politics in Private Policy Definitions of Asian Pacific Americans." *Asian American Policy Review* 8: 17–43.
———. 2004. *Identifying Talent, Institutionalizing Diversity: Race and Philanthropy in Post–Civil Rights America*. Durham, N.C.: Duke University Press.
Shibutani, Tamotsu, and Kian M. Kwan. 1965. *Ethnic Stratification: A Comparative Approach*. New York: MacMillan.
Shutika, Debra Lattanzi. 2008. "The Ambivalent Welcome: Cinco de Mayo and the Symbolic Expression of Local Identity and Ethnic Relations." In *New Faces in New Places: The Changing Geography of American Immigration*, ed. Douglas Massey. New York: Russell Sage Foundation.
Silverman, Carol, Arleda Martinez, Jamie Rogers, Gene Waddell, Lina Morin-Calderon, and Jeanne Bell. 2009. *San Francisco's Nonprofit Sector: Contributions, Diversity, Challenges*. San Francisco: University of San Francisco, Institute for Nonprofit Organization Management (April).
Singh, J. 2000. "Political Expression in an Immigrant Community." In *Asian American Studies: A Reader*, ed. JY-WS Wu and M. Song. New Brunswick, N.J.: Rutgers University Press.
Singh, Jitendra V., David J. Tucker, and Robert J House. 1986. "Organizational Legitimacy and the Liability of Newness." *Administrative Science Quarterly* 31(2): 171–93.
Skocpol, Theda, and Morris P. Fiorina, eds. 1999. *Civic Engagement in American Democracy*. Washington, D.C.: Brookings Institution Press.
Skrentny, John D. 2002. *The Minority Rights Revolution*. Cambridge, Mass.: Harvard University Press.
Smith, David H. 1992. "National Nonprofit, Voluntary Associations: Some Parameters." *Nonprofit and Voluntary Sector Quarterly* 21: 81–94.

Smith, Jackie, John D. McCarthy, Clark McPhail, and Boguslaw Augustyn. 2001. "From Protest to Agenda Building: Description Bias in Media Coverage of Protest Events in Washington, D.C." *Social Forces* 79: 1397–423.

Sonenshein, Raphael J. 1989. "The Dynamics of Biracial Coalitions: Crossover Politics in Los Angeles." *Western Political Quarterly* 42: 333–53.

———. 1993. *Politics in Black and White: Race and Power in Los Angeles.* Princeton, N.J.: Princeton University Press.

———. 2001. "When Ideologies Agree and Interests Collide, What's a Leader to Do? The Prospects for Latino-Jewish Coalition in Los Angeles." In *Governing American Cities: Inter-Ethnic Coalitions, Competition, and Conflict,* ed. Michael Jones-Correa. New York: Russell Sage Foundation.

Song, Miri. 2003. *Choosing Ethnic Identity.* Malden, Mass.: Blackwell.

Soule, Sarah. 1992. "Populism and Black Lynching in Georgia, 1890–1900." *Social Forces* 71: 431–49.

Soule, Sarah A., Doug McAdam, John McCarthy, and Yang Su. 1999. "Protest Events: Cause or Consequence of State Action? The U.S. Women's Movement and Federal Congressional Activities, 1956–1979." *Mobilization* 4(2): 239–55.

Soule, Sarah A., and Nella Van Dyke. 1999. "Black Church Arson in the United States, 1989–1996." *Ethnic and Racial Studies* 22(4): 724–42.

Spilerman, Seymour. 1971. "The Causes of Racial Disturbances: Tests of an Explanation." *American Sociological Review* 36(3): 427–42.

Stewart, Frances. 2008. *Horizontal Inequalities and Conflict.* London: Palgrave Macmillan.

———. 2010. "Horizontal Inequalities in Kenya and the Political Disturbances of 2008: Some Implications for Aid Policy." *Conflict, Security & Development* 10(1): 133–59.

Stryker, Sheldon. 1974. "'A Theory of Middleman Minorities': A Comment." *American Sociological Review* 39(2): 281–82.

Suga, Miya Shichinohe. 2004. "Little Tokyo Reconsidered: Transformation of Japanese American Community Through the Early Redevelopment Projects." *Japanese Journal of American Studies* 15: 237–55.

Sun, Wei, and William J. Starosta. 2006. "Perceptions of Minority Invisibility Among Asian American Professionals." *Howard Journal of Communications* 17(2): 119–42.

Sutton, John, Frank Dobbin, John W. Meyer, and W. Richard Scott. 1994. "The Legalization of the Workplace." *American Journal of Sociology* 99: 944–71.

Suzuki, Bob H. 1989. "Asian-American as the Model Minority." *Change* (November): 13–19.

Taing, Susan. 2005. "Lost in the Shuffle: The Failure of the Pan-Asian Coalition to Advance the Interests of Southeast Asian Americans." *Berkeley La Raza Law Journal* 16: 23–52.

Tajfel, Henri, and Jonathan C. Turner. 1979. "An Integrative Theory of Intergroup

Conflict." In *The Social Psychology of Intergroup Relations*, ed. William G. Austin and Stephen Worchel. Monterey, Calif.: Brooks/Cole.

Takagi, Dana Y. 1992. *The Retreat from Race: Asian-American Admissions and Racial Politics*. New Brunswick, N.J.: Rutgers University Press.

Takaki, Ronald. 1989. *Strangers from a Different Shore: A History of Asian Americans*. Boston: Little, Brown and Co.

———. 1993. *A Different Mirror: A Multicultural History of America*. Boston: Little, Brown and Co.

———. 1994. *From the Land of Morning Calm: The Koreans in America*. New York: Chelsea House Publishers.

———. 2000. *Iron Cages: Race and Culture in the Nineteenth Century*. New York: Oxford University Press.

Takeda, Okiyoshi. 2001. "One Year after the Sit-in: Asian American Students' Identities and Their Support for Asian American Studies." *Journal of Asian American Studies* 4(2): 147–64.

Takei, Isao, and Arthur Sakamoto. 2008. "Do College-Educated, Native-Born Asian Americans Face a Glass Ceiling in Obtaining Managerial Authority?" *Asian American Policy Review* 17: 73–85.

Tang, Joyce. 1996. "To Be or Not to Be Your Own Boss? A Comparison of White, Black, and Asian Scientists and Engineers." *Current Research on Occupations and Professions* 9: 129–65.

Tarrow, Sidney G. 1989. *Struggle, Politics, and Reform: Collective Action, Social Movements and Cycles of Protest*. No. 21. Ithaca, N. Y.: Center for International Studies, Cornell University.

Taylor, Verta. 1989. "Social Movement Continuity: The Women's Movement in Abeyance." *American Sociological Review* 54(5): 761-775.

Telles, Edward E. 2014. *Race in Another America: The Significance of Skin Color in Brazil*. Princeton, N.J.: Princeton University Press.

Telles, Edward, and Vilma Ortiz. 2008. *Generations of Exclusion: Mexican Americans, Assimilation, and Race*. New York: Russell Sage Foundation.

Tropp, Linda R., and Thomas F. Pettigrew. 2005. "Relationships Between Intergroup Contact and Prejudice among Minority and Majority Status Groups." *Psychological Science* 16(12): 951–57.

Tuan, Mia. 1998. *Forever Foreigners or Honorary Whites? The Asian Ethnic Experience Today*. New Brunswick, N.J.: Rutgers University Press.

Turnbull, Spencer K. 2003. "Wen Ho Lee and the Consequences of Enduring Asian American Stereotypes." In *Asian American Politics: Law, Participation, and Policy*, ed. Don T. Nakanishi and James S. Lai. Lanham, Md.: Rowman and Littlefield.

Umemoto, Karen. 1989. "'On Strike!' San Francisco State College Strike 1968–1969: The Role of Asian-American Students." *Amerasia Journal* 15: 3–41.

U.S. Census Bureau. 2006. *American Community Survey*. Washington: U.S. Department of Commerce, Economics, and Statistics Administration.

———. 2010. *Profile of General Population and Housing Characteristics: 2010 Demographic Profile Data.* Washington: U.S. Department of Commerce, U.S. Census Bureau.

U.S. Department of Commerce, Bureau of the Census. 1995. *Census of Population and Housing, 1990 Public Use Microdata Sample: 5-Percent Sample* [computer file]. Washington: U.S. Department of Commerce, Bureau of the Census.

U.S. Department of Homeland Security. 2010. "Yearbook of Immigration Statistics: 2010." Available at: http://www.dhs.gov/yearbook-immigration-statistics-2010 (accessed July 22, 2013).

U.S. Office of Management and Budget. 1977. *Race and Ethnic Standards for Federal Statistics and Administrative Reporting.* Statistical Policy Directive No. 15. Washington: U.S. Office of Management and Budget.

Van Dyke, Nella, Sarah A. Soule, and Verta A. Taylor. 2004. "The Targets of Social Movements: Beyond a Focus on the State." *Research in Social Movements, Conflicts, and Change* 25: 27–51.

Vergara, Vanessa B. M. 1997. "Broken Promises and Aging Patriots: An Assessment of U.S. Veteran Benefits for Filipino World War II Veterans." *Asian American Policy Review* 7: 163–82.

Vo, Linda Trinh. 2004. *Mobilizing an Asian American Community.* Philadelphia: Temple University Press.

Waldinger, Roger. 1994. "The Making of an Immigrant Niche." *International Migration Review* 28(1): 3–30.

———, ed. 2001. *Strangers at the Gates: New Immigrants in Urban America.* Berkeley: University of California Press.

Waldinger, Roger, and Cynthia Feliciano. 2004. "Will the New Second Generation Experience 'Downward Assimilation'? Segmented Assimilation Re-assessed." *Ethnic and Racial Studies* 27(3): 376–402.

Waters, Mary C. 1990. *Ethnic Options: Choosing Identities in America.* Berkeley: University of California Press.

———. 1999. *Black Identities: West Indian Immigrant Dreams and American Realities.* New York and Cambridge, Mass.: Russell Sage Foundation and Harvard University Press.

Weber, Max. 1968. *Economy and Society.* New York: Bedminster Press.

Wei, William. 1993. *The Asian American Movement.* Philadelphia: Temple University Press.

Wilson, William Julius. 1986. *The Truly Disadvantaged: The Inner City, the Underclass, and Public Policy.* Chicago: University of Chicago Press.

Wimmer, Andreas. 2008. "The Making and Unmaking of Ethnic Boundaries: A Multilevel Process Theory." *American Journal of Sociology* 113: 970–1022.

Winant, Howard. 2000. "Race and Race Theory." *Annual Review of Sociology* 169–85.

Wong, Janelle. 2006. *Democracy's Promise: Immigrants and American Civic Institutions.* Ann Arbor: University of Michigan Press.

Wong, Janelle, Karthick Ramakrishnan, Taeku Lee, and Jane Junn. 2011. *Asian American Political Participation: Emerging Constituents and Their Political Identities*. New York: Russell Sage Foundation.

Wong, Kent. 2000. "Building an Asian Pacific Labor Movement." In *Legacy to Liberation: Politics and Culture of revolutionary Asian Pacific America*, ed. Fred Ho. Oakland, Calif.: AK Press Pages.

Woo, Deborah. 2000. *Glass Ceilings and Asian Americans: The New Face of Workplace Barriers*. Lanham, Md.: Rowman & Littlefield Publishers.

Wu, Ellen D. 2013. *The Color of Success: Asian Americans and the Origins of the Model Minority*. Princeton, N.J.: Princeton University Press.

Xie, Yu, and Kimberly Goyette. 2004. *Asian Americans: A Demographic Portrait*. New York: Russell Sage Foundation and Population Reference Bureau.

Yancey, William L., Eugene P. Ericksen, and Richard N. Juliani. 1976. "Emergent Ethnicity: Review and Reformulation." *American Sociological Review* 41: 391–403.

Yang, Kou. 2001. "Research Note: The Hmong in America: Twenty-Five Years After the U.S. Secret War in Laos." *Journal of Asian American Studies* 4(2): 165–74.

Yip, Steve. 2000. Serve the People—Yesterday and Today." In *Legacy to Liberation: Politics and Culture of Revolutionary Asian Pacific America*, ed. Fred Ho, with Carolyn Antonio, Diane Fujino, and Steve Yip. San Francisco: AK Press.

Yoshikawa, Yoko. 1994. "The Heat Is on Miss Saigon Coalition: Organizing Across Race and Sexuality." In *The State of Asian America: Activism and Resistance in the 1990s*, ed Karin Aguilar-San Juan. Boston: South End Press.

Young, Crawford. 1976. *The Politics of Cultural Pluralism*. Madison: University of Wisconsin Press.

Zeng, Zhen, and Yu Xie. 2004. "Asian Americans' Earnings Disadvantage Reexamined: The Role of Place of Education." *American Journal of Sociology* 109(5): 1075–108.

Zhang, Qingsong. 1998. "The Origins of the Chinese Americanization Movement: Wong Chin Foo and the Chinese Equal Rights League." In *Claiming America: Constructing Chinese American Identities During the Exclusion Era*, ed. K. Scott Wong and Sucheng Chan. Philadelphia: Temple University Press.

Zhao, Dingxin. 1998. "Ecologies of Social Movements: Student Mobilization During the 1989 Prodemocracy Movement in Beijing." *American Journal of Sociology* 103(6): 1493–529.

Zhou, Min. 1992. *Chinatown: The Socioeconomic Potential of an Urban Enclave*. Philadelphia, Pa.: Temple University Press.

———. 2000. "Social Capital in Chinatown: The Role of Community-Based Organizations and Families in the Adaptation of the Younger Generation." In *Contemporary Asian America: A Multidisciplinary Reader*, ed. Min Zhou and James V. Gatewood. New York: New York University Press.

———. 2004. "Are Asian Americans Becoming White?" *Contexts* 3(1): 29–37.

———. 2009. "How Neighbourhoods Matter for Immigrant Children: The Formation of Educational Resources in Chinatown, Koreatown and Pico Union, Los Angeles." *Journal of Ethnic and Migration Studies* 35(7): 1153–79.

Zhou, Min, and Carl L. Bankston. 1998. *Growing Up American: How Vietnamese Children Adapt to Life in the United States*. New York: Russell Sage Foundation.

Zhou, Min, Yen-Fen Tseng, and Rebecca Y. Kim. 2008. "Rethinking Residential Assimilation: The Case of a Chinese Ethnoburb in the San Gabriel Valley, California." *Amerasia Journal* 34(3): 53–83.

Zia, Helen. 2000. *Asian American Dreams: The Emergence of an American People*. New York: Farrar, Straus, and Giroux.

Zolberg, Aristide R., and Long L. Woon. 1999. "Why Islam Is Like Spanish: Cultural Incorporation in Europe and the United States." *Politics and Society* 27: 5–38.

Index

Boldface numbers refer to figures and tables.

AAAE (Asian American Architects and Engineers), **57,** 81
AAFRC (American Association of Fund Raising Council) Trust for Philanthropy, 162
AAJA (Asian American Journalists Association), 81–82
AAMA (Asian American Manufacturers Association), 61, 81
AAPA (Asian American Political Alliance), 42
AAPIP (Asian Americans and Pacific Islanders in Philanthropy), 79–80
ACC (Asian Cultural Center), 136
accommodation, 130
advocacy: of ethnic vs. panethnic organizations, **167**; pan-Asian activities, 46, 70, 143; Pew Report dispute, 1. *See also specific organizations*
affirmative action, 48
AFL (American Federation of Labor), 29–30
African Americans: collective action efforts, 88–89; interracial coalitions with Asian Americans, 139–41; negative stereotypes of, 8; racism against, 46. *See also* blacks

African identity, 8, 155
Agnone, Jon, **89**
agriculture, 29, 30, 32–33, 37–39, 66
AIWA (Asian Immigrant Women's Advocates), 78
Alba, Richard, 8, 176*n*31
Alien Land Laws, 33, 35, 36, 181*n*7, 183*n*42
Almaguer, Tomas, 182*n*11
American Association of Fund Raising Council (AAFRC) Trust for Philanthropy, 162
American Citizens for Justice, 61, 92
American Community Survey, **18**
American culture and identity, 4, 45, 53
American Federation of Labor (AFL), 29–30
American Legion, 30
anti-Asian attacks: Chin murder, 10–11, 59, 92, 102, 105; and ethnic organization formation, 39; measurement of, 161–62; and panethnic collective action, 105; and panethnic organization formation, 74; segregation effects, **104**; Yew incident, 91
antiwar movement, 41, 43–44

APALA (Asian Pacific American Labor Alliance), 54, 61, 78–79
APEN (Asian Pacific Power Network), 79
Arab Americans, 132, 156
arts organizations, 57, 80–81, **167**
ascription, 10–11
Asia Foundation, **57**
Asia Institute, **57**
Asian American Alliance, 99
Asian American Architects and Engineers (AAAE), **57,** 81
Asian American Arts Alliance, **57**
Asian American Convenience Stores Association, 61
Asian American Journalists Association (AAJA), 81–82
Asian American Justice Center, 92
Asian American Legal Defense and Educational Fund, **57**
Asian American Manufacturers Association (AAMA), 61, 81
Asian American Political Alliance (AAPA), 42
Asian American Real Estate Association, 61
Asian Americans: diversity of, 3, 16, 18, 80; metropolitan areas with largest populations, **63**; origins of label, 2–3, 41–42; Pew Research Center report, 1–2, 80; population statistics, **12,** 16–17, **30**; racial category, 48–50; relations among, 3, 32, 33, 34–35; socioeconomic status, 17–19; survey respondents' identification with label, 152–53. *See also specific groups*
Asian Americans and Pacific Islanders in Philanthropy (AAPIP), 79–80
Asian and Pacific Islander Health Forum, **57**
Asian Cultural Center (ACC), 136

Asian Health Care Leaders Association, 61
Asian Immigrant Women's Advocates (AIWA), 78
Asian Law Caucus, 54
Asian Media Collective, 44
Asian Pacific American Labor Alliance (APALA), 54, 61, 78–79
Asian/Pacific American Librarians Association, 61
Asian Pacific Americans for Progress, 61
Asian Pacific Dance Festival, 94
Asian/Pacific Islander census category, 47–48, 59
Asian Pacific Policy and Planning Council rally, 106–7
Asian Pacific Power Network (APEN), 79
Asian Women United, 44
assimilation, 8–9, 32, 42, 45, 128–31, 157
Association of Sri Lankans in America, 59
Atlanta, Ga.: labor market segregation and competition, **69**; pan-Asian organizations, 62
attacks. *See* anti-Asian attacks
auto industry, 92

Baltimore, Md., labor market segregation and competition, **69**
Barth, Fredrik, 6, 179*n*57
Bay Area Asian Coalition Against the War, 44
Bhagat Singh Thind; United States v., 26
black power movement, 41, 42
blacks: panethnic identity, 8, 155; panethnic organizations, 56–57; San Francisco population, **116**. *See also* African Americans
Boston, Mass.: Chinatown, 36; Free Chinatown Committee, 98; pan-Asian organizations, 62

Index 235

boundaries, ethnic or cultural: blurring of, 201n45; crossing of, 26–27, 156; durability of, 28–36; of ethnic organizations, 119–25; layered nature of, 85, 157; literature review, 6–7; panethnic organization formation and, 76–82; segregation vs. competitive model, 148; shifts or expansion of, 2–3, 9–13, 68–69, 156–58. *See also* historical context of ethnic group boundaries
Budget of the U.S. Government: Historical Tables, 162
Bulgarians, 46

CAC (Chinese American Coalition), 199n42
CACA (Chinese American Citizens Alliance), 117–18
CACC (Chinese American Citizens Council), 138–39
California: Chinese immigrants, 28–29; Secret War recognition in school curriculum, 96. *See also specific cities*
California Building Trades Council, 30
California Joint Immigration Committee, 30
Cambodian Americans, 67, 122, 137–38
Cambodian Family Association (CFA), 122
CARES (Coalition Against Racial and Ethnic Scapegoating), 109
Caribbean Americans, 155
CBS News, 196n66
CCR (Chinese for Civil Rights), 140–41
celebrations, 93–94, 99–100. *See also* collective action
census data, 47–48, **49**, 107, 156
Center for Asian American Media, 80–81
Central Intelligence Agency (CIA), 109

CFA (Cambodian Family Association), 122
Chan, Jeff, 136
Chicago, Ill.: pan-Asian organizations, 62; Spanish Coalition for Jobs, 177–78n45
Chicago Tribune, 21, **90**
Chicano movement, 42
Chin, Vincent, 10–11, 59, 92, 102, 105
China: boycotts against American products, 37; economic transformation, 19; Japan's occupation of, 34–35, 97; spying, 108–9; Tiananmen Square massacre, 96; U.S. relations with, 58
Chinatown Community Development Center, 119, 187n129
Chinatowns, 36, 184n59
Chinese Alliance for Democracy, 96
Chinese American Citizens Alliance (CACA), 117–18
Chinese American Citizens Council (CACC), 138–39
Chinese American Coalition (CAC), 199n42
Chinese Americans: census category, 47; collective action, 90–91, 96–97; early immigrants, 25, 28–29, 32; educational attainment, **18**; ethnic enclaves, 36–37; ethnic identity, 2, 45; household income, **18**; immigration statistics, **48**; interethnic competition, 66; International Hotel anti-eviction movement, 44–45, 59; New Year celebrations, 99; panethnic organization formation, 73; Pew Research Center report, 1; population statistics, **12**, **30**; poverty rates, **18**; relations with Japanese, 34–35, 96–97; San Francisco population, **116**; socioeconomic hierarchy, 18; during WWII, 40. *See also specific organizations*

236 Index

Chinese Citizens Council, 50
Chinese Consolidated Benevolent Association, 36
Chinese Exclusion Act of 1882, 29, 37, 40
Chinese for Affirmative Action, 57, 118
Chinese for Civil Rights (CCR), 140–41
Chinese Progressive Association, 118
Chinese-Western Daily, 35
churches, 38
CIA (Central Intelligence Agency), 109
citizenship, 11, 26–27, 40, 41
City University of New York–Hunter College, 108
Civil Liberties Act, 95
Civil Rights, U.S. Commission on, 70
Civil Rights Act of 1964, 41
civil rights organizations, 11, 61, 92, 135, **167**
Cleveland Foundation (CF), 49
clothing, 32
Coalition Against Racial and Ethnic Scapegoating (CARES), 109
coalitions, 35, 125–26
collective action, 85–111; of college students, 42–43, 107–8; data collection, 170–71; history of, 89–97; introduction, 85–86; panethnic-ethnic organizing relationship, 87–89, 97–103
college education, 19
college students: early Filipino immigrants, 182*n*24; newspapers, 44; protests by, 42–43, 107–8
colonialism, internal, 148–49
Columbia University, 108
Committee Against Anti-Asian Violence in New York, 61
community: definition of, 24; of early immigrants along ethnic lines, 36–40
community-based organizations (CBOs), 80. *See also specific organizations*

community centers, 118, 119, 124
community development, 62, **167**
competition, interethnic: early immigrants, 31–34; group boundary formation, 76–77; literature review, 76; model of, 13–14, 64, 65, 76, 148; and panethnic collective action, 100–105, 148, **164–67**; and panethnic organization emergence, 63–67, 70–73, **163**
Cornell, Stephen, 179*n*57
cross-cultural organizations, 57–58
Cuban Americans, 2
cultural boundaries. *See* boundaries, ethnic or cultural
cultural celebrations, 93–94, 99–100. *See also* collective action
cultural community, 8
cultural competency, 118, 123–24, **125**, 126–27
cultural division of labor, 148–49
cultural exchanges, 57–58
cultural narratives. *See* narratives
culture, importance for understanding boundary processes, 179*n*57

data collection, 169–73. *See also specific sources of data*
demographics, 1–2, 114–15, 121
demonstrations. *See* collective action
Denver, Colo., pan-Asian organizations, 62
Detroit, Mich., pan-Asian organizations, 62
Deutch, John, 109
DiMaggio, Paul, 187*n*132
discrimination, 11, 39, 41, 81, 157
domestic violence, 123

Ebert, Kim, 188*n*8
education, 58, 96
educational attainment, **18**

Index 237

Encyclopedia of Associations (EA), 21, 55–56, 169–70
enumeration, 107
Espiritu, Yen Le, 10–11, 74, 180*n*69, 188*n*153
ethnic, definition of, 24
ethnic boundaries. *See* boundaries, ethnic or cultural
ethnic collective action efforts: history of, 89–91, 95–97; number of, 87, **89**; panethnic activity impact, 15–16, 97–103; vs. panethnic efforts, 87–89
ethnic enclaves: of early immigrants, 36–37, 38, 53; interethnic competition in, 66; opportunities in, 77, 148; protests against redevelopment efforts threatening, 91; in San Francisco, 115
ethnic events, 16, 88, 101–2
ethnicity: as boundary process, 6–7; definition of, 6
ethnic organizations, 112–44; characteristics of, **167**; data sources, 55–56; ethnic focus, 120–25, 142, **167**; importance in panethnicity emergence, 16, 85–86; interracial coalitions, 139–41, 143–44; introduction, 112–14; name changes, 136–39; panethnic practices, 112–13, 117, 119–20, 125–35, 142–43, 149–50; in San Francisco, 114–19, 171–72. *See also* panethnic organizations
ethnic segregation: definition of, **73**; and panethnic collective action, **104**; panethnic organization formation probability, **73**, 74–75, **164**. *See also* segregation, occupational or labor market
European immigrants, 2, 155, 178*n*49
exclusionary immigration policy, 28–31

FACF (Filipino American Community Foundation), 123

FactFinder, **116**
family reunification, 59, 67
FBI (Federal Bureau of Investigation), 193*n*24
FCDL (Filipino Community Development League), 122–23
Federal Bureau of Investigation (FBI), 193*n*24
festivals, 93–94, 99–100. *See also* collective action
Filipino American Community Foundation (FACF), 123
Filipino Community Development League (FCDL), 122–23
Filipinos: census category, 47; collective action, 91, 95, 96; early immigrants, 30–31, 33, 182*n*24; educational attainment, **18**; ethnic enclaves, 38; Hawaii sugar plantation laborers, 31–32; household income, **18**; immigration quotas, 182–83*n*27; immigration statistics, **48**; International Hotel anti-eviction movement, 44–45, 59; naturalization rights, 41; panethnic organization formation, 73; Pew Research Center report, 1; population statistics, **12**, **30**; poverty rates, **18**; San Francisco population, 116; socioeconomic hierarchy, 18–19; during WWII, 40–41. *See also specific organizations*
Filipinos for Affirmative Action/Filipino Advocates for Justice, 118
film industry, 61
first-generation immigrants, 17, 118, 123, 128–30
foreign-born population, 17
foreigners, Asian Americans racialized as, 108–9
foundations, 48, 49, 112, 116, 162
frame alignment process, 151
fraternal organizations, 36

Free Chinatown Committee, 98
Friends of Free China, 58
funding, 116, 130, 162, **163,** 191*n*59

Gadar Party, 39
Gale Research Company, **57,** 169
gambling, 32
garment industry, 67
Gentlemen's Agreement, 30, 33, 37, 182*n*22
geographic dispersion, of ethnic population, 121
geographic variation, in panethnic organization formation, 62–69
Gibson, Campbell, **12, 30**
Giving USA: The Annual Report on Philanthropy, 162
Goyette, Kimberly, **68**
grants, 116, 162, **163**
Greek Americans, 2
group solidarity, 14, 68, 146, 148
guilds, 36

H-1B visas, 190*n*42
Harvard University, 108
hate crimes, 92, 94, 112, 157, 193*n*24
Hawaii: migrant laborers, 31–32, 184*n*47; Pearl Harbor bombing, 40
health organizations, **57,** 58, 67, 118, 130, **167**
hierarchies: occupationally based, 68, **160,** 161, **163–65,** 191*n*52; racially based, 18–19, 32–34, 71, 76
highly skilled immigrants, 67
Hindus, 39, 47. *See also* Indian (Asian) Americans
Hindustani Welfare Reform Society, 39
Hispanics: ethnic groups, 2; interracial coalitions with Asian Americans, 139–41; panethnicity vs. Asian Americans, 154–55; panethnic organizations, 56–57; San Francisco population, **116**
historical context of ethnic group boundaries, 26–52; ethnic competition, 31–34; interethnic relations among Asian-origin groups, 34–36; introduction, 26–28; labor demand, 28–31; organizations, 36–40; panethnic activity emergence, 41–46; racialization, 46–51; World War II impact, 40–41
Hmong Americans, 67, 95, 96
homeland countries, organizations promoting solidarity with, 34–36, 39, 58
Homeland Security, U.S. Department of, **47, 48**
Hong Kong, 97
household income, 17, **18**
Houston, Tex., pan-Asian organizations, 62
Hsiang, Bob, 44
Huen, Floyd, 43

identity: blacks, 8, 155; and boundary shifts, 2; Chinese, 2, 45; national origin basis, 45, 85, 155; in New York City, 8; and panethnic collective action, 152–53, **168,** 173; racialization's role in formation, 3–6, 9–13, 27, 156
Immigration Acts: (1917), 33; (1924), 27, 33
Immigration and Nationality Act of 1965, 41, 46, 67
Immigration and Naturalization Service (INS), 159
immigration conditions, 18
immigration law, 26–27, 29, 40–41. *See also specific legislative acts*
immigration reform, 93
immigration trends, 18, 46–48, 59–60, 73–74

income, household, 17, **18**
India, economic growth, 19
Indian (Asian) Americans: early immigrants, 29–30, 33; educational attainment, **18**; ethnic organizations, 39; household income, 17, **18**; immigration statistics, **48**; naturalization rights, 41; occupations, 38–39; Pew Research Center report, 1; population statistics, **12, 30**; poverty rates, **18**; San Francisco population, **116**
inequality: panethnic identification and, 15, 180*n*69; panethnic organizations' narratives, 79, 105–10, 147–48; Pew Research Center report omission, 1–2
in-migration rate, 160–61
INS (Immigration and Naturalization Service), 159
institutions, treatment of individuals based on race, 4. *See also* ethnic organizations
intergenerational relations, 122–23
intergroup contact, 13, 72, 103–4, 146–47, 149
intermarriage, 173
International Hotel, 44–45, 59
interracial coalitions, 139–41, 143–44
interviews, 22–23
Italian Americans, 2, 46

JAA (Japanese Association of America), 37–38, 118, 133–34
JACA (Japanese Americans Creating Action), 139–40
JACCR (Japanese American Center for Civil Rights), 127, 131–32
JACL (Japanese American Citizens League). *See* Japanese American Citizens League (JACL)
Jacobs, David, **89**

JAJ (Japanese Americans for Justice), 137
Japan: colonization of Korea, 34*n*47, 38, 184; occupation of China, 34–35, 97; World War II, 40, 96–97
Japanese American Center for Civil Rights (JACCR), 127, 131–32
Japanese American Citizens League (JACL): assimilation advocacy, 45; census category, 47; founding and mission of, 118, 119; Japanese internment investigation and reparations, 95, 98, 125–26; membership vs. Latino organizations, 57
Japanese Americans: agricultural associations, 37–38; agricultural laborers, 32–33; assimilation, 32, 45; collective action, 91, 95, 97; early immigrants, 26, 29–30, 32, 33; educational attainment, **18**; ethnic enclaves, 37; ethnic identity, 2; foreign-born population, 17; Hawaii sugar plantation laborers, 31–32; household income, **18**; immigration statistics, **48**; interethnic relations with other Asian-origin groups, 32, 33, 34–35; nationalism, 35; panethnic organization formation, 73; Pew Research Center report, 1; population statistics, **12, 30**; poverty rates, **18**; San Francisco population, **116**; San Francisco school segregation, 182*n*22; socioeconomic hierarchy, 18; WWII internment, 40–41, 95, 97, 98, 125–26. *See also specific organizations*
Japanese Americans Creating Action (JACA), 139–40
Japanese Americans for Justice (JAJ), 137
Japanese and Korean Exclusion League, 29

Japanese Association of America (JAA), 37–38, 118, 133–34
Japanese Chamber of Commerce, 35
Japanese Cultural and Community Center of Northern California, 119
Japan Institute, 58
Jenkins, J. Craig, **89**
Johnson Reed Act of 1924, 27, 33
journalists, 81–82
J-Town Collective, 98
Jung, Kay, **12, 30**
Jung, Moon-Kie, 183*n*32

KASC (Korean Americans for Social Change), 121
KCA (Koreans for Community Action), 123
Kim, Claire Jean, 34
Kim, Dora Yum, 38
KNA (Korean National Association), 38
Korea, Japan's colonization of, 34, 38, 184*n*47
Korean American Association of Mid-Queens, 99
Korean American Coalition, 57
Korean Americans: census category, 47; classification of immigrants as Japanese during WWII, 41; collective action, 96, 97; early immigrants, 29–30; educational attainment, **18**; ethnic identity, 2; foreign-born population, 17; grocers and merchants, 66; in Hawaii, 184*n*47; household income, 17, **18**; immigration statistics, **48**; interethnic competition, 66–67; panethnic organization formation, **73**; Pew Research Center report, 1; population statistics, **12, 30**; poverty rates, **18**; relations with Japanese immigrants, 34; San Francisco population, **116**; small business owners, 38; socioeconomic hierarchy, 18–19. *See also specific organizations*
Korean Americans for Social Change (KASC), 121
Korean Center, 118, 119
Korean Community Center of the East Bay, 119
Korean Methodist Church, 38
Korean National Association (KNA), 38
Koreans for Community Action (KCA), 123
Kwok, Daphne, 109

laborers, 28–32, 36
labor unions, 29–30, 61, 78–79
language, 58, 93
Lao Mutual Association (LMA), 129–30
Laos, Secret War in, 95, 96
Laotian Americans, 67
Latinos. *See* Hispanics
lawful permanent residence (LPR) status, 190*n*42
laws and legislation, 26–27, 29, 40–41. *See also specific legislative acts*
Le, Khoa Van, 94
leaders: interviews of, 22–23; panethnic activity role, 77–82, 87, 105–10, 150–51; Pew Report criticism, 1–2. *See also* narratives
Leadership Education for Asian Pacifics (LEAP), **57, 62**
League of Revolutionary Struggle, 98
LEAP (Leadership Education for Asian Pacifics), **57, 62**
Lee, Wen Ho, 108–9
Little Tokyo People's Rights Organization (LTPRO), 91, 98
LMA (Lao Mutual Association), 129–30
Los Angeles, Calif.: Asian Pacific Dance Festival, 94; Asian Pacific

Policy and Planning Council rally, 106–7; Chinatown, 36; Chinese Americans' protest against textbooks inaccurately portraying Japan's occupation of China, 97; interethnic competition, 67; Japanese in, 37; labor market segregation and competition, **69**; Little Tokyo People's Rights Organization (LTPRO), 91; pan-Asian organizations, 62; panethnic collective action, 193*n*21; protest against redevelopment plan threatening Little Tokyo, 91; riots (1992), 97; U.S. Census Bureau postenumeration survey protest, 107

Los Angeles Times, 21, **90**

low-skilled or low-wage work, 67–68, 72, 78, 80

LTPRO (Little Tokyo People's Rights Organization), 91, 98

magazines, 44

Malay, 177*n*38

media: Asian American newspapers and magazines, 44; diversity in film and television industry, 61; news coverage of Asian American issues and events, 82, 87–88, 109, 171; Pew Report coverage, 1, 145; portrayals of Asian Americans, 80–81, 85, 92–93

melting pot, 100

Mexican Americans, 2, 177–78*n*48

Middle Eastern Americans, 156

Mien Americans, 95

model minority stereotype: and Asian American identity, 158; and ethnic boundaries, 19; narratives counter to, 15, 79–80, 84, 105–6, 107; Pew Research Center report, 1–2, 145

Movement for a Free Philippines, 58

multiculturalism, 133

Muslims, 39, 132, 156

NAAAP (National Association for Asian American Professionals), 81

NAACP (National Association for the Advancement of Colored People), 137

NAAPAE (National Association for Asian and Pacific American Education), 58

NAAS (National Asian American Survey), 152–53, 173

NAATA (National Asian American Telecommunications Association), 61

NABE (National Association for Bilingual Education), 58

name changes, 136–39

Narasaki, Karen, 109

narratives: of assimilation, 128–35; and panethnic activity, 77–82, 105–10, 145, 147–48, 150–51; racialized boundary framework, 13, 15, 16; San Francisco ethnic organizations, 124–25; of social justice, 140

National Asian American and Pacific Islander Mental Health Association, 61

National Asian American Survey (NAAS), 152–53, 173

National Asian American Telecommunications Association (NAATA), 61

National Asian American Theatre Company, 80–81

National Association for Asian American Professionals (NAAAP), 81

National Association for Asian and Pacific American Education (NAAPAE), 58

National Association for Bilingual Education (NABE), 58

National Association for the Education and Advancement of Cambodian, Laotian, and Vietnamese Americans, 57

National Association of Asian American Law Enforcement Commanders, 61
National Association of Japan-America Societies, 58
National CAPACD (National Coalition for Asian and Pacific American Community Development), 61, 62
National Coalition for Asian and Pacific American Community Development (National CAPACD), 61, 62
National Coalition for Redress and Reparations (NCRR), 95, 98
National Council for Japanese American Redress (NCJAR), 95
nationalism, 148–49, 177*n*37
National Network of Asian and Pacific Women, 61
national origin, definition of, 24
national-origin identity, 45, 85, 155
National Origins Quota Act of 1921 (NOQA), 181*n*6
Native Americans, 42, 178*n*45
Native Sons of the Golden State, 117
Naturalization Act of 1870, 26
NCJAR (National Council for Japanese American Redress), 95
NCRR (National Coalition for Redress and Reparations), 95, 98
Nee, Victor, 8, 176*n*31
newcomer services, 39, **115**, 120–21, 128–30
newspapers, 21, 44, 161–62, 170–71. *See also specific newspapers*
New Year celebrations, 99–100
New York City: Chinatown, 36; Chinese New Year celebration, 99–100; collective action efforts following Yew beating, 90–91; interethnic competition, 66–67; labor market segregation and competition, **69**; pan-Asian organizations, 58, 62; panethnic collective action, 99, 193*n*21

New York Times, 21, **90**, 109
Nichibei Shinbun, 33
Nigerians, 8, 155
nonprofit sector, 115–16. *See also* ethnic organizations
Northwestern University, 108

Oakland, Calif., interview participants, 22–23
Obama, Barack, support for bill granting payment to Filipino WWII veterans, 96
occupational attainment, 19, 38–39, 67–68, 71
occupational hierarchy, 68, **160,** 161, **163–65,** 191*n*52
occupational segregation. *See* segregation, occupational or labor market
Omi, Michael, 9
Orange County, Calif., pan-Asian festival, 93–94
Organization of Chinese American Women, 58
organizations, panethnic. *See* panethnic organizations
organizing. *See* collective action
Oriental, rejection of label, 41–42
others, Asian immigrants as, 108–9, 184*n*60
Ozawa v. United States, 26

panethnic collective action efforts: barriers to, 86–89; Chin case's impact, 92, 102, 105; vs. ethnic efforts, 87–89; and identity, 152–53, **168,** 173; introduction, 85–86; number of, 87–88, **89;** reasons for emergence, 103–10; relationship with ethnic organizing efforts, 97–103; rise of, 92–95
panethnicity: American context, 2; definition of, 2, 7–9, 24; emergence of,

11–13, 41–46; factors leading to, 14–16, 146; racialized boundary framework for, 5–6, 13–16, 63–67; research considerations, 4
panethnic organizations, 53–84; emergence of, 55–60, 112; formation patterns, 69–75, **164**; geographic variations, 62–69; group boundary establishment, 76–82; introduction, 53–55; number of, 56–57; types of, 57–59
panethnic practices of ethnic organizations: adoption of, 112–13, 117, 125–35; continuum of, 119–20; ethnic program link, 142–43; importance of, 149–50
panracial coalitions, 139–41, 143–44
Pearl Harbor, 40
Pew Research Center, 1–2, 80, 145
Philadelphia, Penn.: pan-Asian organizations, 62; Yellow Seeds, 98
philanthropic funding, 191n59
Philippines, independence of, 30–31
Polish Americans, 2, 46
political opportunity, 162, **163**
political participation, 7, 93, 106–7, 153, **168**
population statistics, **12**, 16–17, **30**, 115, **116**
Portland, Ore., Chinatown in, 36
Portuguese, Hawaiian sugar plantation laborers, 31–32
poverty rates, **18**
Powell, Walter, 187n32
professional organizations, 61, 81
professionals, 67–68, 71–72, 190n42
protests. *See* collective action
Puerto Rican Americans, 2, 8, 31–32, 177–78n48
PUMS (public use microdata samples), 159
Punjabis, 39

Quon, Merilynne Hamano, 98
quotas, 41, 46, 181n6, 182–83n27, 187n139

race riots, 39
racial categories, 47–51, 158
racial formation, 9–10
racial groups, definition of, 24
racial hierarchy: early immigrants, 32–34; and panethnic collective action, 76; and panethnic organization formation, 71; in U.S., 18–19
racial ideology, 33
racialization: identity and group formation role, 3–6, 9–13, 27, 156; origins of, 46–51; panethnic collective action impact, 105, **163**
racialized boundary framework, 5–6, 13–16, 63–67, 146, 153–56
racial segregation: definition of, **72**; and panethnic collective action, 103, **104, 147,** 154–55; panethnic organization formation probability, **72,** 74–75. *See also* segregation, occupational or labor market
racism, 43, 46
radical politics, 42–43
Rape of Nanking, 175n10
redevelopment, 91
Refugee Act of 1980, 67
refugees, 18, 59–60, 67, 128
religion, 38, 198n34
reparations, 95, 98, 125–26
research methodology: data collection, 169–73; variable construction and tables, 159–68
research organizations, 58, 59
residential segregation, 77, 115, 148
resistance, 8
The Rise of Asian Americans (Pew Research Center), 1–2, 80
Roosevelt, Franklin D., Japanese internment, 40

Roosevelt, Theodore, Gentlemen's Agreement, 182*n*22

Sacramento, Calif., labor market segregation and competition, 69
San Francisco, Calif.: Chinatown, 36; ethnic organizations in, 114–19, 171–72; interview participants, 22–23; Japanese in, 37; J-Town Collective, 98; labor market segregation and competition, 69; pan-Asian organizations, 58, 59, 62, 78; population statistics, 115, **116**; school segregation, 182*n*22
San Francisco Chronicle, 29
San Francisco Foundation (SFF), 49
San Francisco State College, 43, 114
San Gabriel Valley, Calif., interracial competition, 66
SAWU (South Asian Women United), 123, 124
Seattle, Wash.: Japanese in, 37; pan-Asian organizations, 62
second-generation immigrants, 17, 118, 123, **129**, 132–34
Secret War, 95, 96
segmented assimilation, 8
segregation model, 14–15, 64, 76, 148
segregation, occupational or labor market: ethnic segregation, **73**, 74–75, **104, 164**; measurement of, 161; by metropolitan area, 68–69; and narrative creation, 82; and panethnic activity, 4–5, 103; and panethnic collective action, 14, 103, **104**, 146–49, **165, 166**; and panethnic organization formation, 64–65, 67–75, **164**
segregation, residential, 77, 115, 148
September 11, 2001, 132
shared identity, 37, 149
Sikhs, 39, 96
social conditions, 15–16, 27–28, 54

social justice organizations, 61, 135, 140, 141
social movements, 11–12, 41–46
social services, 118–19, 130
socioeconomic status, 17–19
South Asians, 18–19, 132, **167**, 180*n*64. *See also* Indian (Asian) Americans
South Asian Women United (SAWU), 123, 124
Southeast Asian Community Center, 118, 119
Spanish Coalition for Jobs, 177–78*n*45
spies, 108–9, 196*n*66
Sri Lankans, 59
Stanford University, 108
state, racialization by, 11–12
stereotypes, 92–93. *See also* model minority stereotype
strikes, 31–32
structural conditions, 6, 103, 145. *See also* collective action; segregation, occupational or labor market
suburbs, 66, 77
Supreme Court, 26–27, 156
symbolic support, 125–26

Taiwanese-American Society, 58–59
temporary worker visas, 190*n*42
textbooks, 38, 97
theoretical considerations, 5–6, 13–16, 63–67, 146–51
Third World Liberation Front (TWLF), 42–43
threat, 13–14
Tiananmen Square massacre, 96
Tibetan Aid Project, 58
Tibetans, 96
Tibet Fund, 96
tongs, 36
transformative ethnic organizations, 130, 134–35, 142
Tufts University, 108

TWLF (Third World Liberation Front), 42–43
Tydings-McDuffie Act, 30–31

unemployment, 68–69, **71**, 159, **160**, **163–66**
unions, 29–30. 61, 78–79
United Japanese Deliberative Council of America, 37
University of California, Berkeley, 42, 43, 114
University of California, Davis, 108
University of California, Irvine, 108
University of Illinois at Chicago, 108
U.S. Census Bureau, 47–48, **49**, 107, 156
U.S.-China Peoples Friendship Association, 58
U.S. Pan-Asian American Chamber of Commerce, **57**

VCA (Vietnamese Community Association), 137–38, 139
Vietnamese Americans: collective action, 95; educational attainment, **18**; employment, 67; household income, **18**; immigration statistics, **48**; interethnic competition, 66; Pew Research Center report, 1; population statistics, **12**; poverty rates, **18**; San Francisco population, **116**. *See also specific organizations*
Vietnamese Community Association (VCA), 137–38, 139
Vietnamese Community Center, 119, 124

Vietnamese Youth Development Center, 118
Vietnam Foundation, 58
Vietnam Outreach (VO), 128–29
Vietnam War, 43–44
violence, 74. *See also* anti-Asian attacks
voting, 153

wages and earnings: Hawaii sugar plantation laborers, 32; professionals, 81
Washington, D.C., pan-Asian organizations, 62
Weber, Max, 6
white ethnics, 2
whites: Asian categorization as, 156; group boundary defense, 76; panethnicity vs. Asian Americans, 155; San Francisco population, **116**
Winant, Howard, 9
women's rights movement, 41, 42
World War II, 40–41, 95, 96, 98, 126

xenophobia, 29, 103
Xie, Yu, **68**

Yale University, 108
Yearbook of Immigration Statistics, 159
Yellow Seeds, 98
Yew, Peter, 90–91
Young Koreans United, 96
youth programs, 133–34, **167**
Yugoslavia, 177n37